Key Concepts in
Corporate Social
Responsibility

Recent volumes include:

Key Concepts in Work
Paul Blyton & Jean Jenkins

Key Concepts in Governance
Mark Bevir

Key Concepts in Marketing
Jim Blythe

Key Concepts in Public Relations
Bob Franklin, Mike Hogan, Quentin
Langley, Nick Mosdell & Elliott Pill

**Key Concepts in Human Resource
Management**
John Martin

**Key Concepts in Operations
Management**
Michel Leseure

**Key Concepts in Critical Management
Studies**
Mark Tadajewski, Pauline Maclaran,
Elizabeth Parsons and Martin Parker

The SAGE Key Concepts series provides students with accessible and authoritative knowledge of the essential topics in a variety of disciplines. Cross-referenced throughout, the format encourages critical evaluation through understanding. Written by experienced and respected academics, the books are indispensable study aids and guides to comprehension.

SUZANNE BENN AND DIANNE BOLTON

Key Concepts in
Corporate Social
Responsibility

Los Angeles | London | New Delhi
Singapore | Washington DC

First published 2011
Reprinted 2011, 2013

SAGE Publications Ltd
1 Oliver's Yard
55 City Road
London EC1Y 1SP

SAGE Publications Inc.
2455 Teller Road
Thousand Oaks, California 91320

SAGE Publications India Pvt Ltd
B 1/I 1 Mohan Cooperative Industrial Area
Mathura Road
New Delhi 110 044

SAGE Publications Asia-Pacific Pte Ltd
3 Church Street
#10-04 Samsung Hub
Singapore 049483

Library of Congress Control Number: 2010929684

British Library Cataloguing in Publication data

A catalogue record for this book is available from the
British Library

ISBN 978-1-84787-928-8
ISBN 978-1-84787-929-5 (pbk)

Typeset by C&M Digitals (P) Ltd, Chennai, India
Printed and bound in Great Britain by
CPI Group (UK) Ltd, Croydon, CR0 4YY
Printed on paper from sustainable resources

contents

contents

v

key concepts in corporate
social responsibility

list of figures and tables

FIGURES

TABLES

list of figures and tables

acknowledgements

We would like to acknowledge the willing and talented assistance we have received from Jessica North and Anna Knutszelius in the Graduate School of the Environment at Macquarie University, Australia in assembling this work. We are also grateful to Clare Wells and her team at Sage for their patience and support. Suzanne would like to thank her partner Andrew, whose ongoing personal support and professional expertise in environmental law and corporate sustainability has been invaluable. Dianne would like to express her appreciation of the ongoing personal and professional support of her colleagues at Swinburne University of Technology, Australia and especially Terry Landells for his expertise and advice in the area of business and sustainability.

key concepts in corporate social responsibility

preface

WHY STUDY CSR?

Does business have responsibilities to society broader than making profits for business owners and investors? Over the last fifty years the long history of debate around this question has been focussed through increasing interest in the concept of 'corporate social responsibility' (CSR). At various times, debates about CSR have surfaced in response to social, environmental, economic and political pressures. For example, in the 1950s even the legality of corporate philanthropy was questioned, the concern being whether it transgressed business responsibilities to shareholders. Subsequently interest arose as to whether and how business might benefit commercially from 'doing good'. This in turn generated debate concerning whether such a 'bolt-on' approach to CSR focused on corporate profit maximisation might contradict the higher moral obligations that business had to society. Ongoing debate concerning the multiplicity of business purposes broader than mere financial outcomes had been consistent in the academic and practitioner communities.

However, in the 1990s the coining of the term 'triple bottom line' (TBL) helped popularise an understanding of the need for business to account to a constituency broader than shareholders. By purporting that business should report on its financial, social and environmental outcomes as a matter of course, the framework improved clarity around the interface of business with society. Later, governance and political impact were also suggested as additional and desirable areas for business reporting. Since that time there has been a burgeoning interest in the nature of corporate responsibility and accountability, driven to a large extent by an increasing social awareness of the impact of commercial practices, products and services on the natural environment. These pressures are currently polarising the political debate at a national and global level and creating an environment of dynamic complexity for business around stakeholder relationships, pathways to sustainable business practices, global citizenry responsibilities and risk management.

HOW WILL THIS BOOK ASSIST YOUR UNDERSTANDING AND PRACTICE?

This book presents students, researchers and practitioners with a cross-disciplinary perspective around the core theme of CSR. It addresses three broad areas of inquiry: 'What is CSR?', 'Why would firms undertake CSR?', and 'How are businesses implementing CSR in context?' As a nascent and dynamic area of research and study, we draw broad conceptual boundaries around CSR that include social, economic and environmental dimensions. The 50 entries focus on definitions, the relevance of topics to CSR, development of the concept and related constructs, the key debates and tensions (academic and practical) and some evidence of practice. The book will be useful for researchers/readers in concept mapping their own areas of interest in an informed and holistic manner and facilitating their cross-disciplinary research and study.

This is an increasingly important and urgent area for business and management studies. Traditionally managers have been required to draw upon a range of perspectives through the 'lenses' of different disciplines. New business models that incorporate social responsibility or sustainability concepts have extended the scope of management concerns and accountability across even broader disciplinary areas, particularly in relation to the way business uses resources (both physical and human) and the ensuing environmental impacts. The intention of this book is to help the reader identify these critical CSR issues and make better decisions in the current complex and shifting business environment. We do this by presenting entries from multiple disciplines illustrating CSR as a dynamic and contextual response to internal and external environmental pressures and shifts in community expectations concerning the roles, responsibilities and accountabilities of business.

WHAT IS AGENCY THEORY?

Agency theory is concerned with the governance of the firm. It assumes that the governance function administers delegations on behalf of the firm's owners (principals) to rational actors (agents) who, by undertaking managerial roles, will seek to maximise their individual utility (or their access to desirable goods and services) on economic grounds. The principal, as the owner of the firm, enters into contracts with agents to manage the principal's firm; an executive manager (the agent of the principal) accepts the responsibility to shareholders to maximise shareholder utility. In appointing the agent the owner knows that the agent's role offers opportunities to maximise the agent's utility whilst managing the principal's wealth in the form of investments. Thus agency theory suggests that 'in the modern corporation agents and principals are motivated by opportunities for their own personal gain' (Davis et al., 1997: 22).

Agency theory suggests that if the 'utility functions' of self-serving agents and principals are aligned, then both parties will benefit. However, if they are not, then what are described as 'agency costs' will arise. For example, managers might protect their jobs by promoting unnecessarily risk averse strategies that reduce shareholder value. It is assumed that governance frameworks that determine both the mechanisms of and control over delegations will minimise agency costs. Davis et al. (1997) note that although agency costs can arise from factors such as poor information or managerial skill deficits, agency theory has focused mainly on 'motivation' to pursue self-interest as the main cause of agency costs. An example is the well publicised debate about whether effective governance can be achieved by providing incentive pay to managers to pursue strategic targets of the organisation, rather than to engage in self-serving behaviours. There is much evidence to suggest that these incentives can be perverse and encourage self-serving behaviours by managers.

CRITIQUE OF AGENCY THEORY

Jensen and Meckling (1976) critique agency theory from a perspective relevant to emerging theories of CSR. They suggest that agency theory falsely simplifies human nature (to facilitate modelling exercises) by only describing principal–agent relationships that are at odds. Agency theory is seen as incomplete in comparison with other evolving governance models of stakeholder theory and stewardship theory, both of which suggest that the manager now has broader stakeholder obligations which are not necessarily at odds with short or longer term shareholder interests. In this context, Jensen (2000) introduces the term 'enlightened value maximisation' to specify the firm's intent to seek longer term value maximisation. This approach is also used to determine tradeoffs amongst stakeholder interests and claims.

Caldwell et al. (2006) have produced a conceptual framework around 'principal theory' and 'principle theory' as a way of understanding relationships between agency theory, stakeholder theory and stewardship theory. The assumption behind their principal theory is that in practice it is the principal who often pursues 'self interest with guile rather than the agent'. In other words, 'organizational owners and shareholders can often be ethically opportunistic and take advantage of employees who serve them' (2006: 207). This is illustrated by such activities as downsizing in 'the absence of much planning or strategic thought' (Pfeffer, 1998). Caldwell et al. note that employees often view principal theory as embodying an organisational ethic of power, the rationale for decision-making being 'because we can' rather than the pursuit of long-term outcomes for the organisation. In contrast, principle theory suggests that firms adhere to guiding principles embodying 'core values and sense of purpose beyond just making money – that guides and inspires people through the organization and remains relatively fixed for long periods of time' (Collins and Porras, 1994: 77).

Thus, Caldwell et al. (2006) broaden the debate about organisational governance and its ethical assumptions through employing a critique of agency theory. To do this they illustrate the relevance of principal theory and principle theory, comparing them with other theories of governance including agency theory. In this respect, they question the relevance of agency theory on the basis of arguments around: the open-ended nature of the likely increase in transaction costs to incentivise the agent to act ethically; the possible impact of this policy on a desirable organisational culture of trust and followership; the lack of evidence that a self-interested focus on profit maximises shareholder wealth; and, finally the negative impact on employees who are treated as commodities and are therefore less likely to give their best efforts or engage. Other governance models compared with principal theory and principle theory include stakeholder theory and stewardship theory, which are covered in separate entries.

See also: Employee Engagement, Governance, Stakeholder Theory, Stewardship

REFERENCES

Caldwell, C., Karri, R. and Vollmar, P. (2006) 'Principal Theory and Principle Theory: Ethical Governance from the Follower's Perspective', *Journal of Business Ethics*, 66: 207–223.

Collins, J.C. and Porras, J.I. (1994) *Built to Last: Successful Habits of Visionary Companies*. New York: Harper Business.

Davis, J.H., Schoorman, F.D. and Donaldson, L. (1997) 'Towards a Stewardship Theory of Management', *Academy of Management Review*, 22 (1): 20–47.

Jensen, M.C. (2000) 'Value Maximization, Stakeholder Theory, and the Corporate Objective Function', *Business Ethics Quarterly*, 12 (2): 235–256.

Jensen, M.C. and Meckling, W.H. (1976) 'Theory of the Firm: Managerial Behaviour, Agency Costs and Ownership Structure', *Journal of Financial Economics*, 3: 306–360.

Pfeffer, J. (1998) *The Human Equation: Building Profits by Putting People First*. Boston, MA: Harvard Business.

Business at the Bottom of the Pyramid

A NEW BUSINESS MODEL

The term 'bottom of the pyramid' (BoP) refers to the poorest people in the world who live on less than US$2 per day. There are around 2.7 billion people in this situation, more than half the population of the developing world (see http://web.worldbank.org/). Some economists conceptualise the wealth and earning capacity of the world's population as a pyramid, where those in the bottom quartile are not only the worst off financially but also account for the largest sector of the pyramid. The people categorised as at the bottom of the pyramid often live in rural areas, with little access to education or technology.

Several leading business scholars have researched business activities that could achieve the dual purpose of eradicating this poverty-stricken demographic while at the same time making profits for the companies who can devise products to sell into this market (see Hart, 2005; Prahalad 2006). These writers see the BoP group as a problem in terms of social equity, but a problem that provides an opportunity for phenomenal growth in the private sector in which these 2.7 billion people represent untapped potential for multinationals. They claim that if products such as mini water purifiers or household detergents in disposable minipacks are designed to be affordable for this market and also provide human health and environmental benefits, the firm will be contributing to the overall wellbeing of this sector. Hence BoP proponents claim that if businesses take on the challenges of servicing this demographic, they can assist in alleviating social decay and environmental degradation while also delivering returns on investments by the corporation.

London and Hart's (2004: 361) empirical research on appropriate business strategies to apply to BoP suggests that there are three key strategies of successful BoP market entries:

1. **Collaborating with non-traditional partners**

   • recognising the value of both corporate and non-corporate partners
   • proactively establishing relationships with non-profit and other non-traditional partner organisations
   • relying on non-corporate partners for expertise on the social infrastructure and local legitimacy

2. **Co-inventing custom solutions**

   • linking with multiple distributors, who may modify product differently before selling to the final user
   • allowing for user innovation and modification
   • allowing for the product and business model design to co-evolve
   • viewing the product in terms of the functionality it provides

3. **Building local capacity**

   • recognising the value of existing local institutions
   • providing training to local entrepreneurs and other partners
   • seeing gaps in the local infrastructure or missing services as potential opportunities

These business strategies have been widely supported by the World Business Council for Sustainable Development and other global business networks. According to one of its leading proponents, the only way large corporations can work towards the betterment of society and the natural environment and remain economically viable is through targeting markets at the base of the pyramid (Hart, 2005). BoP can be thought of as a systems approach to change for social good because it emphasises the relationships between the various elements of the global socio-economic system rather than the elements themselves. For instance, it would appear that the success of the model is dependent upon cooperation between governments and consumers, NGOs, business, research and development organisations and other facets of the global socio-economic system.

The Aspen Institute provides three case examples to illustrate this phenomenon (see www.beyondgreypinstripes.org/pdf/BOP.pdf):

- The Grameen Bank was started by Nobel laureate Muhammed Yunus in Bangladesh to offer mini-loans to entrepreneurs who wouldn't qualify for the traditional form of bank loans that are based on collateral.
- PlayPumps sell a water pump that runs on the energy created from children playing on a merry-go-round. Advertising space on the pump's storage tank generates revenue that covers maintenance costs.
- Cell phone providers have developed the means to sell relatively cheap units to remote villages, thus allowing farmers, as just one example, to check grain prices at the nearest market before deciding to take their product into town.

THE ROLE OF INNOVATION

There are many problems and challenges in ensuring these types of business models are ethical, requiring high levels of innovation to ensure that the products or processes they deliver are sustainable. Providing single doses of hair shampoo in plastic containers obviously is problematic in sustainability terms if the country where it is distributed has weak governance systems for waste. Currently, Dow Chemical is experimenting with a totally biodegradable plastic that would enable a sustainable BoP market for this product but would also have positive implications for other sectors of the economy.

As Porritt (2006: 254) points out, a particularly important example refers to the BoP providing support for new technologies designed to generate electricity at the point of use, whether it be the home, factory, school or hospital. This 'distributed generation' or micro-technology capacity would include mini wind turbines, biogas boilers and digesters that would operate independent of the grid. It is these technologies that could be sold into this market, enabling economic, social and environmental benefits. Getting multinationals to market such technologies could help address the dependence of the rural poor in many countries on forest products as a source of energy.

While small local entrepreneurs can target this market, BoP proponents argue that multinational firms have a greater resource and research capacity to develop innovative products and supply the infrastructure required for social, environmental and economic benefits to be obtained. Multinational corporations also have the bridging capacity to transfer knowledge and work across the different regions of the world where these markets are to be found.

Prahalad (2006), originator of some key ideas of BoP, coined the phrase 'inclusive capitalism' to describe the pursuit of profit-making business opportunities which deliver social benefits in developing countries. The BoP model is also linked to other emergent business models, such as social entrepreneurship. That is, starting with social or environmental issues and then applying a business model that addresses the issues while also delivering economic benefits.

CRITICAL PERSPECTIVES ON BOP

While there is wide recognition that governments alone cannot address the problem of global poverty, there are also critics of BoP and associated models such as inclusive capitalism and microfinance. For example, Karnani (2006) argues that we need to view the poor as producers, and emphasise buying from them, rather than selling to them. Questions can also be raised regarding the level of profit companies should be making from selling such products if their overall aim is to do good as well as to make money. Other concerns refer to the role of marketers for the companies selling such goods – are some of these goods essential or are they simply creating a demand for unnecessary products? While companies such as Proctor and Gamble might provide employment for some local people as distributors of these goods, do BoP activities then remove the livelihood of many local vendors? Davidson (2009) argues that these dilemmas can only be resolved if the multinational involved has a clear understanding of CSR and business ethics. At core, such initiatives must deliver value to the poor as the highest priority. This is in contrast to other writers in the field who argue that BoP must not be confused with 'charity' or 'philanthropy', stating that above all BoP is a business concern.

Clearly there are ethical and CSR issues that are important for multinational companies working with these markets to understand and observe. Some of the most successful boycotts of our time have been targeted at companies which have ignored these principles when dealing with the world's poor. For example, Nestlé's promotion of milk products in less economically developed countries resulted in a decrease in breast feeding and the use of dirty water in infant formula, leading to a rise in health problems and deaths among infants. This resulted in the boycotting of Nestlé's baby milk products. Companies now appear to be more aware of such damaging reputational issues and hopefully can work with this new business model to deliver on its expectations for poverty alleviation as well as corporate returns.

See also: *Corporate Citizenship, Corporate Social Responsibility, Corporate Sustainability, Intergenerational Equity, Intragenerational Equity, Social Entrepreneurship, Systems Approaches*

REFERENCES

Aspen Institute (2010) 'A Closer Look at Business Education', available at www.beyondgreypinstripes.org/pdf/BOP.pdf, accessed 3 April 2010.
Davidson, K. (2009) 'Ethical Concerns at the Bottom of the Pyramid: Where CSR meets BOP', *Journal of International Business Ethics*, 2: 22–33.
Hart, S. (2005) *Capitalism at the Crossroads*. Pennsylvania, PA: Wharton School Publishing, University of Pennsylvania.
Karnani, A. (2006) 'Misfortune at the Bottom of the Pyramid', *Greener Management International*, 51: 99–110.
London, T. and Hart, S. (2004) 'Reinventing Strategies for Emerging Markets', *Journal of International Business Studies*, 35: 350–370.
Porritt, J. (2006) *Capitalism as if the World Matters*. London, Sterling, VA: Earthscan.
Prahalad, C.K. (2006) *The Fortune at the Bottom of the Pyramid*. Fruehauf: Wharton School Publishing.

DEFINITION AND EVOLUTION OF A BUSINESS CASE FOR CSR

The business case for CSR draws upon the argument that the market will economically and financially reward organisations that engage in CSR activities (Carroll and Shabana, 2010: 101). Although a widely accepted business case for CSR exists (Vogel, 2005; Lindgreen and Swaen, 2010), the argument that there is no business case (in that CSR takes resources away from the firm's principal economic functions) is also well documented. The debate is complicated further by Wood (2010), who argues that the results of research demonstrating a business case for corporate social performance are generally 'wishy-washy', such an approach being flawed theoretically and ethically because it treats CSR as an add-on to the business function rather than as a moral imperative that underpins business's right to operate.

SO HOW HAS THE BUSINESS CASE FOR CSR EVOLVED?

Lydenberg (2005) suggests that until the late 1970s, CSR was not treated seriously by the investment and business community. This was not helped by Friedman's fierce (1972) advocacy that CSR imposed inappropriate costs on shareholders, and that managers often invested shareholder funds in activities unrelated to core business and core capabilities to further their ego and status whilst creating little social benefit for other stakeholders. However, both Vogel (2005) and Lee (2008) conclude that by the 1990s, discourse around CSR had shifted towards demonstrating how its adoption might be linked to explicit market outcomes and measurable benefits to business.

BUILDING A BUSINESS CASE AROUND AN EVOLVING DEFINITION OF CSR

Lee (2008) notes that the 1960s witnessed an increase in corporate social responsiveness and business awareness about the social and ecological impact of business, but there was little attempt to link social responsibility to financial performance. For example, in 1978 Frederick noted that companies were beginning either to take responsibility for the social environment (CR_1) or to respond to the social environment (CR_2). Carroll and Shabana (2010) describe how in the 1970s a focus on corporate social performance (CSP) emerged that attempted to reconcile the approaches of CR_1 and CR_2, moving the direction of the debate around CSR much more closely to the idea of a business case. The 1980s witnessed increasing academic interest in the business case for social performance. By 1991 Wood was seeking to add clarity to such debates by refining the concept of CSP as 'a business organization's configuration of principles of social responsibility, processes of social responsiveness, and policies, programs and observable outcomes as they relate to the firm's societal relationships' (1991: 697). Carroll and Shabana remind us that by the 2000s the corporate scandals and the GFC were shifting the focus of debate towards business ethics and away from CSP or CSR, with tension emerging between a voluntaristic approach to CSP and calls for more regulation to curb the worst excesses of corporate risk-taking. Dahlsrud's (2006) factor analysis of CSR practices suggests approaches to CSR include a voluntariness in addressing discrete functions, and ethical and regulatory frameworks pertinent to the development of business sustainability, covering society's required and expected business behaviours.

Kurucz et al. (2008) suggest that despite the diverse definitions of CSR, the rationale for the business case commonly includes its capacity to: reduce cost and risk; build a reputation in the market and the broader community; create competitive advantage in an environment experiencing increasing community expectations of firms to act in a socially responsible manner; build synergy and innovation for broad stakeholder benefit through the creation of social capital across stakeholder groups. Wood (2010) also includes claims concerning increased employee motivation, and the possibility of reducing the threat of increased regulation through self-regulation.

ECONOMIC ISSUES UNDERPINNING THE DEBATE

Key debates that impact on the business case for CSR concern the function and level of profit required to ensure long-term business success. Emphasis in this debate has shifted along with changing social expectations on business. In 1962, Friedman maintained the role of business to be that of optimising profits for shareholders. Four decades on, Barnett

(2007) suggests that an excessive focus on profits decreases an essential capability of the firm to influence and manage stakeholders. Although tension between these viewpoints remains, there is increasing activity amongst academics and practitioners to demonstrate that companies can improve their performance economically and financially by undertaking their core business in a manner that considers its impact on the broader society. There is evidence that stakeholders increasingly appreciate the benefits of a more strategic approach to CSR, i.e. its positive financial and economic impacts as well as social benefit. As Lee (2008) and Vogel (2005) have noted, we are shifting towards CSR frameworks that are more financially performance-oriented and witnessing a gradual acceptance by companies that CSR influences profit.

Wood (2010) questions whether CSR should be seen as an organisational function of a closed system, and therefore as an add-on, or as a role within an open system in which an appreciation of complex interactions with society underpins its business case. Carroll and Shabana (2010) differentiate between a narrow business case that looks for direct links between individual CSR activities and corporate financial performance (CFP) and broader approaches that justify direct and indirect linkages that can enhance collaborative and innovative stakeholder relationships based on trust and a commitment to longer term and mutual benefits.

DOES A RELATIONSHIP BETWEEN CFP AND CSP CONSTITUTE A BUSINESS CASE?

Margolis and Walsh (2003), drawing on 127 studies on the relationship between CSP and CFP, suggest that a majority of these support the business case, there being very little evidence of a negative relationship between CSP and CFP. However, they also identify strong grounds for questioning these results on the basis of research methodology. They appear to support Wood's (2010) concerns that an empirical approach relating CSP to CFP might by its very nature legitimise the economic contractual model of the firm (that assumes that the firm is nothing more than a series of contracts undertaken to maximise profits), stating that a 'preoccupation with instrumental consequences renders a theory that accommodates economic premises yet sidesteps the underlying tensions between the social and economic imperatives that confront organizations' (2003: 280). They also purport that this approach understates the need for a new normative theory of the firm concerning how business organisations might 'respond to human misery while also sustaining their legitimacy, securing vital resources and enhancing financial performance ...' (2003: 284). They conclude that a useful starting point for researchers might be to get a better idea of how organisations actually benefit society, before pursuing a scientific analysis of the relationship between CFP and CSP.

Salzmann et al. (2005) also acknowledge severe shortcomings in the methodologies of existing studies supporting the business case, including poor measures of social performance and financial performance, a lack of testing of definitions and concepts, and inadequate sampling techniques, with few comparative studies undertaken at an organisational level. Despite these limitations, scholars, consultants and think-tanks have not hesitated to make broad recommendations for actions and have developed valuation tools to quantify the business case. Salzmann et al. (2005) argue further that what is needed is more descriptive research on specific target groups using comparative studies. In other words, a basic understanding of rationales, practices and impacts of CSP is required before other research methodologies are employed to assess the financial returns of a variety of CSR initiatives that are by their very nature contextually specific.

CONCLUSION

There seems to be broad support for the view that there is a business case to be made for CSR. Even critics of the CSP–CFP research focus such as Wood (2010) would acknowledge that this positive connection is well established. But there is also broad concern around the complexities of developing such business cases and a plea for more attention to building business cases that will recognise situational contingencies and the complexities associated with diverse CSR agendas. Every initiative will not be a winner in narrow financial terms. However, the literature suggests that some initiatives will in fact deliver broader stakeholder value that is recognisable in the market and in the wider community. Vogel (2005) makes this case strongly by saying 'the effort to demonstrate through statistical analysis that corporate responsibility pays may be not only fruitless, but also pointless and unnecessary, because such studies purport to hold corporate responsibility to a standard to which no other business activity is subject'. He exemplifies this by reminding us that although it is unlikely that a direct positive relationship can be demonstrated between advertising expenditures and profit levels, it is equally unlikely that the case for advertising would be disputed.

See also: Business at the Bottom of the Pyramid, Corporate Social Responsibility, Risk Management, Social and Societal Marketing, Triple Bottom Line

REFERENCES

Barnett, M.L. (2007) 'Stakeholder Influence Capacity and the Variability of Financial Returns to Corporate Social Responsibility', *Academy of Management Review*, 32: 794–816.

Carroll, A.B. and Shabana, K.M. (2010) 'The Business Case for Corporate Social Responsibility: A Review of Concepts, Research and Practice', *International Journal of Management Reviews*, 12 (1): 85–105.

Dahlsrud, A. (2006) 'How Corporate Social Responsibility is Defined: An Analysis of 37 Definitions', *Corporate Social Responsibility and Environmental Management*, September, available at www.csr-norway.no/papers/2007_dahlsrud_CSR.pdf, accessed 12 May 2010.

Frederick, W.C. (1978) 'From CSR1 to CSR2: The Maturing of Business and Society Thought', *Working Paper 279*. Pittsburgh, PA: Graduate School of Business, University of Pittsburgh.

Friedman, M. (1962) 'The Social Responsibility of Business is to Increase its Profits', *New York Times*, September, 126.

Friedman, M. (1972) 'Milton Friedman Responds', *Business and Society Review*, 1: 5–16.

Kurucz, E., Colbert, B. and Wheeler, D. (2008) 'The Business Case for Corporate Social Responsibility', in A. Crane, A. McWilliams, D. Matten, J. Moon and D. Seigel (eds), *The Oxford Handbook of Corporate Social Responsibility*. Oxford: Oxford University Press, pp. 83–112.

Lee, M.P. (2008) 'A Review of the Theories of Corporate Social Responsibility: Its Evolutionary Path and the Road Ahead', *International Journal of Management Reviews*, 10 (1): 53–73.

Lindgreen, A. and Swaen, V. (2010) 'Corporate Social Responsibility', *International Journal of Management Reviews*, 12 (1): 1–7.

Lydenberg, S.D, (2005) *Corporations and the Public Interest: Guiding the Invisible Hand*. San Francisco, CA: Berret/Koehler.

Margolis, J.D. and Walsh, J.P. (2003) 'Misery Loves Companies: Rethinking Social Initiatives by Business', *Administrative Science Quarterly*, 48: 268–305.

Salzmann, O., Ionescu-Somers, A. and Steger, U. (2005) 'The Business Case for Corporate Sustainability: Literature Review and Research Options', *European Management Journal*, 23 (1): 27–36.

Vogel, D.J. (2005) 'Is there a Market for Virtue? The Business Case for Corporate Social Responsibility', *California Management Review*, 47 (4).

Wood, D.J. (1991) 'Corporate Social Performance Revisited', *Academy of Management Review*, 16: 691–718.

Wood, D.J. (2010) 'Measuring Corporate Social Performance: A Review, *International Journal of Management Reviews*, 12 (1): 50–84.

key concepts in corporate
social responsibility

Business Ethics

WHAT IS BUSINESS ETHICS?

Ethics is concerned with the nature of morality, or a society's norms, values and beliefs about right and wrong, and the philosophies, principles, guidelines and conditions that influence moral choices. Wines highlights the complexity and uncertainty that typifies ethical concerns, defining ethics as 'the cognitive, analytical, systematic and reflective application of moral principles to complex, conflicting or unclear situations' (2008: 487).

Crane and Matten define business ethics as 'the study of business situations, activities and decisions where the issues of right and wrong are addressed ... mean[ing] morally right and wrong as opposed to, for example, commercially, strategically, or financially right or wrong' (2007: 52). Business ethics embraces the study of ethics *for* business and *in* business, which Wines (2008) purports should go beyond a concern with moral philosophy, ethical dilemmas and CSR to examine moral psychology, corporate culture, the impact of authority and organisational design, motivation, and the historical and contemporary interactions between society, business and the law. This account places an emphasis on the relationship between business ethics, the law, moral philosophies, CSR and the risks to business.

DEVELOPMENT OF BUSINESS ETHICS

Sauser (2005: 346) has noted that business ethics cannot be distinguished from ethics in general because 'an ethical person behaves appropriately in all societal contexts'. This position was acknowledged by Adam Smith who, in 1759, in *The Theory of Moral Sentiments*, argued that both understanding one's obligations to society and maintaining a sense of justice were preconditions for effective business and commerce. Barnard, in his seminal (1938) work *The Functions of the Executive*, also emphasised the importance of individual actions in organisations and the need for leadership to consider the economic, legal, moral, social and physical elements of the environment when making decisions. Simon's (1945) *Administrative Behaviour* built on Barnard's work by further exploring the influence of

13

the organisation on individual actions and vice versa. In so doing, he noted that businesses were broadening their notion of responsibility towards the community beyond mere legal compliance. Drucker's (1954) *The Practice of Management* extended this moral and ethical focus beyond individual behaviour in organisations, focusing more on CSR and including it as an area in which businesses should set objectives. However, Svensson and Wood (2007) pointed out that business ethics as an academic discipline in the USA was not formalised until 1974.

Sauser (2005) notes that while law is a significant source of ethical guidance, other sources include; authority derived from organisational policies; professional codes of behaviour; the community's conceptualisation of morality or social mores; and standards derived from the individual conscience.

BUSINESS ETHICS AND THE LAW

Ethics and morality have broader application than the law, the law being the codified set of a particular society's acceptable behavioural standards. Joyner and Payne (2002) suggest the concept of legality accords with the 'letter' of the law whereas the concept of morality (and ethics) accords with the 'spirit' of the law. Sauser goes further by suggesting that 'while few business philosophers question the role of law as a *necessary* standard of business morality, there is a raging debate over whether the law is a *sufficient* standard of ethicality in business' (2005: 347). He questions whether it is appropriate for a business person to merely obey the law or to meet higher standards of morality. Many businesses seek adherence to higher ethical standards through developing codes of conduct which enshrine normative expectations of employee conduct, often over and above the law.

ETHICAL FRAMEWORKS AND CSR

According to Crane and Matten, business ethics serves as an analytical tool that can help managers evaluate different possibilities and develop 'moral imagination for the consequences of their actions for the human beings affected by those decisions' (2007: 54). Joyner and Payne consider the concepts of business ethics and CSR to be highly aligned, CSR being defined as 'categories or levels of economic, legal, ethical and discretionary activities of a business entity as adapted to the values and expectations of society' (2002: 300).

The following major ethical theories have been identified as applicable to business decision-making around CSR:

- *Ethical egoism* maintains that what is right is what is in one's own interests. Whilst this approach is often seen as individually-oriented, it can include a rational appraisal of a corporation's long-term interests, including the need to be broadly socially responsive.
- *Virtue ethics* maintains that an individual's character will influence behaviour that is aligned with the 'good life'. Virtues can include honesty, integrity, fairness, prudence and courage. In some instances virtues may conflict, creating dilemmas for business managers, e.g. courage may lead to recklessness rather than prudence. The aspirational nature of virtue ethics can limit the cross-cultural relevance in that virtues may have different cultural priorities. However, it would appear to suggest appropriate guidance about socially responsible behaviour in local societies, if not more generally in a global society.
- *Deontological ethics* (the Greek 'deon' meaning obligation or duty) is concerned with the universal moral nature of an action, regardless of the preferences or desires of the actor, or of the circumstances in which the action takes place. This approach also encounters difficulties in determining universal 'absolutes'. However, situations such as the global financial crisis (GFC) that began in 2007 and ongoing concerns about human-induced climate change (and associated transitions from fossil fuel based energy) might have highlighted possible moral 'absolutes' in a global economy.
- *Consequentialist ethics* maintains that the ethics of an action are determined by its consequences. Utilitarianism is one such approach that maintains an action is right if it generates the greatest good for the greatest number of people, with the notion of 'good' traditionally defined in terms of 'happiness', 'pleasure' or 'satisfaction'. The pragmatic nature of this ethical framework facilitates decision making based on perceived consequences. Its weakness is in defining what constitutes 'good', e.g. in determining a corporation's social responsibilities.
- *Rights-based ethics* is concerned with the rights that people have by virtue of being human, e.g. breathing clean air or freedom of association. Rights-based ethics (along with justice-based ethics) appears to have underpinned much of the early debates around CSR, especially around the 'social' impact of business decisions.
- *Justice-based ethics* is concerned with fairness and equity in the application of rules, laws and codes of conduct. Justice-based ethics can

perhaps be identified in CSR debates around the challenge to inter-generational equity posed by the environment-related spill-over effects of business activity.

- *Cultural relativism* maintains that the different values inherent in different cultures can only be understood relative to those cultures, and that ethical positions exist as a result of the dominant cultural influences on the way people think and act. Cultural relativists might assert that national or ethnic groupings of people are entitled to follow their own sets of cultural norms. Such circumstances can create dilemmas for business decision-makers, e.g. policies around wage setting in developing economies.
- *Postmodern ethics* recognises that a society's dominant ways of thinking influence ethical approaches but would question if it is possible for rational argument to provide acceptable solutions to all dilemmas. Bauman suggests that 'Human reality is messy and ambiguous – and so moral decisions, unlike abstract ethical principles, are ambivalent' (1993: 32).

Garriga and Melé (2004) categorise ethical approaches to CSR as normative stakeholder theory, universal rights and sustainable development. Normative stakeholder theory is distinguished from pragmatic approaches to stakeholder management, suggesting that 'a socially responsible firm requires simultaneous attention to the legitimate interests of all appropriate stakeholders ... balance[ing] a multiplicity of interests' (2004: 60) and requiring a 'normative core' of ethical principles to create such a balance. Universal human rights approaches to CSR have been significant, e.g. the UN Global Compact stipulates human rights, labour, environmental and anti-corruption principles for business. The third area, that of sustainable development, demands a values-based corporate response to the issues of intergenerational and intragenerational equity. This approach is discussed more fully in the specific entry on sustainable development.

ETHICS AND RISK

Changing community attitudes to the economic, social and environmental responsibilities of business, especially in relation to the negative externalities of its operations, can represent discernible risks to business continuity (a negative externality occurs when a firm does not pay the full cost of a decision, i.e. the costs to society are more than the cost to the consumer). It appears that acceptable responses to these shifting community expectations, e.g. responses to the GFC, may require action that is increasingly underpinned by universally acknowledged and locally relevant ethical principles.

See also: Codes of Conduct, Corporate Social Responsibility, Human Rights, Intergenerational Equity, Intragenerational Equity, Risk Management, Stakeholder Theory, Stewardship

REFERENCES

Barnard, C.I. (1938) *The Functions of the Executive*. Cambridge: Harward University Press.
Bauman, Z. (1993) *Postmodern Ethics*. Malden, MA: Blackwell.
Crane, A. and Matten, D. (2007) 'Business Ethics', in W. Visser, D. Matten, M. Pohl, and N. Tolhurst (eds), *The A To Z Of Corporate Social Responsibility*. Chichester: Wiley.
Drucker, P.F. (1954) *The Practice of Management*. New York: Harper & Row.
Garriga, E. and Melé, D. (2004) 'Corporate Social Responsibility Theories: Mapping the Territory', *Journal of Business Ethics*, 53: 51–71.
Joyner, B.E. and Payne, D. (2002) 'Evolution and Implementation: A Study of Values, Business Ethics and Corporate Social Responsibility, *Journal of Business Ethics*, 41: 297–311.
Sauser, W.I. (2005) 'Ethics in Business: Answering the Call', *Journal of Business Ethics*, 58: 345–357.
Simon, H.A. (1945) *Administrative Behavior*. New York: Macmillan.
Smith, A. (1759) *Theory of Moral Sentiments*. London: A. Millar.
Svensson, G. and Wood, G. (2007) 'A Model of Business Ethics', *Journal of Business Ethics*, 77: 303–322.
Wines, W.A. (2008) 'Seven Pillars of Business Ethics: Toward a Comprehensive Framework', *Journal of Business Ethics*, 79: 483–499.

Business Networks

VOLUNTARY NETWORKS FOR RESPONSIBILITY ASSURANCE

Prompted by increasing concern over the negative impacts of global economic activity on the health of society and the planet, voluntary networks comprising organisations from different business and other sectors have emerged that are concerned with establishing an infrastructure to progress and standardise CSR initiatives. To some extent these networks attempt to redress the absence of a global structure that could provide internationally recognised governance for CSR. Industry-specific initiatives include the chemical industry's Responsible Care and the Carbon Disclosure Project.

More generic initiatives include the World Business Council for Sustainable Development (WBCSD), which represents 200 leading companies from different industry sectors and taps into partner networks representing government and NGOs. For instance, it promotes and publicises a wide range of sustainable development initiatives that emerge from the NGO sector to business. WBCD reports focus on how business can prompt market changes that will support more sustainable forms of development – the recent *Vision 2050* report (WBCSD, 2010), for example, provides suggestions for incorporating the costs of externalities, starting with carbon, ecosystem services and water, into the structure of the marketplace; doubling agricultural output without increasing the amount of land or water used; halting deforestation and increasing yields from planted forests: promoting energy efficiency initiatives and providing universal access to low-carbon mobility. Vision 2050 was developed as a cooperative venture by 29 companies, supported by the WBCSD and a number of other external contributors such as the Global Footprint Network.

Numerous other multiple stakeholder groups have emerged in this context. Overall, their basic intent is to encourage greater transparency and more responsible behaviour on the part of corporations. According to Waddock (2008), such networks support the three elements of responsibility assurance: the development of codes of conduct and standards; verification and certification; and legitimate reporting systems.

STANDARDS, PRINCIPLES AND CODES

One of the best known of these networks associated with the development of standards, principles or codes for responsible behaviour is the Global Compact. The Global Compact is described as 'the world's largest corporate citizenship and sustainability initiative' (see www.unglobalcompact.org). Established by the UN in 2000, at the time of writing the initiative has more than 7,700 participants, including 5,300 businesses from 130 countries. It enshrines 10 principles concerning human rights, labour rights, environmental sustainability and corruption and involves a diverse range of participants including companies, governments, NGOs, labour and the UN itself.

Other standards, principles or codes include the Caux Roundtable Principles for Business that provide a measurable global standard for responsible business, the CERES principles that provide a 10-point code concerned with environmental performance, and the Equator Principles that set benchmarks for companies in the financial sector to assess social and environmental issues in project financing. Each of these standards or sets of principles has been set by organisations from different sectors working together to establish frameworks for responsible behaviour. The Global Compact also provides a scaffold for other networks designed to foster a business awareness of its social and environmental responsibilities. The Globally Responsible Leadership Initiative, for example, is a network of business schools and corporations, established under the auspices of the Global Compact.

VERIFICATION AND CERTIFICATION

The verification and certification networks include organisations such as Fair Trade, Social Accountability International and the Forest Stewardship Council (FSC). The FSC was established in 1993 as a certification system that provides standard-setting, trademark assurance and accreditation services to companies, organisations and communities interested in responsible and sustainable forestry. It is an independent organisation whose members include various environmental and social NGOs, the timber trade and the forestry profession, indigenous people's organisations, business organisations, community forestry groups and forest product certification organisations from around the world. At the time of writing, more than 135 million ha of forest worldwide are certified to FSC standards, distributed in over 80 countries. In order for a forest manager to buy FSC certification, they must abide by a set of environmental and social standards, often requiring changes in forest management practices.

The FSC certification is accepted by the leading Green Building Councils, which themselves have various certification systems. A number of countries have versions of the US LEED (Leadership in Energy and Environmental Design) programme that draws together different organisations in the building sector to provide an accreditation system for green building.

REPORTING

The most utilised example of the reporting functional network is the Global Reporting Initiative (GRI). Ceres, a coalition of investors and environmentalists, launched the GRI in 1997. Two years later, in 1999, the United Nations Environment Programme (UNEP) joined the GRI, which was separately incorporated in the Netherlands in 2002. GRI was an effort to establish standards for reporting on sustainability and other corporate social responsibility efforts and outcomes in a way that paralleled financial reporting. As of today, the GRI database included 201 reports from 106 entities using some or all of the GRI Guidelines. The list included such entities as Ben & Jerry's, General Electric, General Motors, Cinergy, Sunoco and DuPont.

Hence the GRI can be thought of as a multi-stakeholder network made up of many experts, across a number of countries worldwide, who participate in GRI's working groups and governance bodies, use the GRI Guidelines to report, or who work to contribute to develop the Reporting Framework in other ways – both formally and informally. This global network has developed a reporting framework through a consensus-seeking process with participants drawn globally from business, civil society, labour and professional institutions. It sets out indicators for each of the major sectors that can assist companies in measuring and reporting social, environmental, economic and governance performance. The Stakeholder Council of GRI is the democratically elected body that provides policy and strategy advice to the Board of Directors, helps in the selection of Directors, and has a concur/non-concur role in approving major changes in GRI's Guidance documents. The GRI allows for cross-company comparisons to be made and is now utilised by thousands of companies across the world. It is supported by a network that comprises auditors, NGOs, academics, corporations, governments, investors and labour organisations – all of whom have contributed to its development and use.

HOW EFFECTIVE ARE THE NETWORKS?

Clearly, these networks can bring about change through providing a way to leverage the capacity of business to influence market direction in a more responsible and sustainable fashion, while still securing economic benefits. In a recent survey, Cetindamar (2007) found that participation in the Global Compact was viewed positively by companies in terms of both securing network opportunities and improving corporate image. The results indicate that companies who have participated the longest and to the greatest extent as members of the Global Compact network also regard their CSR involvement as having had a strong, positive influence on their market performance. This research seems to indicate that companies obtain both ethical and economic benefits from joining the Global Compact.

Yet compared to an effective global governance system supported by democratic principles such networks present many problems and inadequacies. Waddock (2008), for example, identifies two key problems with this emergent infrastructure and its multiple stakeholder's decision-making processes. First, there is a confusing array of behaviours and principles to be assessed. Second, these networks tend to be driven by Europe and North America, raising issues concerning inclusiveness and the rights of indigenous peoples.

A further issue is that many of these arrangements do not enable closure around a means of addressing sustainability or responsible business challenges, but rather are pointed towards the more restricted goals of fostering dialogue and sharing best practices. On the positive side, as discussed in the Social Partnerships entry, such networks can be interpreted as self-regulation instruments where CSR acts as a new governance framework, and where inter-sector alliances may increasingly enable public accountability mechanisms for private actors (Albareda, 2008).

See also: *Fair Trade, Globalisation, Governance, Human Rights, Social Partnerships, Voluntary Regulation*

REFERENCES

Albareda, L. (2008) 'Corporate Responsibility, Governance and Accountability: From Self-regulation to Co-regulation', *Corporate Governance*, 8 (4): 430–439.

Cetindamar, D. (2007) 'Corporate Social Responsibility Practices and Environmentally Responsible Behavior: The Case of The United Nations Global Compact', *Journal of Business Ethics*, 76 (2): 163–176.

Waddock, S. (2008) 'Building a New Institutional Infrastructure for Corporate Responsibility', *The Academy of Management Perspectives*, 22 (3): 87–108.

World Business Council for Sustainable Development (2010) *Vision 2050: The New Agenda for Business*. Conches-Geneva and Washington, DC: World Business Council for Sustainable Development.

business networks

21

Civil Society

WHAT IS CIVIL SOCIETY?

The term 'civil society' draws historically and intellectually from a diversity of contributions and perspectives captured in the following working definition by the Centre for Civil Society (CCS) at the London School of Economics:

> Civil society refers to the arena of uncoerced action around shared interests, purposes and values. In theory, its institutional forms are distinct from those of the state, family and market, though in practice, the boundaries between ... [them] ... are often complex, blurred and negotiated. Civil society commonly embraces a diversity of spaces, actors and institutional forms, varying in their degree of formality, autonomy and power. Civil societies are often populated by organisations such as registered charities, development non-governmental organisations, community groups, women's organisations, faith-based organisations, professional associations, trades unions, self-help groups, social movements, business associations, coalitions and advocacy groups. (CCS, 2004)

Data gathered by the Index on Civil Society project supported by the World Alliance for Citizen Participation (CIVICUS) that compares civil society in 22 countries suggest that during the twentieth century there was a 200-fold increase in the number and variety of civil society organisations operating globally, with around $7 billion per year of government funding being dispersed through them (see Keane, 2003: 4–5 for details on their composition and roles).

HISTORY OF THE TERM

The term 'civil society' has been associated historically with the philosophical notion of 'the good society'. Socrates represented a good society as one in which the use of dialectically based public discourse would ensure a truthful disclosure of social issues and their resolution by civil society. Aristotle believed that the political community would flourish as an 'association of associations' that promoted citizen autonomy, allowing citizens to develop and prosper as individuals and together as a

key concepts in corporate social responsibility

22

society, and furthering the 'eudaimonia' of citizens (i.e. their happiness, virtue and wellbeing). Cicero's *societas civilis* purported to be a 'good society' in that the state, shaped by the collective voice of the citizens, promoted the wellbeing of citizens and civil peace (Edwards, 2004). Thus classical political thinkers conceptualised civil society as the inter-relationship between the state as the civil form of society and the characteristics of good citizenship manifest in its people.

Two major political philosophers offered contrasting views that helped define the relationship between the state and civil society. Hobbes believed that civil society could only persist when people were controlled by the state to limit their natural rights in a manner that did not harm others. Locke, on the other hand, regarded civil society as the overarching condition of human existence in which people led a more peaceful and fruitful life in the state of nature. This 'lesser' level of state administration derived its legitimacy from the people. In other words, for Locke 'the 'civility' in social life was prior to the birth of the state ... Locke advocated the primacy of society over the state' (CCS, 2004: 3).

In the nineteenth century, Hegel redefined civil society 'as a realm that was separate from the family ... and from the state ... view[ing] ... civil society not [only] as a sphere of instrumental needs and wants, but also of human and social recognition' (Hurrell, 2007: 100). Marx argued that civil society constituted the 'substructure' of society where productive forces and social relations came together in social formations, whereas political society was the 'superstructure'. In the capitalist state, both the state and civil society represented the interests of the dominant class, i.e. the bourgeoisie. Gramsci's view differed from that of Marx in that he saw civil society as being embedded in the political superstructure, constituting the seat of cultural and ideological capital that contributed to the hegemony of capitalism (Ehrenberg, 1999). The political superstructure was a political space in which both the state and the market could be challenged by the people. Consequently, from the 1990s onwards the term 'civil society' was often used to identify a position for opposing Communist and authoritarian regimes. This position was aligned with the post-modernist approach to deconstructing political action by using the term 'civil society' rather than that of 'political society'. The CCS (2004) notes that in the 1990s, the emergence of NGOs and new social movements led to the conceptualisation of civil society as a third sector which was a platform for activities aimed at creating an alternative social and world order.

civil society

23

CIVIL SOCIETY AND DEMOCRACY

Alexis de Tocqueville, the nineteenth-century philosopher, contributed significantly to the identification and critique of the relationship between civil society and liberal democratic politics. More recently, Almond and Verba (1989), noting the critical role of political culture in the democratic process, argued that activities around voluntary organisations produced more empowered and informed citizens whose political awareness and potential contribution to political agendas were enhanced by their engagement in cross-sectoral activities in civil society.

Cardoso reminds us that, theoretically and practically, 'democracy' has been a national construction and that '[t]he patterns of relationship between State and civil society ... vary hugely from country to country. In some the question is not even present at the national agenda' (2003: 4), i.e. in those situations civil society organisations have no legitimate external mandate. He concludes that '[t]he power of civil society is a soft one. It is their capacity to argue, to propose, to experiment, to denounce, to be exemplary ... not ... to decide' (2003: 4).

GLOBAL CIVIL SOCIETY

It has been said that the 'resurrection' of civil society occurred as part of the 'democratisation' movements that took place in the 1970s and 1980s (Hurrell, 2007). Specifically, in relation to 'global civil society', Keane explains that this neologism emerged in the 1990s as a result of overlapping concerns associated with:

> the military crushing of the Prague Spring; a heightening appreciation of the revolutionary effects of the new galaxy of satellite/computer-mediated communications ... ; the new awareness, stimulated by the peace and ecological movements, of ourselves as members of a fragile and potentially self-destructive world system; the widespread perception that the implosion of Soviet-type communist systems implied a new global political order; the world-wide growth spurt of neo-liberal economics and market capitalist economies; the disillusionment with the broken and unfulfilled promises of post-colonial states; and the rising concern about the dangerous and misery-producing vacuums opened up by the collapse of empires and states and the outbreak of uncivil wars. (2003: 1–2)

Against this background, the UN established a High-Level Panel on UN-Civil Society in 2003. The Panel's paper on *Civil Society and Global*

key concepts in corporate social responsibility

Governance identifies the importance and influence of civil society in the management of global change, recognising that 'global governance ... is a highly contested process where the space for political action by states and non-state actors is greatly extended' (Cardoso, 2003: 1). Given the increasing complexity of the challenges of global governance and concern for the wellbeing of future generations, Cardoso suggests that 'greater consistency and coherence must be introduced into the rules of engagement with civil society' (2003: 7) if civil society is to influence the various approaches and processes associated with the different forms of global governance.

CRITIQUE OF THE TERM

Critics have commented on the ambiguity of the term 'civil society', and more recently 'global civil society'. Cardoso (2003: 3) warns against failing to recognise the significance of internal divisions in civil society, in that certain community groups may support and advocate for causes that are not compatible with universally accepted principles and values.

Edwards (2004) agrees that the term is problematic when used to represent so many and often contradictory stances. He attempts to deconstruct what he calls the 'civil society puzzle' or the confused dialogues around civil society by exploring:

- civil society and voluntary associations as the 'gene carriers' of the good society, bearing in mind that that many good values are developed elsewhere through the family, the educational system, the workplace, etc.
- how civil society sees the contributions of voluntary associations in a broader context by acknowledging the need for coordinated action with other institutions, i.e. aligning the contributions of government, business and citizens.
- how civil society supports the 'public' as a whole polity that cares about the common good, deliberates about it democratically, and facilitates reform across interested parties or stakeholders (Edwards, 2005).

CIVIL SOCIETY AND CSR

So what might business corporations take away from this debate on global civil society? The *school of social capital* (Putnam, 2000) provides support for maximising associational and volunteering activity with the broader community. The *comparative associational school* (Skocpol, 2003) sees value in the broadening of community associations so that they can better enter into a policy dialogue with government. Both of these perspectives can inform debates on the shifting role of business as part of global civil society, e.g. in relation to the reduction of world poverty and carbon pollution.

Edwards (2004) recommends that a civil society ought to go further by promoting an active citizenry around issues that highlight and address forms of social inequality. He also suggests an area of focus on associational life might identify the increasing challenges people face in playing an active part in civil society (many resulting from a less supportive social infrastructure). This provides an opportunity for corporations, as part of their CSR, to support their employees and other stakeholders in their pursuit of active citizenry.

The 2008 meeting of the World Economic Forum (WEF) closed with an appeal to leaders in business, government and civil society to develop a 'new brand' of collaborative and innovative association to address globalisation challenges including climate change and water conservation. At the WEF in 2009 the global financial crisis gave a new sense of relevance and urgency to this appeal for new forms of collaborative action in the realm of global civil society to inform global and national policy.

See also: Community Relations, Corporate Citizenship, Social Capital, Social Partnerships

REFERENCES

Almond, G. and Verba, S. (1989) *The Civic Culture: Political Attitudes and Democracy in Five Nations.* London: Sage.

Cardoso, F.H. (2003) *Civil Society and Global Governance. High-Level Panel on UN-Civil Society.* Available at www.un.org/reform/civilsociety/cardosopaper.shtml, accessed 2 May 2010.

Centre for Civil Society (2004) *What is Civil Society?* Available at http://w.lse.ac.uk/collections/CCS/what_is_civil_society.htm, accessed 2 May 2010.

Edwards, M. (2004) *Civil Society.* Cambridge: Polity.

Edwards, M. (2005) *Civil Society, the Encyclopaedia of Informal Education.* Available at www.infed.org/association/civil_society.htm, accessed 2 May 2010.

Ehrenberg, J. (1999) *Civil Society: The Critical History of an Idea.* New York: New York University Press.

Hurrell, A. (2007) *On Global Order: Power, Values and the Constitution of International Society.* Oxford: Oxford University Press.

Keane, J. (2003) *Global Civil Society?* Cambridge: Cambridge University Press.

Putnam, R.D. (2000) *Bowling Alone: The Collapse and Revival of American Community.* New York: Simon and Schuster.

Skocpol, T. (2003) *Diminished Democracy: From Membership to Management in American Civic Life.* Norman, OK: University of Oklahoma Press.

Codes of Conduct

TYPES OF CODES OF CONDUCT

Codes of conduct are statements of the required behaviours and responsibilities of members of an organisation or association that contribute to the welfare of its stakeholders. They usually focus on ethical or socially responsible issues and are an example of the self-regulation of industry.

Codes of conduct are but one example of the many types of codes operating at the corporate level – others include the business code of practice and business principles. The particular benefit of this form of code is that it articulates the norms and values of the organisation, differing from mission statements which focus on the aspirations and goals of the organisation or association (Stevens, 2008).

The rapid expansion of the numbers of these codes has been linked to the impact of globalisation on industry standards. Bondy et al. (2007) argue that higher levels of public scrutiny are pushing multinationals to self-regulate in association with high levels of global competition where governments may hesitate to impose stricter environmental and social standards. NGO pressures, along with support from some governments, have resulted in numerous codes of conduct emerging since the mid-1990s, in line with an increasing interest in CSR.

Codes may be voluntary or mandatory. Codes such as the Responsible Care code are mandated by the various chemicals industry associations on their members, yet are voluntary in that they are not set by government regulation. Groups of NGOs also often require their members to sign a code.

Codes of conduct for suppliers are useful in setting down explicit and transparent guidelines in order to manage the relationship between

codes of conduct

corporation and supplier. They define the rules of conduct towards clients, stakeholders, suppliers, advisors and the public. For example, Westpac Banking Corporation, a leading bank as measured by sustainability and CSR indices, has a Sustainable Supply Chain Code that aims to ensure that:

> suppliers are aware of the specific environmental, social and ethical issues and risks and opportunities of relevance to their operations and products, that they have management systems in place to address these issues, risks and opportunities, and that these systems are delivering effective performance management and improvement. (The Westpac Group, 2010)

Recently developed codes of conduct include the Principles of Responsible Investment, promoting socially responsible investing. There are many individual codes of conduct developed by particular corporations (such as Nike) or associations (such as the International Federation of Accountants). Codes can be classified according to the author, their content, or their intent. Table 1, adapted from Bondy et al. (2007), gives examples of codes according to this classification system.

CODE EFFECTIVENESS AND CSR

The debate around codes of conduct hinges on the fact that many codes are developed by the corporation itself, and are vaguely defined and not externally audited or checked in any way. They are criticised as mere window dressing, and as meaningless in comparison with sector rules or laws. On the positive side, they can offer a way for companies to manage their moral responsibilities. Overall, research to date shows that a code is meaningless unless it is integrated into a stakeholder management culture developed in consultation with those on whom it will impact. This can be problematic given the global supply chain. Apple Inc., for example, recently acknowledged that it was finding it difficult for foreign contractors to take its code of labour rights seriously. In another case, TESCO, which has a code of conduct with specific provisions around environmental protection, has recently been named as complicit in environmental damage caused by the palm oil industry. The WWF has recently disclosed that TESCO was one of a number of leading companies that had not bought any oil certified sustainable by the Roundtable on Sustainable Palm Oil – which sets environmental standards for the

Table 1 Categories of codes of conduct

Code types	Example of criteria used	Real world example of codes
Author organisation	Company Industry association Model (acts as an example – created by variety or organisations) Inter-governmental Multi-stakeholder (negotiated between numerous stakeholders)	Nike Code of Conduct Responsible Care (chemical industry) International Code of Ethics for Canadian Business OECD Guidelines for Multinational Enterprises CERES Principles
Content	Regulatory Philosophical Social responsibilities Management philosophy High road (aspirational)/ Low road (rules of behaviour)	Vodafone Code of Ethics Global Compact (quasi-code) Social Venture Network Standards of Corporate Responsibility Nike Code of Conduct Global Sullivan Principles/ Glaxosmithkline Code of Conduct
Code function	Guide or restrict corporate behaviour Influence other actors/ carry out self-regulation Operational or subscription	Virtually all codes Ethical Trade Initiative Base Code Social Venture Network Standards of Corporate Responsibility

Source: Adapted from Bondy, K. Matten, D. and Moon, J. 'Codes of Conduct as a Tool for Sustainable Governance in MNCs', in Benn, S. and Dunphy, D. (eds), *Corporate Governance and Sustainability*, London and New York: Routledge, 2007, pp. 167. Reprinted with permission.

£16bn-a-year industry, the most important being a ban on planting new oil palms in virgin forests (Hickman, 2009).

Such findings highlight the wide-ranging debate on the effectiveness of codes of conduct as a means of implementing or encouraging CSR within organisations. A web-based study of 150 organizations across three different countries found that the motivations for taking up the code have little to do with CSR, but are more likely to be adopted for reputational or other business reasons (Bondy et al., 2008). This research shows that codes are more useful as a means of ensuring compliance and appropriate employee behaviour rather than as an implementation tool for CSR.

codes of conduct

CODES OF CONDUCT AND EMPLOYEE BEHAVIOUR

While there are concerns about the ability of voluntary codes to ensure responsible corporate behaviour, as shown by the passing of the US Sarbanes-Oxley Act requiring increased disclosure of information to improve accountability and transparency, there is some recent evidence that voluntary initiatives such as codes do have an impact (Stevens, 2008). Codes can moderate employee behaviour if certain parameters are in place, such as being identifiably embedded in organisational systems and practices. Enron illustrates that an organisation can have a code of conduct yet be highly irregular in its conduct as a result of a culture that is risk-taking and aggressive. Codes are effective if the organisational culture is cooperative and supportive of the norms and values it enshrines and also if it is embraced by supervisors, managers and leaders. Recent research indicates the importance of an employee taking ownership of the code through a full understanding of how the code relates to their own role in the organisation.

The question is raised, however, as to how much the code of conduct enforces particular sets of behaviour, norms and values. The limitations of codes relate to their lack of accountability provisions, such as sanctions and measurement specifications, and whether they are either very general and thus meaningless or very targeted, such as those developed by the Ethical Trading Initiative, which deals only with labour issues (Bondy et al., 2007).

THE EXAMPLE OF COFFEE: COMMON CODE FOR THE COFFEE COMMUNITY (4C)

The example of the coffee industry highlights the potential CSR benefits of industry-wide codes, as compared to codes for specific organisations. Coffee is grown in developing countries but consumed in the West. Smallholders are suggested to supply 70 per cent of the world's coffee, while much of the buying is done by large multinationals. During the 1990s the coffee market became more and more a buyer-driven commodity chain. Producer incomes dropped while consumer spending on coffee increased.

As a code, the Common Code for the Coffee Community (4C) is unusual because its participative decision-making processes involve a tripartite structure consisting of coffee producers, the coffee trade and industry, and civil society organisations. This structure has the potential to lead to a shared recognition of the coffee industry problem (Kolk, 2005). The 4C code was drawn up with participation from representatives from public and private sectors, coffee producers and NGOs such as OXFAM, with the support of the German Federal Ministry for Economic Cooperation and Development (BMZ). The 4C aims to enable coffee producers to increase their income by means of a range of organisational methods. The code also aims to exclude unacceptable social, environmental and economic practices. While it may act as a model for future developments, current performance shows it holds only 4 per cent of the world's coffee, suggesting that the impact of this code is still limited.

See also: *Fair Trade, Socially Responsible Investment, Voluntary Regulation*

REFERENCES

Bondy, K., Matten, D. and Moon, J. (2007) 'Codes of Conduct as a Tool for Sustainable governance in MNCs', in S. Benn and D. Dunphy (eds), *Corporate Governance and Sustainability*. London and New York: Routledge, pp. 165–186.

Bondy, K., Matten, D. and Moon, J. (2008) 'Multinational Corporation Codes of Conduct: Governance Tools for Corporate Social Responsibility?', *Corporate Governance*, 16 (4): 294–311.

Hickman, M. (2009) 'The Palm Oil Scandal: Boots and Waitrose Named and Shamed', *The Independent*, 28 October.

Kolk, A. (2005) 'CSR in the Coffee Sector: the Dynamics of MNC Responses and Code Development', *European Management Journal*, 23 (2): 228–236.

Stevens, B. (2008) 'Corporate Ethical Codes: Effective Instruments for Influencing Behavior', *Journal of Business Ethics*, 78: 601–609.

Westpac Group, The (2010) 'Sustainable Supply Chain Management'. Available at www.westpac.com.au/docs/pdf/aw/SSCMFAQ.pdf, accessed 31 March 2010.

Community Relations

COMMUNITY IN A GLOBALISED WORLD

The origin of the term 'community' is the Latin word *munus* which describes, amongst other things, the principles of service, office and duty.

Communitas, a broader Latin term for 'fellowship' or 'organised society', suggests that these services are delivered by a group that embraces various levels of intent, shared values and needs, resources and levels of risk. In a globalised world, supported by online communications, these communities can exist across national boundaries, regions and sectors, and are increasingly supported by complex networks of groups and partnerships directed towards shared and often transient goals.

Corporations operating internationally and globally extend their influence into the community as a matter of course, by playing a role in community development that is broader than their business function. This has led to questions about the extent of social responsibility that might be expected from a corporation, e.g. how might direct foreign investment by corporations be channelled to support, or at times lead, community relations programmes or other forms of aid invested in the community (Goddard, 2005)? This latter approach reflects a shift away from government and community-based efforts promoting human rights and ethics in corporations, towards the involvement of corporations in tri-sectoral partnerships (government, corporate and community) aimed at achieving shared development targets. Corporations might achieve this by 'weav[ing] their expert knowledge base, economies of scale, and community relations function into the rich solutions for community development' (2005: 270).

FROM PHILANTHROPIC TO STRATEGIC CORPORATE INITIATIVES

Carroll and Buchholtz (2006) note that business philanthropic activities are both discretionary and voluntary. These have evolved significantly in response to community expectations of business. Corporate responses to social emergencies or needs have tended to shift corporations towards a more strategic involvement in communities through corporate strategic initiatives (CSIs). However, Hess et al. suggest that CSIs 'are more commonly associated with corporate strategy than community relations' (2002: 110). They note that many corporations are becoming key providers of aid to communities in need, often associated with their core business. This might include transport services to support aid agencies (e.g. United Parcel Services), Intel's provision of technology and teachers to school students in the Philippines, or MacDonald's commitment to developing entry-level employees to build up human capital in local communities.

These initiatives deliver advantages to corporations (Hess et al., 2002) by using CSIs to gain a significant competitive advantage in the process of trialling new products and services in new markets, and by enhancing their reputation by acknowledging and responding to concerns around public morality embedded in consumer preferences, particularly in international markets. In addition, an involvement in CSIs can also provide the opportunity to demonstrate a comparative advantage over the public sector (including NGOs and not-for-profits) through the delivery of products and services that are core to their capabilities.

PARTNERSHIPS TOWARDS SUSTAINABLE COMMUNITIES

Given that there appears to be clear rationales for benefits for the private sector, how might these multi-sectoral partnerships work to promote specific goals at a community level? In other words, what might be the nature of the interactions between government, business and community in developing more sustainable communities?

At the Earth Summit of the United Nations Conference on Environment and Development (UNCED) in Rio de Janeiro in 1992, world leaders adopted a global action plan for sustainability, known as Agenda 21. It called on all countries to develop a plan of action for sustainability, with the latter term defined as: 'Development today must not undermine the development and environment needs of present and future generations'. The Local Agenda 21 (LA21), which constitutes Chapter 28 of the Agenda 21 document, embraces this definition and directs local governments to adopt and adapt plans of action around their responsibilities for planning, developing and maintaining an economic, social and environmental infrastructure. Chapter 30 of Agenda 21 is concerned with strengthening the role of business. It suggests programme areas for business, such as promoting cleaner production and responsible entrepreneurship. Chapter 30 also focuses on government's role in educating and supporting business to carry out this brief.

This approach has stimulated many national and global government initiatives, including regulatory measures, and economic incentives and has streamlined administrative processes towards this end. The International Council for Local Environmental Initiatives (ICLEI), an international body representing local authorities, drafted the LA21 chapter and coordinates the international LA21 campaign. A 2002 survey found that more than 6,400 local governments in 113 countries had become involved in LA21 activities over a 10-year period.

More recently the focus has been around the contributions of different partners from government, industry and other community players to work collaboratively from their individual strengths to optimise sustainable development at the community level. (More detail is provided on these social partnerships in the specific entry on that topic.)

HOW MIGHT THESE PARTNERSHIPS WORK?

Davies provided a useful insight into this question. By drawing from the example of environmental governance for sustainable development in the UK, she noted that

> multi-sector partnerships, despite their inherent slipperiness in terms of definition, distinction and containment are seen as an important mechanism whereby sustainable development can be operationalised and in particular local governance structures can be strengthened. (2002: 190)

Davies adapted actor network theory (ANT) to analyse sustainable community partnerships supporting Going for Green (GfG) projects in Huntingdonshire in the mid-to late-90s. A key concern was whether such partnerships allowed the redistribution of power to broader local groups. Davies' findings suggested that major challenges existed, and these were worth consideration in the quest for sustainable community partnerships. Specifically, she noted that multi-sectoral partnerships did not operate in a governance vacuum and that other top-down institutional interests could impose barriers and boundaries on partnership innovation. Another finding was that partnerships needed to innovate, but to do so they required a clear understanding of aims and objectives, together with agreed norms underpinning group expectations. These developments took time, and sometimes the timeframes for grants inhibited a sustained commitment to projects.

Some case studies, such as the Magadi Soda Company in Magadi, Kenya (Muthuri, 2007), illustrate a shift in corporation philosophy and stance on CSR from a philanthropic approach to one which champions a participatory and interactive community development process. Muthuri presented a model of multi-sector collaboration of possible interest to other corporations wanting to contribute to their local communities through helping to address poverty and development challenges.

HOW MIGHT CONTRIBUTIONS BE EVALUATED?

Use of multi-sector partnerships in community development poses questions about how we might evaluate progress towards a more sustainable society through indicators around social, environmental and economic goals. Although there has been prolific activity in the last decade towards such ends, many say that there is little to show from such energy. Reed et al. (2006) reflect the concerns of Davies (2002) noted above about the challenge of top-down interpretations of sustainability informing many existing indicators, an example being the Environmental Sustainability Index (ESI) developed by American academics. They argue that this runs contrary to the intention of LA21 'that puts local involvement at the front of any planning process and challenges policy makers to allow local communities to define sustainability for themselves' (Reed et al., 2006: 407).

Hess et al. (2002) suggest that CSIs require a better organisational measurement of the effectiveness of social initiatives within the broader community, noting that such bodies as the Council on Foundations and the London Benchmarking Group are working on indicators that will inform both organisational stakeholders and local communities about these outcomes. Acknowledging local community groups as stakeholders seeking meaningful influence and involvement in the setting of goals and outcomes for CSI initiatives might be a fruitful starting point for business.

CONCLUSION

As a result of globalisation strategies, the capability of governments to resolve social and economic problems is being challenged, raising the question as to whether a more effective (and perhaps unavoidable) strategy is to involve business as a player in community-wide solutions for more sustainable development. Such a solution might influence the organisational cultures of industry players by making them more aware of the local impacts of their economic activity and the consequences for sustainable development. In addition, the skill-sets acquired by corporations in championing broader strategic projects built on multi-sector collaboration will add to their own social capital resources as well as to those of the community. The local community would also appear to benefit from the efforts of businesses to redress some of the existing imbalances in current models of community relations, especially those concerning the identification of agendas around sustainable communities.

See also: Corporate Citizenship, NGOs, Social Capital, Social Partnerships, Sustainable Development

REFERENCES

Agenda 21: Earth Summit – The United Nations Programme of Action from Rio. Geneva: United Nations.

Carroll, A.B. and Buchholtz, A.K. (2006) *Business and Society: Ethics and Stakeholder Management.* Mason, OH: Thomson South-Western.

Davies, A.R. (2002) 'Power, Politics and Networks: Shaping Partnerships for Sustainable Communities', *Area*, 34 (2): 190–203.

Goddard, T. (2005) 'Corporate Citizenship and Community Relations: Contributing to the Challenges of Aid Discourse', *Business and Society Review*, 110 (3): 269–296.

Hess, D., Rogovsky, N. and Dunfee, T.W. (2002) 'The Next Wave of Corporate Community Involvement: Corporate Social Initiatives', *California Management Review*, 44 (2): 110–125.

Muthuri, J.N. (2007) 'Corporate Citizenship and Sustainable Community Development: Fostering Multi-Sector Collaboration in Magadi Division in Kenya', *The Journal of Corporate Citizenship*, 28: 73–84.

Reed, M.S., Fraser, E.D.G. and Dougill, A.J. (2006) 'An Adaptive Learning Process for Developing and Applying Sustainability Indicators with Local Communities', *Ecological Economics*, 59: 406–418.

Complexity Theory

CHANGE AND COMPLEXITY

The pace of change affecting corporations is increasing rapidly partly due to globalisation, technological innovation, growing community awareness of a corporation's societal impacts and shifting community standards concerning corporate social responsibility. Organisational dynamics in response to these conditions are complex. Many researchers purport that in such environments top-down control is becoming less effective and that new systemically oriented approaches that recognise the complexity of interactions between individuals and stakeholder groups are required. It has been suggested that complexity theories, including Chaos Theory, Dissipative Structures, Complex Adaptive Systems and Complex Responsive Processes, provide models of complex interactions and reactions that create order in dynamically changing environments. Some have suggested that these models are useful in conceptualising organisational change and related leadership issues.

WHAT ARE COMPLEXITY THEORIES?

Complexity theories have arisen from the study of the behaviour of complex natural living systems. Burnes (2005) has summarised the literature on complexity theories and its application to organisational change. He defines complexity theories as those

> concerned with the emergence of order in dynamic non-linear systems operating at the edge of chaos: in other words, systems which are constantly changing and where the laws of cause and effect appear not to apply ... Order in such systems is seen as manifesting itself in a largely unpredictable fashion, in which patterns of behaviour emerge in irregular but similar forms through a process of self-organisation, which is governed by a small number of simple order-generating rules. (2005: 77)

The dynamic, non-linear nature of interaction within natural systems means that the outcomes of actions are unpredictable, order being created at the 'edge of chaos' or 'far from equilibrium' through the operation of a set of simple order-generating rules. An often quoted example is Reynolds' (1987) model replicating the flocking behaviour of birds through adherence to simple order generating rules of interaction. Examples of complexity theories that have helped shape the debate about complexity, management and leadership include the following.

Chaos theory

Lorenz (1993) describes chaotic systems as dynamic systems of interdependent entities or elements connected in non-linear ways that are constantly and irreversibly transforming themselves. They are very sensitive

complexity theory

to initial conditions. For example, a small change in the initial condition of the weather system in one part of the world has the potential to set off a chain of amplifying events eventually leading to a very large weather event, prompting Lorenz (1993) to ask the now widely recognised question 'Does the flap of a butterfly's wings in Brazil set off a tornado in Texas?'. Lorenz found that chaotic systems were not subject to the conventional laws of cause and effect. Rather, the effects of small events were amplified by chaos, thus 'causing the instability necessary to transform an existing pattern of behaviour into a new, more appropriate one' (Burnes, 2005: 78). This model has been seen as representing certain developments, processes and mindsets that can occur in intense and complex organisational change environments with largely unpredictable risks.

Stacey notes limitations on the application of chaos theory to organisations, arguing that it 'cannot be directly applied to human action … [and] … cannot offer analogies for human action' (2003: 302). This is because the so-called 'chaotic' systems are at some level ordered, in that they produce a predetermined outcome. They therefore do not fully represent what happens in systems that experience various forms of human freedom and choice.

Dissipative structures

Nobel Prize winner Ilya Prigogine (1980) found that under appropriate conditions certain living systems maintained their high level of organised complexity 'far from the state of equilibrium'. For example, certain natural phenomena pass through states of randomness and instability to reach critical points at which they 'bifurcate' or spontaneously change into a new structure or behaviour that could not have been predicted from knowledge of the previous state. 'Convection' is an example of a dissipative structure: as heat is applied to liquid, molecules move from random order to a new structure in which the molecules move in a regular direction setting up hexagonal cells (steam) constituting a 'dissipative structure' that could not be predicted from its prior random state but is determined by its own internal dynamic.

Some writers have suggested that the characteristics of dissipative structures and chaos theory may help conceptualise an organisation's response to overwhelmingly complex environmental conditions operating in new ways through transformations and metamorphoses (Leifer, 1989).

Complex adaptive systems

An example of how complexity theories have contributed to an understanding of organisational dynamics is reflected in complex adaptive systems (CAS) theory. Olson and Eoyang (2001: 7) suggest that in CAS order emerges, as opposed to being determined through hierarchy. Occurrences within CAS are irreversible and its future is unpredictable. Agents (the basic building blocks of CAS) are semi-autonomous units or individual players, groups or systems that seek to maximise their fitness of purpose within CAS through emerging, adapting or evolving over time.

Whilst chaos theory and dissipative structures theory seek to explain the behaviour of *whole* systems or populations through mathematical modelling, CAS theory 'attempts to model the same phenomena ... using an agent based approach ... [which] ... seeks to formulate rules of interaction for the [*largely autonomous*] individual entities making up a system or population as a whole' (Burnes, 2005: 79). Advocates of CAS believe that the most effective processes for change exist at the 'micro' level, purporting that large-scale change occurs through the integration of changes that emerge from the interactions within and the evolution of small groups.

Complex Responsive Processes

Stacey (2003) contends that 'process thinking' (as opposed to systems thinking) is more congruent with the open-endedness and unpredictability of human interaction. The notions of system 'wholes' and system 'boundaries', typical of systems thinking, are absent from 'complex responsive processes'. Iterative exchanges between people produce emerging patterns of interaction that eventually amplify differences of human behaviour and cognition into novelty. In complex responsive processes, participation does not mean participating in a system or 'whole' but rather directly interacting with people in local situations occurring in the present.

IMPLICATIONS OF COMPLEXITY THEORIES FOR ORGANISATIONS AND FOR CSR

Complexity theories have been seen as useful by some commentators (Burnes, 2005) as metaphorical devices for creating new insights into managing change by illustrating that:

- creativity, growth and self-organisation may be optimal when a complex system operates at the 'edge of chaos', employing simple order generating rules
- a self-organising process expedites continual reorganisation, often manifest in rapid new product or service development and increased efficiency
- cause-effect, top-down, command and control styles of management are less effective in constantly changing environments
- managing continuous change requires a deployment of democratic principles (i.e. the freedom to self-organise) and influence at a local level.

These features of complexity theories perhaps offer insights into ways of achieving ordered and creative CSR responses within complex and dynamic interfaces between business, society and the natural environment.

IMPLICATIONS FOR LEADERSHIP IN COMPLEX ENVIRONMENTS

Stacey and Griffin (2005) specifically consider the implications of complexity for leadership. They note that in complexity, local leadership emerges. Leaders are required to interact skilfully with others in influential ways to transform values and norms of groups in context, needing enhanced sensitivity to potentially negative forces in teams that are dealing with ambiguity and change. Leaders might offer support in complexity by articulating emerging themes and sense-making the way forward. Other relevant attributes drawn from Stacey and Griffin and other commentators include: a high capacity for empathy; emotional awareness of group dynamics; a capacity to think both rationally and intuitively; a capacity for spontaneity, imagination and reflection; a sensitivity to the dynamics of inclusion and exclusion in the process of creating social capital; a tolerance for high levels of anxiety and uncertainty; and a capacity to apply ethical judgements in new and ambiguous situations. Stacey and Griffin suggest that this approach contrasts with more traditional models of leadership in which the leader as a change agent stands outside the system, designing and manipulating inputs and using power to stay in control.

See also: Responsible Leadership, Stakeholder Theory, Systems Approaches

REFERENCES

Burnes, B. (2005) 'Complexity Theories and Organizational Change', *International Journal of Management Reviews*, 7 (2): 73–90.

Leifer, R. (1989) 'Understanding Organizational Transformation Using a Dissipative Structure Model', *Human Relations*, 42 (10): 899–916.

Lorenz, E. (1993) *The Essence of Chaos*. London: UCL Press.

Olson, E.E. and Eoyang, G.H. (2001) *Facilitating Organization Change: Lessons from Complexity Science*. San Francisco, CA: Jossey-Bass Pfeiffer.

Prigogine, I. (1980) *From Being to Becoming*. San Francisco, CA: Freeman.

Reynolds, C.W. (1987) 'Flocks, Herds and Schools: A Distributed Behaviour Model', Proceedings of the SIG-GRAPH '87', *Computer Graphics*, 21 (4): 25–34.

Stacey, R. (2003) *Strategic Management and Organizational Dynamics: The Challenge of Complexity*, 4th edn. Harlow: Pearson Education.

Stacey, R. and Griffin, D. (2005) 'Leading in a Complex World', in Griffin, D. and Stacey, R. (eds), *Complexity and the Experience of Leading Organizations*. London: Routledge.

Corporate Accountability

WHAT IS ACCOUNTABILITY?

'Accountability' is a diffuse and somewhat murky term. Not only does it have many definitions but it also raises the contentious issue of to whom an account is to be made out, to society in general or to the shareholders? Counter to the traditional view that corporations are only responsible to their shareholders and the market should be the ultimate source of control, more recent interpretations are that accountability is due to a range of stakeholders. CSR and corporate citizenship are often described as a way of increasing corporate accountability as they are based on an understanding that corporations are responsible to society as well as to their shareholders. On the other hand, critics of the voluntary and discretionary nature of CSR see corporate accountability supported by regulation as the only viable means of ensuring responsible corporate behaviour.

Drawing from the literature on political accountability, corporate accountability can be defined as 'corporate control; that is, the establishment of clear means for sanctioning failure' (Valor, 2005: 196). Luo gives a more expansive definition:

> Corporate accountability is the extent to which a company is transparent in its corporate activities and responsive to those it services. Broadly, corporate accountability consists of (1) financial reporting accountability and (2) strategic decision transparency. Accountability is essentially a matter of disclosure, transparency, and of explaining corporate policies and actions to those whom the company is beholden. (2005: 12)

The evident escalation in corporate power and influence combined with a series of corporate scandals, including Enron, WorldCom, AOL/Time Warner, Adelphia, Citigroup, Dynegy, Global Crossing, IMClone and Tyco, have resulted in an escalation of calls for more corporate accountability for the social and environmental costs of operations and to ensure the separation of accounting and consulting practices. Increasing pressure for more corporate accountability has been exerted by consumer activism (as described in the entry on Ethical Consumerism), the social and ethical investment movement and through the work of NGOs such as Transparency International. The passing of legislation such as the US Sarbanes-Oxley Act of 2002 builds more corporate accountability into the US law by specifying what records companies must keep and for how long. Most importantly, it may act as a source of influence upon the governments of other countries. It signifies recognition by the legislature of a leading economy of the importance of protecting shareholders and the general public from the potentially fraudulent activities of business operators and their advisers.

THE EMERGENCE OF THE CORPORATE ACCOUNTABILITY MOVEMENT

The corporate accountability movement that emerged at the end of the 1990s was and still is one of the most influential social movements of recent times. CSR, corporate citizenship and corporate sustainability are linked to this shift because they are associated with new voluntary or regulatory enforcement mechanisms regarding corporate practices. The focus now is on how civil society can work with the corporate world in developing a series of co-regulatory arrangements. As described in other entries such as Business Networks, these can be through global networks such as the Global Reporting Initiative (GRI) and the Global Compact, or through public private partnerships between business and NGOs such as the Forest Stewardship Council (FSC), or by interfirm collaborations such as the World Business Council for Sustainable Development (WBCSD) (Albareda, 2008). However, such mechanisms do have limitations given the dependence of many NGOs on these partnerships for their survival, and the still low level of support coming from consumer groups in terms of higher environmental or social product standards.

RELATIONSHIP BETWEEN CORPORATE GOVERNANCE AND ACCOUNTABILITY

Accountability is closely linked to corporate governance, i.e. the system by which the organisation is directed and controlled. Corporate governance involves corporate fairness, transparency and accountability. As an aspect of corporate governance, accountability is seen in terms of answerability and responsibility and underpinned by inclusivity – that is, responsibility to all stakeholder groups. Hence corporate governance and corporate accountability can be thought of as interdependent and integral to each other.

Multinational organisations provide many accountability and governance challenges. They include managing direction and control across different national contexts and working with a mix of legislative and voluntary mechanisms. In the USA for instance, in the aftermath of so many corporate scandals, there have been calls for US corporations to adhere to US legislation on labour and environmental laws when operating overseas (see www.corpwatch.org/article.php?id=4668).

Capital markets are now incorporating these concepts of wider social accountability through the use of such tools as socially responsible investment and various social indices. This has increased transparency and therefore accountability, although how to obtain full disclosure remains a problem. For this reason, a number of commentators continue to argue that accountability is a governmental concern, and in some countries accountability to the wider society is enshrined in corporate law. An example would be legislation that requires managers to take citizens' views into account in their decision making. The business case underlying this argument is that citizen consultation can be a valuable source of new ideas as well as generating trust.

FOSTERING ACCOUNTABILITY

The increasing demand for transparency in corporations' reports in regard to social and environmental impacts is a result of the increased pressure on organisations to be accountable for their actions. Reporting is a mechanism that should foster corporate accountability, but unless it is associated with a means for facilitating action by organisational stakeholders it is not going to result in more accountability (Cooper and Owen, 2007). Nor is accountability something that can just be taught as a formal training module, for instance as a course in an MBA degree; rather, it needs to be incorporated through a multifaceted lens that integrates formal, informal, objective, and subjective–interpretive aspects of accountability. In this way, accountability is more likely to become an aspect of the employee's 'felt' or subjective experience, alongside formal performance appraisal systems, finance and accounting systems, and rules and regulations. In that sense, accountability is an aspect of the wider agenda of fostering ethical behaviour in organisations. Researchers argue that this is dependent upon participative dialogue and discourse and the fostering of a culture that supports open questioning (Rhodes et al., 2009). Overall, as with the other multiple stakeholder processes described in the entry on Business Networks, progressing accountability depends on the extent to which the organisation employs transparent and democratic mechanisms of engagement, decision making, monitoring and evaluation.

ACCOUNTABILITY STANDARDS

Because the definition of accountability is so diffuse, standardisation involving the setting of reference points around which accountability performance can be evaluated is critical to embedding it meaningfully in corporate behaviour. AccountAbility (the Institute of Social and Ethical AccountAbility) is an international NGO established in 1996 by corporate businesses whose members promote accountability in pursuit of sustainable development. AccountAbility's AA 1000 series are principles-based standards for helping organisations become more accountable, responsible and sustainable. These standards are the AA 1000 AccountAbility Principles Standard (2008) (AA 1000APS), the AA 1000 Assurance Standard (2008) (AA 1000AS) and the AA 1000

Stakeholder Engagement Standard (2005) (AA 1000SES). The Principles Standard refers to The Foundation Principle of Inclusivity, The Principle of Materiality and The Principle of Responsiveness. The Assurance Standard is used to provide assurance on publicly available sustainability information, particularly CSR/sustainability reports, while the Stakeholder Engagement Standard provides a framework to help organisations ensure stakeholder engagement processes of all types, including both macro and micro engagement processes, are robust and deliver results.

These standards are for use by any type of organisation from multi-national businesses to small and medium enterprises (SMEs), governments and civil society organisations, and they are developed by a consultative process incorporating representatives of those stakeholder groups that the standards will have an impact on. Licensing is now required for all commercial use of the Assurance Standard, and the Stakeholder Engagement Standard can be used as an integral element of other standards. Although various international bodies such as the Global Compact have emerged to enshrine these standards, little has been developed in the way of binding international treaties that would support accountability.

See also: Business Networks, Corporate Citizenship, Corporate Social Responsibility, Governance, Social Partnerships

REFERENCES

AA Series of Standards, AccountAbility, at http://www.accountability.org/aa1000series accessed 13 July 2010.

Albareda, L. (2008) 'Corporate Responsibility, Governance and AccountAbility: From Self-regulation to Co-regulation', *Corporate Governance*, 8 (4): 430–439.

Cooper, S. and Owen, D. (2007) 'Corporate Social Reporting and Stakeholder Accountability: The Missing Link', *Accounting, Organizations and Society*, 32 (7–8): 649–667.

Luo, Y. (2005) 'Corporate Governance and Accountability in Multinational Enterprises: Concepts and Agenda', *Journal of International Management*, 11: 1–18.

Rhodes, C., Pullen, A. and Clegg, S. (2009) 'If I Should Fall From Grace ...': Stories of Change and Organizational Ethics, *Journal of Business Ethics*, 91 (4): 535–551.

Valor, C. (2005) 'Corporate Social Responsibility and Corporate Citizenship: Towards Corporate Accountability', *Business and Society Review*, 110 (2): 191–212.

corporate accountability

HOW HAS THE TERM EMERGED?

The notion of corporate citizenship (CC) has extended the debates around the roles and responsibilities of business in society, embedded in concepts such as corporate social responsibility (CSR), corporate social responsiveness and corporate social performance. Valor defines CC as a process and ultimately a reality that 'connect[s] business activity to broader social accountability and service for mutual benefit' (2005: 193). Whereas CSR and other related concepts listed above have received more attention in the academic literature, CC appears to have been introduced into the academic debate by the interests and actions of corporate players (Matten and Crane, 2005). In the preamble to the UN's Global Compact initiative of 2002, the need for the pursuit of good corporate citizenship in an increasingly globalised world is acknowledged.

Matten and Crane (2005) have suggested that despite the addition of the term 'CC' to CSR literature, it had not, up to the time of their writing, helped clarify the different levels of understanding of the social role of business. From the existing literature, they identified two conventional approaches to CC, arguing that these approaches did not constitute new terminology nor offer conceptual clarity. They argued that the 'limited view' of CC shifts the notion of corporate philanthropy from a discretionary form of CSR to that of strategic philanthropy (i.e. companies seeing CC as a means of social investing or building reputational capital in anticipation of economic returns to the firm). The 'equivalent view' of CC merely melds the notion of CC into the legal, economic, ethical and philanthropic dimensions of CSR as noted by Carroll (1998).

AN 'EXTENDED' VIEW OF CC: A 'RIGHTS' PERSPECTIVE

Matten and Crane's (2005) contribution to the conceptual enrichment of the term 'CC' is largely reflected in their analysis of the term 'citizenship' concerning the social, civil and political rights of the individual. Citing Wood and Logsdon (2001), they suggest that in adopting CC, corporations take on corporate citizenry responsibilities through a respect for the individual rights of citizens. A consensus has emerged that this form of corporate citizenry reflects the reality that in a globalised economy, nation-states cannot solely guarantee social, political and civil rights, thus creating opportunities for corporate sector leadership 'to act as agents of change that create community through positive social action' (Goddard, 2005: 271). Matten and Crane identify instances in which corporations might pick up citizenship responsibilities in the vacuums left where governments cease to administer or have not yet administered citizenship rights, or even where the administration of such 'rights' may be beyond 'the reach' of national governments (2005: 172). In such cases, they argue, corporations might impact positively on social rights within a community through improving health or welfare benefits, working with the state to ensure the civil rights of communities in the face of economic development, or in some cases even providing additional opportunities for communities to exercise political rights, action and citizen responses through facilitating such activities as consumer boycotts.

Van Osterhaut (2005) has suggested that Matten and Crane's (2005) 'extended' theoretical framework is merely explanatory and as such fails to demonstrate empirically their claims to extend and conceptually improve the concept of CC. Matten and Crane disagree but note that van Oosterhaut's critique raised questions worth consideration, including: that the central claim about corporations taking on the administration of citizen rights might be speculative; that the motivation of corporations to take on such responsibilities needs further consideration; and that corporate rights also need to be considered along with their CC responsibilities. However, they contest the extent to which other writers have provided evidence of CC activity to support arguments as to why corporations might assume CC responsibilities, e.g. in relation to the 'licence to operate' theory.

CC AND THE LICENCE TO OPERATE

Goddard (2005) suggests that in global environments corporations constitute significant 'social mechanisms', i.e. their very presence, their impact on communities over time, and the relationships they develop in maintaining their 'licence to operate' make them capable of generating significant positive change. Wulfsun (2001) argues that corporations have a responsibility, not a mere 'capability', to undertake citizenry roles, with business and society being inter-dependent. Thus he maintains that the role of business includes a stewardship of the interests of the general public.

Sobhan (2002) acknowledges difficulties in identifying and extending CC models. For example, although the stakeholder model implies a sense of stewardship by the corporation towards its stakeholders, conceptualising the stewardship role as a possible feature of CC may be difficult in broad constituencies that do not have the same level of connectedness with stakeholder concerns.

However, despite such conceptual challenges, the notion of CC has been considered as a relevant framework to explore the relationship between the corporate sector and the community of which they are part from a perspective of the economic, social, financial and environmental impacts of corporate activity and their consequences for future community development. Goddard (2005) suggests that indicators of social change such as the Human Development Indicator (HDI) and the Indicator of Sustainable Economic Welfare (IESW) are tools that might be adapted to measure the outcomes of corporate engagement and impact.

CC: RIGHTS AS WELL AS RESPONSIBILITIES

Matten and Crane (2005) suggest that identifying corporate rights alongside their responsibilities is a significant area for review in models of CC. It has been considered that a means of articulating 'rights' in context might be to embed them in contracts together with a specification of CC responsibilities. This might be the case particularly in collaborative alliances and partnerships between corporations, community and government.

CC: 'STAGES' OF GROWTH

Mirvis and Googins (2005) reviewed various models of the stages of growth of corporate citizenship, noting the relationship between the path taken and the socio-economic, environmental and institutional pressures on the organisation. They focused on five stages of growth: elementary, engaged, innovative, integrated and transforming. As an example they suggested that BP had demonstrated aspects of citizenship behaviour associated with the 'integrated stage' in that its commitment to sustainability 'builds on the logic of multi-stakeholder capitalism but joins social, environmental and economic sustainability to the long term survival of the firm' (2005: 14). To achieve this it had put in place an integrated governance system 'that includes a Board level Ethics and

Environmental Assurance Committee, Corporate Directors of Social Policy and Business Ethics, group level oversight bodies, corporate and regional co-ordinators and business unit accountability measurements and audits' (2005:114). However BP's efforts, commencing in April 2010, to contain a giant oil leak in the Gulf of Mexico might warrant reflection on the relationships between governance, CC and risk management strategies, particularly when changes in the organisational leadership and ensuing culture occur. The cost of BP's response at the beginning of September 2010 was approximately US$8 billion, 'including the cost of the spill response, containment, relief well drilling, static kill and cementing, grants to the Gulf states, claims paid, and federal costs' (BP, 2010). Mirvis and Googins also suggest that Unilever has demonstrated citizenship behaviour at the 'transformative stage' in that it appears to have made citizenship mainstream within certain business product ranges through investments in commodities, such as iodised salt in India and Africa that address local health problems.

It should be borne in mind, however, that there is often a public relations (PR) dimension to corporate citizenship activities. For example, the Shell Foundation, which supports vulnerable communities in dealing with social problems, was set up in the year 2000 after a community backlash over the sinking of the *Brent Spar* and the execution of protesters against Shell's drilling in the Niger Delta. In late 2006, Shell was negotiating with Gazprom in Russia concerning the £11bn gas project known as the 'Sakhalin-2 scheme', a project that had raised serious environmental concerns. It was disclosed by the *Guardian* newspaper that Shell had used its Foundation to help it lobby the UK Secretary of State for International Development concerning the project. Subsequently, environmental campaigners highlighted that such Foundations were often mere PR vehicles.

IMPLICATIONS FOR MANAGEMENT

In commenting on the developing role of CC, Grit notes that the 'retreat of public administration requires a larger self-steering capacity of society' (2004: 98), inviting private organisations to operate in a public space in which a consideration of political tensions is essential. This notion of corporate citizenship challenges managerial roles and responsibilities to deal with dynamic shifts in accountability within and between institutions (identified as the market, the state and civil society). As further discussed in the entry on Environmental Discourses, Beck

(1994) has described this situation as the rise of 'sub-politics' or the shaping of society from below, requiring the contemporary state to negotiate with private organisations that need to consider and contribute more to the public good. Grit notes that in this climate the notion of corporate citizenship requires contemporary management 'to make a profit and to deliver a contribution to public matters that go beyond self-interest' (2004: 98). He suggests that in this situation the role of the manager could be strengthened to deal with these challenges by: more tightly regulated or 'imposed corporate citizenship' shaping managerial action; improved information flows and clarified professional standards for 'technocratic corporate citizenry'; requiring managers to undertake normative discussion concerning ethics in new business agendas; and enhancing their information dissemination role in stakeholder management to achieve 'societal legitimacy and accountability' with stakeholders. This aligns well with the findings of the Vision 2050 Report of the World Business Council for Sustainable Development released in 2010 that suggests a sustainable future depends on cross-sectoral collaboration, innovation and new ways of conceptualising successful outcomes by leaders and managers across all sectors.

See also: *Agency Theory, Community Relations, Corporate Social Responsibility, Environmental Discourses, Postcolonialism, Stakeholder Theory, Stewardship*

REFERENCES

Beck, U. (1994) 'The Reinvention of Politics: Towards a Theory of Reflexive Modernization', in Beck, U., Giddens, A. and Lash, S. (eds), *Reflexive Modernization: Politics, Tradition and Aesthetics in the Modern Social Order*. Cambridge: Polity Press, pp. 1–55.

BP (2010) 'Update on Gulf of Mexico Oil Spill – 03 September', Press Release, available at http://www.bp.com/gulfofmexicoresponse

Carroll, A.B. (1998) 'The Four Faces of Corporate Citizenship', *Business and Society Review*, 100: 1–7.

Goddard, T. (2005) 'Corporate Citizenship and Community Relations: Contributing to the Challenges of Aid Discourse', *Business and Society Review*, 110 (3): 269–296.

Grit, K. (2004) 'Corporate Citizenship: How to Strengthen the Social Responsibility of Managers?', *Journal of Business Ethics*, 53: 97–106.

Matten, D. and Crane, A. (2005) 'Corporate Citizenship: Towards an Extended Theoretical Conceptualization', *Academy of Management Review*, 30 (1): 166–179.

Mirvis, P. and Googins, B. (2005) 'Stages of Corporate Citizenship', *California Management Review*, 48 (2): 104–126.

Sobhan, R. (2002) 'Aid Effectiveness and Policy Ownership', *Development and Change*, 33: 539–548.

Valor, C. (2005) 'Corporate Social Responsibility and Corporate Citizenship: Towards Corporate Accountability', *Business and Society Review*, 110 (2): 191–212.

van Oosterhaut, J.H. (2005) 'Dialogue', *Academy of Management Review*, 30 (4): 677–681.

Wood, J. and Logsdon, J.M. (2001) 'Theorising Business Citizenship' in Andriof, J. and McIntosh, M. (eds), *Perspectives on Corporate Citizenship*. Sheffield: Greenleaf.

World Business Council for Sustainable Development (2010) *Vision 2050: The New Agenda for Business*. Geneva: WBCSD.

Wulfsun, M. (2001) 'The Ethics of Corporate Social Responsibility and Philanthropic Ventures', *Journal of Business Ethics*, 29: 135–145.

Corporate Responsibility Reporting

REPORTING NON-FINANCIAL PERFORMANCE

Corporate responsibility reporting can be defined as an approach to reporting a firm's activities which identifies, measures and reports on socially or environmentally relevant behaviour. The measurement and reporting of financial data has long been seen as a core plank of corporate accountability. It is only in relatively recent times that organisations have looked to how to account for and report non-financial performance. For accountants and others interested in corporate information systems, the problem has been how to implement accounting systems that will incorporate the intangible nature of many social and environmental costs and benefits as well as identify them in relation to lifecycle analysis aspects of production and manufacturing systems. Traditional measurement and reporting systems for companies were not designed to capture this complex combination of financial, environmental and social metrics. However, companies are increasingly expected to demonstrate transparency and accountability in areas that go beyond financial performance, to embrace reporting on companies' performance against social and environmental 'responsibilities' as a corporate citizen. The result has been a proliferation in the number of companies producing reports that attempt to tabulate aspects of their social and environmental performance, sometimes termed 'sustainability reports'.

In recognition of the fact that measuring the environmental and social aspects of business activity can be a means of improving overall performance and adding corporate value, much recent effort has gone into the development of indicators that enable a comparison across time periods, corporate divisions and other boundaries. This is because many sustainability and corporate responsibility issues, such as the use of water and energy, human rights and community relations, are interconnected and therefore must be considered in an integrated and holistic way.

As described more fully in the entry on Business Networks, in 1997 the Global Reporting Initiative (GRI) was established to encourage companies to develop sustainability reports supporting the inclusion of social and environmental issues and sometimes financial impacts. In an attempt to promote holistic approaches to measuring sustainability, the GRI uses both systemic indicators, which relate an organisation's performance to its broader economic, environmental or social context, and cross-cutting indicators, which relate two or more dimensions of an organisation's economic, environmental and social performance as a ratio. An example would be workplace accidents or emissions per economic performance unit.

RECENT TRENDS

KPMG, a global network of professional service firms, has conducted periodic surveys for more than a decade (e.g. 2002, 2005, 2008) that give a useful overview of changes in sustainability reporting, showing a steady increase. The 2005 KPMG survey also indicated that the GRI was having a positive influence, with more than half the number of companies stating that they were inspired to report by the GRI.

The 2008 KPMG International Survey is the most comprehensive survey conducted on this subject to date. In addition to the Global Fortune 250, the sample also included the 100 largest companies by revenue in 22 countries. It showed that 80 per cent of the Global Fortune 250 now release environmental, social and governance (ESG) data in stand-alone reports or integrated into annual financial reports, up from 50 per cent in the three years since KPMG last conducted its survey in 2005. However, 40 per cent of the Global 250 and 55 per cent of the 100 largest companies in 22 countries do not integrate ESG information into their annual reporting. The KPMG report noted that the number of companies that utilise formal assurance made a significant jump to 40 per cent in 2008 after holding steady at 30 per cent in the 2002 and 2005 versions of the survey – with the large accounting firms leading in terms of their market share of assurance services.

MOTIVATIONS FOR REPORTING

A number of countries now require some form of public disclosure of corporate environmental information or performance. This reflects a shift in corporate environmentalism away from a compliance-driven approach towards the competitive advantage view, and to include considerations of long-term risk management and value creation. For example, the majority of the world's largest companies have environmental policies and obtain certification through ISO 14001 and the EU Eco Management and Audit Scheme (EMAS) – as discussed in the entry on Voluntary Regulation. However, few give specific details on their environmental management systems, indicating the potential business value embedded in these systems. A quarter of these companies now make the investment to externally validate their environmental management practices (Jose and Lee, 2007). As noted above, reporting becomes a means of companies identifying how they can align their sustainability efforts with their objectives by tracking these sources of value.

Although the first separate environmental reports emerged in the late 1980s, it was not until relatively recently that a number of multinationals began to pay more attention to sustainability reporting that included social as well as environmental metrics in order to capture the potential competitive advantage associated with social or environmental initiatives. This trend also reflects an acknowledgment by companies that an effective monitoring of equal opportunities and diversity in the workplace is an important part of improved human capital management and equality practice. As well, sustainability reports are increasingly including a reference to corporate governance issues such as board supervision and the structuring of sustainability responsibilities to compliance, ethics and external verification. Sectoral and national differences are also evident. For example, voluntary disclosure is more prevalent in Europe and Japan than in the USA. Companies with high environmental footprints such as in the resources or automobile industry are more inclined to report, although reporting is increasingly common in the financial sector and particularly with large companies.

The KPMG surveys reveal that innovation and ethical considerations were increasingly important drivers for reporting between 2005 and 2008. Comparatively, risk management reduced in importance. Perceived benefits of this more proactive approach include reputation and a better understanding of stakeholder needs and expectations. Indeed, it is sometimes argued that companies report on their social and environmental performance purely as a strategy to gain legitimacy in the eyes of the public. Deegan et al. (2002), for example, have used their study of BHP to argue that companies will utilise social and environmental reporting as a means of addressing unfavourable media attention.

The academic literature on corporate responsibility and sustainability reporting has focussed on identifying the motivations for reporting with little emphasis on identifying who the actual audiences are for this form of reporting. What research there is seems to indicate that investors and employees are the key targets for this form of reporting and that aside from signalling risk management issues, the reporting serves mainly to inform the organisation about its own activities. Analysis of the impact on wider stakeholders is limited and companies do not seem to be applying a systematic approach to analysing what or to whom it is best to report. The fact that CSR and corporate sustainability are such diffuse concepts, involving numerous stakeholders with diverse needs, is adding to the complexity of assessing appropriate reporting procedures and responses. Reflecting these challenges and associated free-rider issues, recent surveys have found that a majority of investors favoured mandatory sustainability-related reporting and were also in favour of global guidelines being developed towards that end (Kolk, 2005).

CRITICAL ISSUES

The criteria for assessing corporate responsibility reporting include evidence of external verification, the comprehensiveness of any coverage of social and environmental issues, the existence of an environmental management system, whether any environmental or social performance targets have been specified, how these are measured and verified, and how accessible such reporting is to the public. Amid recognition of the difficulty of making comparisons between and across sectors, and between small and large companies, there have been calls for stricter third-party verification procedures and reporting rules. Another limitation is that the majority of reports use lagging metrics, although larger firms are more likely than smaller firms to use future-oriented metrics, and there are noticeable differences across countries and regions in terms of the types of environmental metrics that are used. Another critical issue is that many metrics describe operations performance rather than environmental impact. (These issues are further discussed in the entry on Performance Evaluation and Measurement.)

There are major implications of the shift towards greater transparency and higher levels of public disclosure for the accountancy and financial services profession. Reflecting this shift, many of the accounting professional organisations have taken up membership of the Accounting for Sustainability Forum, an international body sponsored by HRH the Prince of Wales. Building the capacity for business and industry to plan, to adopt appropriate frameworks and tools, and to harness incentives to make changes for more responsible and sustainable behaviour is dependent upon how these professions can work with the business sectors to assist in identifying and reporting on related objectives and impacts.

See also: *Business Networks, Corporate Accountability, Corporate Responsibility Reporting, Performance Evaluation and Measurement*

REFERENCES

Deegan, C., Rankin, M. and Tobin, J. (2002) 'An Examination of the Corporate Social and Environmental Disclosures of BHP from 1983–1997: A Test of Legitimacy Theory', *Accounting, Auditing & Accountability Journal*, 15: 312–343.

Jose, A. and Lee, S. (2007) 'Environmental Reporting of Global Corporations: A Content Analysis based on Website Disclosures', *Journal of Business Ethics*, 72: 307–321.

Kolk, A. (2005) 'Sustainability Reporting', *VBA Journal*. Available at www.basisboekmvo. nl/files/Sustainability%20reporting.pdf, accessed 19 July 2009.

KPMG (2008) 'Corporate Responsibility as a Strategic Factor. Available at www. kpmg.ch/docs/20081027_MR_Sustainability_CR_reporting_ENS.pdf, accessed 19 July 2009.

corporate responsibility reporting

Corporate Social Responsibility

DEFINITION

The question as to whether business has broader responsibilities to society than making profit for shareholders can be traced back for centuries (Carroll and Shabana, 2010). Since the mid-twentieth century many debates of this nature have occurred around the concept of corporate social responsibility (CSR). At different times this term has been appraised as one that is evolving, contextual, pragmatic, multifaceted, integrative and singularly focused; in some cases, all or combinations of these features have existed in tension. Garriga and Melé note that the field of CSR 'presents not only a landscape of theories but also a prolif-eration of approaches which are controversial, complex and unclear' (2004: 51). Theories and practices around notions such as 'society and business, social issues management, public policy and business, stake-holder management, [and] corporate accountability' (2004: 51) have contributed to definitional variations. More recently, related but alterna-tive concepts have gained currency, including corporate citizenship and corporate sustainability. Confronted with this complexity some writers have concluded that a single definition is elusive. Nevertheless, there is broad agreement that social and environmental responsibility is now a core business issue, no matter how it is defined (Montiel, 2008).

FRAMEWORKS FOR DEFINING CSR

There have been many attempts to clarify and simplify this complex concept. Carroll's early modelling of the social responsibility of business was focussed at a broad macro level, defining CSR as 'encompass[ing] the economic, legal, ethical and discretionary expectations that society has of organizations at a given point in time' (1979: 500). Garriga and Melé (2004) note that Frederick (1994, 1998) classified evolutionary shifts in CSR practices between 1987 and 1998, a practice which has since become common in describing the stages of CSR development. Frederick perceived CSR as progressing from being a philosophical-ethical relationship between business and society (what he terms 'CSR1'), towards a more practical organisational response by business to the social environment and related pressures (CSR2), to a further stage at which business developed a normative approach around ethics and values (CSR3). In a final iteration he rejected firm-centric models of CSR in favour of a model that regards the cosmos, or harmonious universe, as the normative reference point for managerial concerns about business impact on society (CSR4), introducing science and religion into the study of CSR.

Dahlsrud (2006) has perceived CSR as a social construction specific to context. Through the use of content analysis of existing CSR definitions he found five emerging categories of CSR: the dimensions of stakeholder, social, economic, voluntariness and environmental. On the basis of these findings he concluded that, despite different uses of terminology, the definitions of CSR are largely congruent, thus diminishing the need for a single definition. He also noted that definitions of CSR tend to describe CSR rather than support an understanding of how to manage it, concluding that 'the problem for business is not so much to define CSR, as it is to understand how CSR is socially constructed in a specific context and how to take this into account when business strategies are developed' (2006: 6).

Garriga and Melé's (2004) model of CSR is informed by Parsons' (1961) assertion that in any social system four elements can be discerned, constituting an 'adaptation to the environment (related to resources and economics), goal attainment (related to politics), social integration, and pattern maintenance or latency (related to culture and values)' (2004: 52). On this basis they hypothesise four groups of CSR theories. The first group, labelled *instrumental,* is focused on the application of CSR as a means of wealth creation or maximising shareholder value through seeking competitive advantage. Such an approach might include leveraging from social investment as a competitive edge, understanding the value of dynamic capability (consistent with the resource-based view of the firm), and perhaps also appreciating strategic opportunities such as meeting the needs of clients at the bottom of the economic and social pyramid and employing cause-related marketing. The second group, identified as *political theories,* relates to a corporation's social and political obligations as a result of its social power and impact on society, calling on social contract theory which surmises that companies who do not use their social power effectively and responsibly will lose it. This grouping includes theories around global corporate citizenry, seen as increasingly significant in an era in which resources at a state level are challenged to meet the basic social, welfare and other infrastructural requirements of citizens. A third theoretical grouping, known as *integrative theories*, explores the alignment of business and society and the desirability for business to respond to community needs, standards and pressures. This area of inquiry includes the processes by which organisations respond to community concerns, often known as 'issues management'; the extent to which management might legitimately be involved in relevant public policy; stakeholder management; and corporate social performance. The fourth group of *ethical theories* deals with the nature of ethical values, perspectives, decisions and responsibilities that underpin the relationship between business and society. Garriga and Melé suggest that this latter grouping might include stakeholder normative theory, human rights, sustainable development, and the common good approach which embeds the ethical notion of working together for the common good.

MOTIVATION FOR ADOPTING CSR

Aguilera et al. suggest that there is enough evidence of both theoretical and practical support for CSR to move on from definitional concerns to a consideration of a more relevant and urgent question, i.e. 'What catalyses organizations to engage in increasingly robust CSR initiatives and consequently impart social change?' (2007: 837). Their model examines CSR from a multidisciplinary perspective at micro (individual), meso (organisational), macro (country) and supra (transnational) levels, suggesting how actors at each level might be motivated to behave in a socially responsible or irresponsible manner. Behaviour at each level is considered from an instrumental, relational and moral perspective with the intention of shifting the debate from a focus on reactive social change associated with CSR, to a consideration of the motives and challenges associated with positive and proactive approaches in context. They explore, amongst other things:

- the *individual* employee's needs for control, belongingness and purpose
- the *firm's* responsiveness to insider and outsider pressure for CSR emphasising the importance of the politics of decision making
- the priorities and motives of *national governments*
- how organisations (including governments) working in a *transnational* space are likely to have a multiplicative rather than additive relationship concerning CSR motives.

A major aim of this comprehensive framework is to explore the motivations of major actors in adopting CSR, taking into consideration cross-national comparisons of cultural contextuality.

TAKE-UP OF CSR

Prolific academic commentary and diverse business practice relating to CSR has added to the complexity of understanding its meaning and boundaries. In the 1980s the concept of CSR moved from being a nonentity in the business world to becoming 'almost universally sanctioned and promoted by all constituents in society from governments and corporations to non-governmental organizations and individual consumers' (Lee, 2008: 53). Major international organisations such as the UN, the ILO, the World Bank and the OECD have now institutionalised the promotion and monitoring of CSR initiatives within their portfolios. By the end of the 1990s, Lee maintained that close to 90 per cent of Fortune 500 firms had included CSR as part of their organisational goals, reporting such activities in their annual reports. In 2009, all but one of the global top 100 companies by revenue had published a report on CSR and sustainability performance (Global 500, 2009).

Matten and Moon draw attention to differences in the take-up and reporting of CSR across countries, noting that 'national differences in CSR can be explained by historically grown institutional frameworks' which in turn influence the characteristics of 'national business systems' (2008: 407). They list these frameworks as being derived from political, financial, educational, labour, cultural, market and governance functions. Of key significance to the issue of perceived take-up of CSR is their differentiation between 'explicit' and 'implicit' CSR. Explicit CSR usually denotes that the firm is taking responsibility for addressing perceived CSR issues through the use of voluntary programmes rather than by responding to governmental or institutional authority. Implicit CSR is not perceived as voluntary. It responds to an institutional environment that codifies what is required of organisations in relation to their social responsibility. In this latter context businesses who act in a manner that is socially responsible do not necessarily claim it as such. Matten and Moon illustrate this duality by drawing attention to differences in emphasis between the reporting of CSR in the USA and in Europe. They give the example that the relatively lesser national institutional frameworks around employment and health often provide greater opportunities for American firms to respond to perceived social agendas, as CSR initiatives, than is available to many European firms that have more stringent legislation in these areas. This

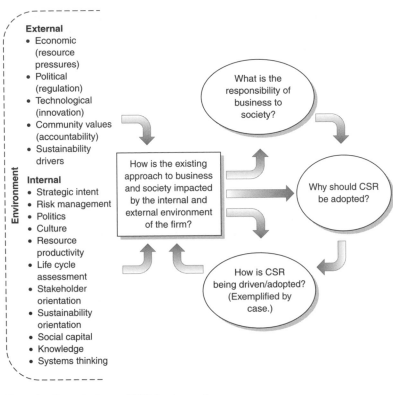

Figure 1 *Dynamic stages of CSR development*

reality constitutes one more complexity in the analysis of a comparative take-up of CSR across nations.

The literature appears to focus on three basic questions, as represented in Figure 1. These are, 'What is CSR?', 'Why would firms undertake CSR?' and 'How are they implementing CSR in context?' Figure 1 is informed by an overview of the literature presented above. Its intention is to show that the concept of CSR is itself dynamic and responsive to internal and external environmental characteristics and pressures. Therefore it might be seen as inappropriate to attempt to define CSR on the basis of finite characteristics or different stages of either incremental or evolutionary shifts outside the context of an open and dynamic corporate cultural adaptation. Thus, if the cycle is envisaged over time, it might represent either an upward or a downward trajectory in its perceived responsiveness to community and environmental pressures for

CSR. The assumption underpinning Figure 1 is that business decisions around CSR will continue to be regarded by the organisation as unique and contextual responses to the internal and external environment, balancing commercial, environmental, social and people sustainability concerns.

WHERE TO NOW?

As demonstrated above, there is ongoing and intense activity around defining and categorising the meaning and scope of CSR, to support debate, deliberation and action at both an academic and practitioner level. Many frameworks are being developed to clarify the thinking around such areas as: the expectations that society has of organisations at a given point in time concerning economic, legal, ethical and discretionary activities; the motives of individuals, firms and governments in promoting CSR; the evolutionary shifts in thinking about CSR in relation to changes in stakeholder perspectives; and the themes that are emerging from data provided by practitioners and academics that might help an understanding of CSR responses in context.

Montiel (2008) suggests that despite the obvious urgency of social and environmental issues, managers remain confused by the flurry of activity around the definition and diverse approaches to the implementation of CSR, particularly concerning its relationship with the increasingly significant notion of corporate sustainability. Although he acknowledges the need to gain clarity through pursuing 'well-defined, clearly bounded and commonly agreed on constructs', Montiel also asks whether we should be recognising the merging and evolving CSR categories as well. For example, he notes the blurring of the boundaries of research between CSR, corporate sustainability (CS) and environmental management (EM). CS now includes both social and environmental issues, and all constructs have a strong overlapping interest in economic responsibility. Montiel attempts to trace the evolution of these different and overlapping phenomena by analysing the number of articles published in the categories of CSR, EM and CS over time, as an indicator of interest in the category. However, he notes the limitations of an approach that aims to identify new and diminishing fields of interest, given that practitioners and researchers use the terms differently and interchangeably. On this basis he argues specifically for a recognition of the convergence between CSR and CS based on their shared environmental and social concerns:

In CSR, environmental issues are a subset of a broader social performance dimensions. In the CS field, the social dimension has become an increasingly important part of the sustainability paradigm ... the conceptualization of CSR that integrates economic, social, and environmental dimensions and the triple bottom line conceptualization of CS, which comprises economic, social and environmental dimensions, are very similar. (Montiel, 2008: 260)

Future research will no doubt be framed by the strength of an institutional response to existing research and the emergence of priority agendas. For example, the World Business Council for Sustainable Development's 'Vision 2050' calls for a commitment to a stable global population that can live well within the limits of the planet. To achieve this overarching goal it emphasises cross-sectoral and interdisciplinary collaborative activity that can forge new definitions of success at an economic and political, national and global level. Such an agenda, and progress toward that agenda, will no doubt influence both practitioner and researcher perspectives on how CSR is conceptualised to achieve a practical benefit and outcome, thus redefining existing debates around the nature of CSR.

See also: *Business Case for CSR, Business Ethics, Corporate Citizenship, Corporate Sustainability, Resource-Based View*

REFERENCES

Aguilera, R.V., Rupp, D.E., Williams, C.A. and Ganapathi, J. (2007) 'Putting the S Back in Corporate Social Responsibility: A Multilevel Theory of Social Change in Organisations', *Academy of Management Review*, 32 (3): 836–863.

Carroll, A.B. (1979) 'A Three Dimensional Conceptual Model of Corporate Performance', *Academy of Management Review*, 4 (4): 497–505.

Carroll, A.B. and Shabana, K.M. (2010) 'The Business Case for Corporate Social Responsibility: A Review of Concepts, Research and Practice', *International Journal of Management Reviews*, 85–105.

Dahlsrud, A. (2006) 'How Corporate Social Responsibility is Defined: An Analysis of 37 Definitions', *Corporate Social Responsibility and Environmental Management*, 15: 1–13.

Frederick, W.C. (1994) 'From CSR_1 to CSR_2: The Maturing of Business and Society Thought,' *Business and Society*, 33 (2): 150–164.

Frederick, W.C. (1998) 'Moving to CSR_4: What to pack for the trip', *Business and Society*, 37 (1): 40–60.

Garriga, E. and Melé, D. (2004) 'Corporate Social Responsibility Theories: Mapping the Territory', *Journal of Business Ethics*, 53: 51–71.

Global 500 (2009) Available at http://money.cnn.com/magazines/fortune/global500/2009/index.html, accessed 21 April 2010.

Lee, M-D.P. (2008) 'A Review of the Theories of Corporate Social Responsibility: Its Evolutionary Path and the Road Ahead', *International Journal of Management Reviews*, 10 (1): 53–73.

Matten, D. and Moon, J. (2008) '"Implicit" and "Explicit" CSR: A Conceptual Framework for a Comparative Understanding of Corporate Social Responsibility', *Academy of Management Review*, 33 (2): 404–424.

Montiel, I. (2008) 'Corporate Social Responsibility and Corporate Sustainability: Separate Pasts, Common Futures', *Organization & Environment*, 21: 245–269.

Parsons, T. (1961) 'An Outline of the Social System', in Parsons, T., Shils, E.A., Naegle, K.D., and Pitts, J.R. *Theories of Society*. New York: Free Press.

Corporate Sustainability

Corporate sustainability (CS) can be thought of as a business approach that creates long-term value for the organisation by incorporating economic, environmental and social dimensions into its core business decisions. More widely, it is referred to as the efficient use of resources and generation of wealth so as to contribute to a healthy economy, society and natural environment.

A number of indices are now established that claim to record corporate performance in sustainability. In the UK, the FTSE4Good index deals with three areas: environmental sustainability, positive stakeholder relationships, and upholding and supporting universal human rights. In the USA, the Dow Jones Sustainability Index claims to be the first global index designed to monitor and assess not only the economic but also the social and environmental performance of leading corporations. It focuses on five corporate sustainability principles: innovative technology, corporate governance, shareholder relations, industrial leadership and social wellbeing, interpreted as a corporation making a positive responsibility to society (see Dow Jones Sustainability Index at www.sustainability-index.com/07_htmle/sustainability/corpsustainability.html).

ELEMENTS OF SUSTAINABILITY

CS has emerged in the corporate lexicon more recently than linked concepts of CSR and corporate citizenship. Distinguishing between these concepts is difficult as they are overlapping and diffuse, but compared to CSR and corporate citizenship, CS evokes both business longevity and a greater emphasis on corporate responsibilities in relation to the natural environment. CS is essentially a business approach that incorporates the risk management of social, economic and environmental aspects into the firm's operations. The basic idea is that corporate longevity can be ensured through incorporating economic, social and environmental logics into corporate values, strategies, operations and relationship management. In other words, it is management associated with a holistic and systems-based approach.

Proponents of the shift to CS argue that three elements of sustainability are required for organisational effectiveness. *Economic sustainability* refers to ensuring that the organisation is financially viable and, if a public company, that it makes adequate returns to investors. *Social sustainability* refers to ensuring that the corporation internally creates a supportive and developmental environment for staff and externally meets the legitimate expectations of key stakeholders. *Environmental sustainability* refers to ensuring that the organisation eliminates any negative impacts on the natural environment and actively contributes to the health of the biosphere. The three pillars of corporate sustainability are often referred to as 'the triple bottom line'. More specific detail on the triple bottom line approach is given in the entry on that topic.

INTERPRETATIONS OF CS

Sustainability is a difficult term for which to set criteria because it refers to the interrelatedness of technological, social, political and environmental systems. Dyllick and Hockerts (2002) classify three types of capital relevant to the concept of CS: economic, natural and social capital. Drawing on this classification, they argue that managers need to satisfy the criteria of eco-efficiency, socio-efficiency, eco-effectiveness, socio-effectiveness, sufficiency and ecological equity. There are strong or weak versions of sustainability depending on whether all forms of capital are maintained intact independent of one another. Strong sustainability requires that each form of capital is kept constant. For organisations, strong sustainability implies that social, environmental and economic objectives must be addressed simultaneously if any one of these objectives is to be of value (Figge and Hahn, 2004).

A relatively new and evolving management paradigm, interpretations of CS draw from the literature on sustainable development and CSR and also rely heavily on stakeholder theory. This is because the capacity of a firm to continue operating over a long period of time depends on the quality of its stakeholder relationships (Perrini and Tencati, 2006). As noted, there are considerable overlaps with other concepts, such as corporate citizenship and CSR, and as a result numerous academics and practitioners have criticised its lack of clarity. Indeed, as the importance of corporate sustainability in the management literature grows, so does the confusion surrounding its definition. According to van Marrewijk (2003), corporate sustainability is not a 'one size fits all' concept – how it is defined and therefore implemented is reliant upon the levels of development, awareness and ambition of organisations.

A number of writers have addressed the problem of classifying CS through a phased approach to the concept. Dunphy et al. (2007), for instance, distinguish the following developmental phases of CS:

Phase 1: rejection
Phase 2: non-responsiveness
Phase 3: compliance
Phase 4: efficiency
Phase 5: strategic proactivity
Phase 6: ideal phase of the sustaining corporation.

Of the phases that go beyond compliance, the efficiency phase is the weakest interpretation of sustainability. Here organisations emphasise the efficient use of finance and other resources internally and through supply chain management; eco-efficiency based on pollution control and the repair and prevention of environmental damage. Both environmental and human resource management policies and approaches are geared to cost reduction. In the strategic proactivity phase, there is an emphasis on product stewardship based in a lifecycle approach and on strategic repositioning and market redefinition to take advantage of an increasing community emphasis on sustainability. This phase represents a moderate version of CS. The sustaining corporation phase is a strong version of CS where sustainability is fully integrated into the business model of the organisation so that it can contribute to ecological renewal and to the development of a just society and the ensuring of human fulfilment. Figure 2 depicts these phases as three waves. The first wave, for example, is made up of organisations still in the phases of rejection or non-responsiveness. The arrows at the bottom of the Figure indicate how the phase affects the value of the organisation.

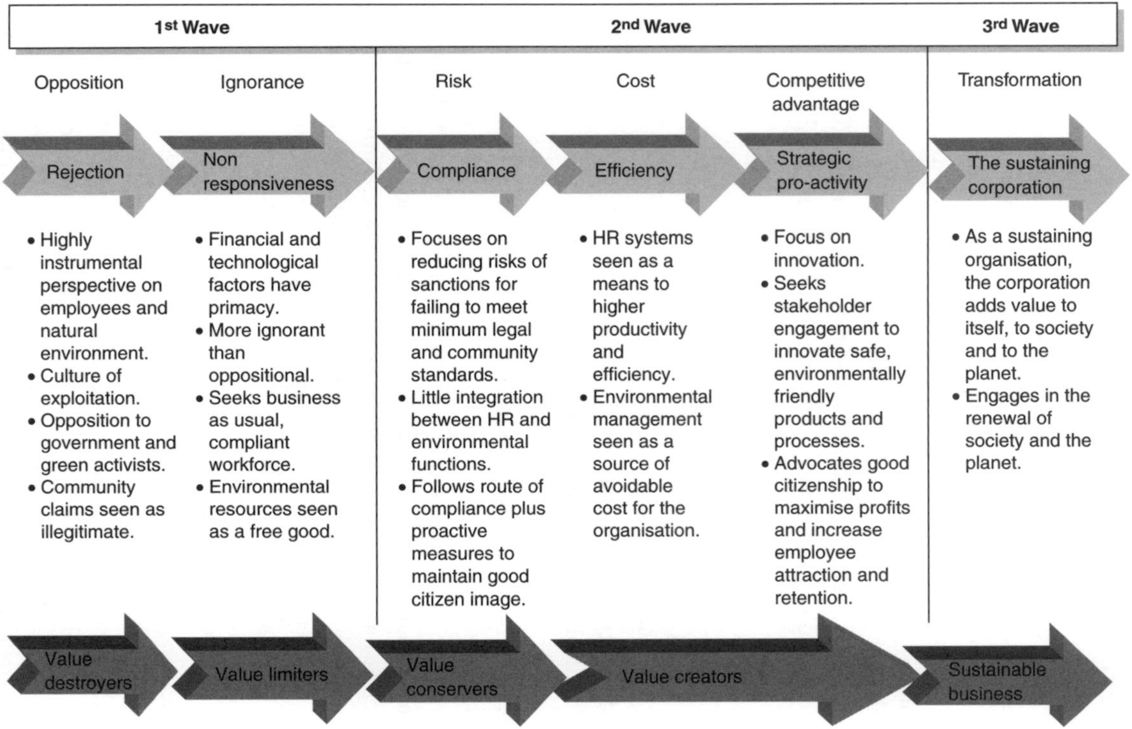

1st Wave		2nd Wave			3rd Wave
Opposition	Ignorance	Risk	Cost	Competitive advantage	Transformation
Rejection	Non responsiveness	Compliance	Efficiency	Strategic pro-activity	The sustaining corporation
• Highly instrumental perspective on employees and natural environment. • Culture of exploitation. • Opposition to government and green activists. • Community claims seen as illegitimate.	• Financial and technological factors have primacy. • More ignorant than oppositional. • Seeks business as usual, compliant workforce. • Environmental resources seen as a free good.	• Focuses on reducing risks of sanctions for failing to meet minimum legal and community standards. • Little integration between HR and environmental functions. • Follows route of compliance plus proactive measures to maintain good citizen image.	• HR systems seen as a means to higher productivity and efficiency. • Environmental management seen as a source of avoidable cost for the organisation.	• Focus on innovation. • Seeks stakeholder engagement to innovate safe, environmentally friendly products and processes. • Advocates good citizenship to maximise profits and increase employee attraction and retention.	• As a sustaining organisation, the corporation adds value to itself, to society and to the planet. • Engages in the renewal of society and the planet.

Value destroyers — Value limiters — Value conservers — Value creators — Sustainable business

Figure 2 *Waves of sustainability*

Adapted from: Dunphy, D., Griffiths, A. and Benn, S. *Organisational Change for Corporate Sustainability*, London and New York: Routledge, 2007, P. 17. Reprinted with permission.

OPERATIONALISING CS

Implementing CS means dealing with a complex and ambiguous concept, involving multiple stakeholders. For instance, from an investment perspective, CS refers to a management focus on future challenges and intangible criteria, such as quality of management, corporate governance structures, reputational risks, human capital management and stakeholder relations.

But overall, an insufficient understanding of management's key arguments or business logic for adopting corporate sustainability strategies has impeded rigorous testing of the CS proposition (Salzmann et al., 2005). As with the related issue of the business case for CSR, research analysing the relationships between the three elements of sustainability has delivered some varying results. The so-called business case for sustainability claims a positive relationship between the financial and the non-financial sustainability objectives, although the many different variables impacting on the relationships between the elements make this claim very difficult to prove. The relationships between the non-financial elements are even less understood. Clearly, companies may trade off elements against each other, for example, compensating for new environmental investments with cuts in human resources. However, there are also synergies between the elements. So for example, progressive human resource practices may contribute to the development of environmental sustainability.

In practical terms, Epstein (2008: 37) suggests nine principles of corporate performance that lead to corporate sustainability:

1. Ethics
2. Governance
3. Transparency
4. Business relationships
5. Financial return
6. Community involvement
7. Value of products and services
8. Employment practices
9. Protection of the environment

According to Epstein, conceptualising CS into such operationalised categories enables it to be quantified and hence facilitates its integration into the day-to-day activities of the organisation.

corporate sustainability

See also: *Business Case for CSR, Corporate Citizenship, Corporate Social Responsibility, Corporate Sustainability Strategies, Sustainable Development, Triple Bottom Line*

REFERENCES

Dunphy, D., Griffiths, A. and Benn, S. (2007) *Organizational Change for Corporate Sustainability*. London and New York: Routledge.

Dyllick, T. and Hockerts, K. (2002) 'Beyond the Business Case for Sustainability', *Business Strategy and the Environment*, 11 (2): 130–141.

Epstein, M. (2008) *Making Sustainability Work*. Sheffield: Greenleaf.

Figge, F. and Hahn, T. (2004) 'Sustainable Value Added – Measuring Corporate Contributions to Sustainability Beyond Eco-Efficiency', *Ecological Economics*, 48: 173–187.

Perrini, F. and Tencati, A. (2006) 'Sustainability and Stakeholder Management: The Need for New Corporate Performance', *Business Strategy and the Environment*, 15 (5): 296–308.

Salzmann, O., Ionescu-Somers, A. and Steger, U. (2005) 'The Business Case for Corporate Sustainability: Literature Review and Research Options', *European Management Journal*, 23 (1): 27–36.

van Marrewijk, M. (2003) 'Concepts and Definitions of CSR and Corporate Sustainability: Between Agency and Communion', *Journal of Business Ethics*, 44: 95–105.

Corporate Sustainability Strategies

WHAT IS MEANT BY CORPORATE SUSTAINABILITY STRATEGIES?

'Corporate sustainability strategies' can be defined as business strategies that are designed to integrate long-term economic, environmental and social aspects into long-term value creation while maintaining global competitiveness and brand reputation. Such strategies are promoted as enabling companies to create sustainable value for their companies. 'Corporate sustainability leaders achieve long-term shareholder value by gearing their strategies and management to harness the market's potential for sustainability products and services while at the same time successfully reducing and avoiding sustainability costs and risks' (Dow Jones Sustainability Index, available at www.sustainability-index.com/07_htmle/sustainability/corpsustainability.html).

According to Baumgartner and Ebner (2010: 78), there are four different types of sustainability strategies:

- *Introverted* – risk mitigation strategy: a focus on legal and other external standards concerning environmental and social aspects in order to avoid risks for the company.
- *Extroverted* – legitimating strategy: a focus on external relationships and licence to operate.
- *Conservative* – efficiency strategy: a focus on eco-efficiency and cleaner production.
- *Visionary* – holistic sustainability strategy: a focus on sustainability issues within all business activities; competitive advantages are derived from differentiation and innovation, offering customers and stakeholders unique advantages.

Despite their differences, each of these approaches involves a demonstrated commitment by the firm to align the overall strategic direction with human and environmental sustainability principles. Achieving strategic sustainability is highly dependent upon value adding and innovation; upon building and institutionalising the key competencies and capabilities that support both human and environmental sustainability; and upon being receptive and responsive to the needs and interests of diverse stakeholders including local communities (Dunphy et al., 2007). A recent innovation in strategic sustainability, the so-called 'business at the bottom of the pyramid' model, for example, covered in more detail in the entry on that topic, focuses on the needs of low-income populations and how operating in these markets can contribute to the social, economic and environmental welfare of these populations as well as firm profitability.

Dunphy et al. (2007) set out five steps to implementing strategic sustainability:

- *Step 1: Top team elaboration of corporate goals relating to sustainability*
  For example, some firms, such as the multinational corporation IKEA and the leading Australian water retailer Yarra Valley Water (Crittenden et al., 2010), put their managers through the Natural Step programme

and then diffuse the programme throughout the organisation. (This step is further described in the entry on Systems Approaches.)

- *Step 2: Development and systematic alignment of measurement systems with corporate goals*
  For example, measurement systems for social and environmental performance can be developed with the assistance of the Global Reporting Initiative (GRI). These measurement systems can help inform overall corporate goals.
- *Step 3: Diagnosis of opportunities*
  At Yarra Valley Water, for instance, a combination of systems approaches based on the Natural Step, lifecycle analysis, stakeholder mapping and stakeholder consultation was used to establish strategic business opportunities for the firm and to support more effective decision making at all levels of the organisation.
- *Step 4: Implementation and diffusion of successful practices both internally and externally*
  This step depends on an investment in organisational learning and development with a focus on sustainability so as to build employee and supplier knowledge and commitment. Westpac, for example, one of Australia's leading banks and one of only two banks to achieve gold status with the Dow Jones Sustainability Index, has developed a series of sustainability objectives that guide knowledge development around sustainability within the organisation and with their suppliers. They include Going Mainstream, Sustainable Products, Treading Lightly and Environmental Footprint, as well as others related to social responsibility, governance and risk management. Each has specific targets to be addressed.
- *Step 5: Review, monitoring and alignment*
  Performance reviews and feedback mechanisms that have third-party assurance are key to this aspect of the sustainability strategy.

Each of these steps requires companies to align their sustainability efforts and impacts with short-and long-term objectives. Berns et al. (2009) suggest that conceptualising these challenges and what they might mean for corporate sustainability strategising is assisted by distinguishing between long-term and short-term approaches. The short-term or 'compliance plus' approach, is driven by the need for companies to include in their considerations changing social and environmental responsibility expectations upon business and industry sectors as a whole. For the long-term, sustainability alignment means working within new institutional frameworks such as partnerships and networks. For the individual company, sustainability strategising means appropriate product redesign, so that, for instance, it can differentiate and gain long-term value creation. As Berns et al. (2009) point out, so few companies understand how to align their sustainability objectives with value creation that those who do have a major competitive advantage.

CASE EXAMPLES

Laszlo (2008) lists a number of firms that are adopting sustainability strategies into their business. They include Du-Pont, Wal-Mart, Unilever, and many others.

Du-Pont

Du-Pont, for example, the US manufacturer of food, healthcare products, clothing, hardware and electronics, is ranked among the 50 largest US industrial/service corporations by *Fortune 500* magazine and employs more than 85,000 people in 70 countries. In the decade from 1995–2005, Du-Pont's reputation spiralled upwards from its label of 'Top US Polluter of 1995' to first in *BusinessWeek*'s list of top green companies in 2005. It did this by means of forming partnerships with NGOs such as the Environmental Defence Fund and the World Resources Centre, by working with other stakeholders such as external scientific advisory boards, and by establishing a clear-cut sustainability strategy of pursuing shareholder and stakeholder value. Like many other leading companies, Du-Pont's reports are included on the Global Reporting Initiative (GRI) register.

Wal-Mart

It is not only manufacturing companies that are now promoting their sustainability strategies. Wal-Mart, for instance, launched its sustainability strategies with a public announcement in 2005 when its CEO announced the chain would take a leadership position in sustainability. As an example, in February 2010 Wal-Mart announced a goal to eliminate 20 million metric tons of greenhouse gas (GHG) emissions from its global supply chain by the end of 2015. According to their press release at the time, this 'represents one and a half times the company's estimated global carbon footprint growth over the next five years and is the equivalent of taking more than 3.8 million cars off the road for a year' (Walmart Corporate, 2010). The programme focuses on product categories with the highest carbon impact (lifecycle GHG emissions by amount of product sold). Action is counted towards the overall goal if GHGs are reduced in these selected products in any aspect of their lifecycle, from the sourcing of raw materials through to disposal. Suppliers and Wal-Mart will account for the reductions and the claims will be assessed by PricewaterhouseCoopers.

Wal-Mart's sustainability strategies have come under fire from a number of environmental and human rights NGOs, such as Friends

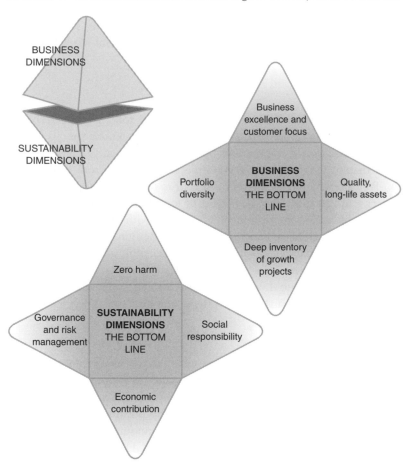

Figure 3   *Sustainability strategy at BHP Billiton*

Source: http://hsecreport.bhpbilliton.com/2006/Sustainability/ourApproach.asp. Reproduced with the kind permission of BHP Billiton. Material was sourced from BHP Billiton Sustainability Report 2006.

of the Earth and the International Labor Rights Forum, on the grounds that its carbon footprint is huge. Critics also point out that that it sources products unethically from factory farming and that its wealth has been built through the exploitation of employees and local communities.

BHP Billiton

BHP Billiton, a global resources company, uses the metaphor of the diamond to describe its sustainability strategy (see Figure 3). As it states on its website: 'An inherently stable structure, with the strength in each dimension contributing equally to an even stronger, stable and more valuable whole, and a robust bottom-line, the diamond is symbolic of our approach to sustainable development' (BHP Billiton, 2006).

In sum, sustainability strategies rely at an operational level in part on the establishment of environmental management systems and on following the prescriptions of various environmentally-related standards, such as ISO14001. Other strategies include meeting shareholders' demands for required levels of financial returns and long-term economic growth; building customer support through high levels of service, product quality and innovation; ensuring accountability and transparency in corporate decision making through good governance; and providing internal and external stakeholders with fair working conditions while building individual skills and capabilities.

See also: Business at the Bottom of the Pyramid, Business Networks, Corporate Sustainability, Systems Approaches

REFERENCES

Baumgartner, R. and Ebner, D. (2010) 'Corporate Sustainability Strategies: Sustainability Profiles and Maturity Levels', *Sustainable Development*, 18 (2): 76–89.

Berns, M., Townend, A., Khayat, Z., Balagopal, B., Reeves, M., Hopkins, M. and Kruschwitz, N. (2009) 'The Business of Sustainability: Findings and Insights from the First Annual Business of Sustainability Survey and the Global Thought Leaders' Research Project', Special Report from MIT Sloan Management Review (2009). Available at www.mitsmr-ezine.com/busofsustainability/2009#pg1, accessed 17 May 2010.

BHP Billiton (2006) 'Licence to Operate', BHP Billiton Sustainability Report. Available at http://hsecreport.bhpbilliton.com/2006/sustainability/ourApproach.asp, accessed 13 April 2010.

corporate sustainability strategies

73

Crittenden, P., Benn, S. and Dunphy, D. (2010) 'Learning for Change at Yarra Valley Water'. Available at www.aries.mq.edu.au/projects/case_study_yarra_valley_water/index.php, accessed 17 May 2010.

Dunphy, D., Griffiths, A. and Benn, S. (2007) *Organizational Change for Corporate Sustainability*. London: Routledge.

Laszlo, C. (2008) *Sustainable Value: How the World's Best Companies are Doing Well by Doing Good*. Sheffield: Greenleaf.

Walmart Corporate (2010) 'Walmart Announces Goal to Eliminate 20 Million Metric Tons of Greenhouse Gas Emissions from Global Supply Chain. Available at http://walmartstores.com/pressroom/news/9668.aspx, accessed 13 April 2010.

Eco-Efficiency

WHAT IS ECO-EFFICIENCY?

Eco-efficiency seeks to reduce the intake of raw materials and energy, reduce emissions of all types into the air, water and soil, and result in smaller amounts of waste. Even small reductions in energy intake, for example, have been shown to have positive implications for the bottom line and will clearly be of much more importance with the emergence of a carbon economy.

BEYOND COMPLIANCE TO EFFICIENCY

A company that is only focused on compliance is interested solely in addressing the legal requirements around issues such as health and safety, product liability, environmental regulations and governance requirements. For a company whose intent is to implement corporate responsibility or sustainability, compliance is just a baseline against which to measure social, economic and environmental performance.

Corporate activity has long been associated with negative impacts on air or water quality and on human health. Such impacts are termed 'negative externalities' – costs that are carried by those who did not create them. The need to comply with tighter regulations designed to reduce externalities while at the same time maintaining profit flows has encouraged the corporate interest in eco-innovation to deliver environmental efficiencies.

Eco-innovation can enable cost savings in a number of ways. For example, eliminating toxic materials can reduce costs associated with training, spill responses, special equipment and disposal fees. Concentrating on green innovation can also lead to better understandings of how to increase product reliability. Phillips Microelectronics, for instance, while investigating how to reduce the content of fire retardant chemicals in their television mountings, discovered a means of reducing hot spots in the unit, thus increasing both product safety and durability (Hitchcock and Willard, 2009). Beyond more environmentally efficient processes or the use of resources, there is increasing emphasis on organisational innovation, such as implementing environmental audits, environmental management systems and systems to enable recycling and remanufacturing. The Fuji Xerox Remanufacturing plant at Zetland in Sydney, for instance, is a total waste management centre for customers sorting returned parts, sub-assemblies, cartridges and packaging for resource recovery. The centre remanufactures approximately 250,000 parts and sub-assemblies annually to 'better than new' condition. It now accounts for 70 per cent by value of Fuji Xerox Australia's spare parts requirements – these parts would have otherwise been scrapped.

According to Dunphy et al. (2007), the key issues for creating eco-efficient organisations include:

- the establishment of auditing and measurement systems to monitor performance in the management of natural resources and quality
- the development of environmental management systems and programmes that can communicate guidelines, tools and strategies across the organisation
- building support across middle management by setting targets and goals, and linking these to performance indicators
- including external stakeholders in the process through supply chain management practices.

ECO-EFFECTIVENESS

The major problem with the approach for eco-efficiency is that it does not address the need to reduce consumption. Consumption is outpacing the gains made in applying eco-efficiency to products and processes, and rebound effects where higher efficiencies lead to more consumption are now evident (Ryan, 2005). Eco-effectiveness, a different concept to eco-efficiency, focuses on this problem. Research in this area emphasises indicator development for low-impact affluence and quality-of-life measures. For example, the cradle-to-cradle approach applies whole systems and lifecycle thinking to design and production processes (Braungart et al., 2007). Designing for eco-effectiveness in fabrics, for example, would involve the requirement that they be fully compostible rather than just 'natural' or 'recyclable'. This approach also emphasises forms of innovation that involve cooperation between companies to sell on wastes as raw materials, as described in the entry on Pollution and Waste Management. In the product service systems that are emerging in the IT industry, the traditional sale/purchase approach is replaced by a product service solution whereby customers are provided with a computing service of which products form a part. The holistic management of a suite of services by the solution provider for the customer differentiates the product service solution from leasing and renting. Such a partnership can be positive for both the solution provider and the customer.

An area of great interest for designers is biomimicry, which involves basing a design on nature, where manufacturing and production exists in a loop with waste from one process becoming food for another (Benyus, 1997). Non-toxic or low-energy solutions such as the passively cooled building in Harare, Zimbabwe, whose structure is modelled on ant heaps found in similar climatic conditions in Africa, and the design features of Japan's Shinkansen 500-Series bullet train inspired by the aerodynamics of birds, are famous examples. The bullet train's overhead pantograph sports serrations modelled on the design of owl plumage to reduce air resistance noise, and the air-piercing nose cone design was inspired by the kingfisher's beak.

Scientists at the University of Manchester have developed a new adhesive, 'gecko tape', comprising billions of tiny plastic fibres, less than a micrometer in diameter, similar to the natural hairs covering the soles of geckos' feet which help it to climb surfaces, including glass ceilings. With no toxic chemicals, a 1 cm square of tape can support a weight of 1 kg. Establishing whole industrial systems that are modelled on the closed systems of nature, such as the famed example of the eco-industrial park at Kalundborg in Denmark, is an example of introducing eco-effectiveness through design.

Clearly, innovation processes toward corporate responsibility, sustainability and sustainable development have received increasing attention in recent years. But these pressures raise issues of high levels of complexity and uncertainty, and managers appear to have problems in addressing them. For example, sustainability and CSR-based innovations typically involve a wider range of stakeholders, and are more ambiguous, as many of the parties have contradictory demands and may involve science that is not accepted at some corporate or governmental levels (Hall and Vredenburg, 2003).

Developing an approach to corporate responsibility that will enable a sustainable society requires working with paradigmatic change in the way our socio-economic system is configured. This involves new ways of working, such as embracing transdisciplinary approaches, continuous innovation and learning, and an ongoing search for strategic business models that are more sustainable and which go beyond eco-efficiency to eco-effectiveness.

See also: Corporate Sustainability Strategies, Pollution and Waste Management, Systems Approaches

REFERENCES

Benyus, J. (1997) *Biomimicry Innovations Inspired by Nature*. New York: William Morrow.

Braungart, M., McDonough, W. and Bollinger, A. (2007) 'Cradle-to-cradle Design: Creating Healthy Emissions – a Strategy for Eco-effective Product and System Design', *Journal of Cleaner Production*, 15 (13–14): 1337–1348.

Dunphy, D., Griffiths, A. and Benn, S. (2007) *Organizational Change for Corporate Sustainability*. London: Routledge.

Hall, J. and Vredenburg, H. (2003) 'The Challenges of Innovating for Sustainable Development', *MIT Sloan Management Review*, 45 (1): 61–68.

Hitchcock, D. and Willard, M. (2009) *The Business Guide to Sustainability*. Sterling, VA: London and Earthscan.

Ryan, C. (2005) 'Integrated Approaches to Sustainable Consumption and Cleaner Production', in K.C. Hargraves and M. Smith (eds), *The Natural Advantage of Nations*. London and Sterling, VA: Earthscan, pp. 407–429.

Employee Engagement

EMPLOYEE ENGAGEMENT AND CSR

The concept 'employee engagement' is of relatively recent interest to the human resource management function, as a factor influencing competitiveness and profitability. Organisations are also beginning to understand that the level of employee engagement might be influenced by employee and wider community perceptions concerning the impact of the organisation's activities on societal and environmental wellbeing.

Collier and Esteban (2007) suggest that, in turn, a company's success in delivering its corporate social responsibility (CSR) initiatives might depend on employee engagement and willingness to support CSR implementation programmes. They ask how employees might be motivated to gain commitment (or achieve a buy-in) to these CSR objectives. Motivation is a key driver of engagement, described as 'the energising force that induces action' (Locke, 1997: 402). Collier and Esteban (2007) suggest that employee motivation and commitment will likely be influenced by an awareness of and involvement in CSR programmes and the associated organisational culture.

They identify various types of CSR programmes and associated organisational cultures that might require different levels and types of employee commitment. These include internal organisational initiatives such as specialised compliance programmes (e.g. the ISO 28000 standard for security management systems in the supply chain) that often exist in parallel with codes of conduct. In addition, Collier and Esteban identify external initiatives or 'social outreach', including corporate philanthropy and broader corporate citizenship agendas, that might encompass, for example, corporate accountability for environmental 'footprints'. A third level of corporate initiative employs the firm's 'core competencies to enhance social welfare', an example being One World Health (OWH) that develops safe and affordable medicine for the developing world through arrangements and partnerships with pharmaceutical firms and research scientists (Collier and Esteban, 2007: 22). This latter approach might increase employee appreciation of the firm's positive impact on society, thus possibly influencing levels of engagement.

A useful model for conceptualising employee commitment to the organisation is that of Mayer and Allen (1991), who noted three forms of organisational commitment: *affective commitment*, based on emotional attachment to the organisation; *normative commitment*, based on a feeling of obligation to remain in the organization; and *continuance commitment*, where the employee stays because of the perceived high costs of leaving. Thus the concepts of motivation and commitment make significant contributions to understanding 'employee engagement'.

CLARIFYING THE TERM

Macey and Schneider have commented on the ambiguity of the term 'employee engagement' for both practitioners and academics, concluding that 'in large part, this can be attributed to the "bottom-up" manner in which the engagement notion has quickly evolved within the practitioner community' (2008: 3). To clarify the term they developed a model that identified three discrete dimensions of the term 'engagement'. The first dimension is *trait engagement*, or the extent to which employee engagement is influenced by personality. This construct is reflected in the second dimension, *psychological state engagement*, when the employee displays certain positive 'affectivity' or 'feelings' towards the experience of organisational involvement. This state in turn influences *behavioural engagement*, which Erickson (2005) has defined as discretionary effort or as certain forms of in-role behaviour that are generally beyond normal effort. Macey and Schneider elaborate on these dimensions:

- *Trait engagement* involves the individual manifesting 'positive affectivity, conscientiousness, the proactive personality, and the autotelic personality' (2008: 24). The autotelic personality is able to set its own goals and become immersed in the resultant activity, undertaking all that is required, including relevant learning, to achieve these goals in a self-directed manner. Trait engagement results in a positive and energetic approach to task, which would perhaps include a readiness for change.
- *State engagement* describes a positive affect 'associated with the job and the work setting connoting or explicitly indicating feelings of persistence, vigor, energy, dedication, absorption, enthusiasm, alertness and pride' (2008: 24). Employees experience certain levels of positive feeling around organisational commitment, job involvement and job satisfaction. These levels of energy, enthusiasm and active involvement go further than 'job satisfaction', i.e. enjoying doing one's job, having the satisfaction that the job is done well and feeling that one's efforts are being rewarded appropriately.
- *Behavioural engagement* is when state engagement, described above, manifests itself as behavioural engagement in which the individual proactively defines a task and the resources and conditions for task achievement, whilst taking responsibility for ensuring its completion, often without direction. This type of behavioural engagement appears to foster adaptive behaviour that is proactive, personally initiated, and open to change, and is valuable to organisations in an increasingly complex and shifting environment.

EMPLOYEE ENGAGEMENT, COMMITMENT AND CULTURE

These models of 'employee engagement', motivation and commitment raise questions about the nature of organisational culture conducive to the development of desirable attributes in employees. Collier and Esteban (2007) note that CSR or corporate citizenship behaviours (including employee commitment and engagement behaviours) can be supported by cultures that are either compliance-oriented or values-based, accepting that the two orientations can be mutually supportive. They concluded that '[c]ompliance based programs [and cultures] were associated with willingness to seek advice, lower observed misconduct and ethical awareness ... [whereas] ... values programs [and cultures] yield outcomes such as commitment, integrity and better organizational communication, and they can thus be seen as a more important influence on effective outcomes' (2007: 26).

Trevino et al. (1999) also emphasise that consistency between ethics, CSR programmes and the values demonstrated by leadership and management will have a significant impact on employee commitment and engagement. On the one hand, employee perceptions and behaviour will be influenced by the fairness of practice through which employees are held to account for breaches of compliance codes; on the other hand, employee perceptions of fairness will also take into account how organisations treat employees. Both insights will affect commitment and engagement behaviours.

Kahn suggests that 'psychological presence [required for employee engagement] can be draining in terms of the personal level of effort required, which, depending on other demands on the individual, may not always be possible to sustain' (1992: 25). Thus the presence of a high-level employee engagement has a risk component attached to it, associated with an organisational breach of trust. Kahn (1990) proposes that a core condition for an enduring engagement outcome is the fostering of psychological safety through a culture of trust. Similarly, Sikora et al. (2004) identify the risks to employee engagement when organisations fail to recognise and monitor accumulated stress in conditions of constant and overlapping change in the workplace, incurring costs as a result of the reduction in employee engagement, commitment and motivation. These outcomes can also manifest themselves externally as burnout and employee sickness that diminish individual and organisational capability in both short- and long-term timeframes, at times incurring broader social costs to family and community around welfare and the stocks of human and social capital. (These concerns are also discussed in the entry on Employee Health and Safety.)

Bolton (2004) argues that organisations should therefore recognise that the energy, enthusiasm and trust that feed employee engagement are finite resources and will perhaps vary with the individual's personal circumstances. Thus in increasingly complex and changing environments, the organisation should not as a matter of course expect consistent or increasing levels of engagement from employees. Rather, it should identify its responsibilities to build resilient cultures that will support and maintain high levels of employee engagement (Bolton, 2004).

Kahn (1992) provided insights into responsibilities for managerial practice and cultural values that might sustain employee engagement. He noted that *state engagement* was increased when people were able to utilise 'their preferred selves' in the workplace in relation to personal interests, values and competencies. This requires a commitment on the part of management to identify individual strengths, gaps, traits, preferences, states and behaviours in order to allocate resources, both human and physical, in heavy change environments in a fair and effective manner. Conditions for supporting such an approach, and perhaps optimising employee engagement, suggest the importance of developing a culture of trust in which 'consistency between policies and actions as well as ethical leadership, fair treatment of employees and open discussion of ethics ... [exists instead of] ... a culture that emphasizes self-interest ... unquestioning obedience to authority and the perception that the ... [CSR or ethics] program exists only to protect top management from blame' (Trevino et al., 1999: 131–132).

Thus employee engagement (embracing employee motivation and commitment) is regarded widely as a key attribute intrinsic to both sustainable management practices in complex and fast-paced environments and also in relation to eliciting employee buy-in into CSR programmes and corporate citizenry behaviours. In turn, the modelling of high levels of CSR and corporate citizenry behaviour appears to influence the level of employee engagement.

See also: *Corporate Citizenship, Corporate Social Responsibility, Intragenerational Equity, Resource-Based View, Social Capital, Sweatshops*

employee engagement

REFERENCES

Bolton, D. (2004) 'Change, Coping and Context in the Resilient Organisation', *Mt Eliza Business Review*, 7 (1): 56–66.

Collier, J. and Esteban, R. (2007) 'Corporate Social Responsibility and Employee Commitment', *Business Ethics: A European Review*, 16 (1): 19–33.

Erickson, T.J. (2005) *Testimony submitted before the US Senate Committee on Health, Education, Labour and Pensions*, May 26.

Kahn, W.A. (1990) 'Psychological Conditions of Engagement and Disengagement at Work', *Academy of Management Journal*, 33: 692–724.

Kahn, W.A. (1992) 'To be Fully There: Psychological Presence at Work', *Human Relations*, 45: 321–349.

Locke, E.A. (1997) 'The Motivations to Work: What We Know', in Maher, M.L. and Pintrich, P.R. (eds), *Advances in Motivation and Achievement*, Vol. 10. Greenwich, CT: JAI Press, pp. 375–412.

Macey, W.H. and Schneider, B. (2008) 'The Meaning of Employee Engagement', *Industrial and Organizational Psychology*, 1: 3–30.

Mayer, J.P. and Allen, N.J. (1991) 'A Three Component Conceptualization of Organizational Commitment', *Human Resource Management Journal*, 1 (1): 61–90.

Sikora, P.B, Beaty, E.D. and Forward, J. (2004) 'Updating Theory on Organizational Stress: The Asynchronous Multiple Overlapping Change (AMOC) Model of Workplace Stress', *Human Resource Development Review*, 3 (1): 3–35.

Trevino, L.K., Weaver, G.R., Gibson, D.J. and Toffler, B.L. (1999) 'Managing Ethics and Legal Compliance: What Works and What Hurts', *California Management Review*, 41 (2): 131–151.

Employee Health and Safety

WORKPLACE RISKS

Both employees and employers have cause to be concerned that working conditions are appropriate to maintain employee health and safety. Many jobs are potentially dangerous and it has become a mark of a responsible organisation and a responsible society that these conditions are controlled and regulated, often by state-based legislation but increasingly by voluntary codes or standards. Examples of risks that are more obvious are those associated with the use of high temperatures or high voltages in manufacturing, while the risks of working with some chemicals may not be obvious until it is too late. That is why many companies now take a more preventative approach.

Occupations such as mining are well recognised as posing particular risks, and good companies will implement training and other preventative programmes to obviate dangers to employees. Manufacturing jobs are riskier than service jobs and younger workers tend to have more accidents, so companies can specifically target these sectors of the workforce with occupational health and safety (OHS) programmes relevant to that workplace. Preventative approaches taken by companies include the formation of worker health and safety teams. Often made up of roughly equal numbers of workers and employees, such teams seem to have reduced the number of accidents and, of course, reduced employee compensation costs.

NEW TRENDS IN OHS

As is occurring in other dimensions of corporate responsibility, the emphasis on employee health and safety is moving to prevention. Decision makers recognise the value of a safe design of workplaces and of products, where hazards are identified and risks assessed early on in the design process to eliminate or minimise the risks. Governments also are increasingly interested in such efforts and are attempting to facilitate this approach. Designers need to address safety at all stages of the lifecycle. For example, a machine might need to be designed with various protections to ensure safe operation, but also to ensure that it can be installed, maintained and disposed of safely.

More recently, other risks associated with the workplace have been recognised. They include repetitive motion disorders and stress-related illnesses and may involve work–life balance issues. Psychologists and industrial physicians recognise an increased work intensity resulting from an excessive workload and stress to be a key factor in contributing to negative employee perceptions of work conditions. There is some suggestion that increases in work intensity result from new approaches to management that encourage high levels of work commitment and a close alignment of employee and company values. According to Hatchuel (2002), such conditions represent a loss of work control or governability so that the boundaries between work and personal life disappear. While assembly line jobs can be regulated and are readily critiqued and monitored by external organisations or employee representatives, unconfined jobs, such as many white-collar occupations, present 'intensity challenges', i.e. to do with balancing self-management with high expectations. Those jobs require senior management to develop solutions such as specific re-confining techniques and support systems. The problem can be compounded by new technologies such as mobile phones and email systems, with many employees feeling pressured to answer emails or respond to clients' and colleagues' needs outside work hours.

Workplace hazards include physical hazards such as noise, vibration, ultra-violet radiation; chemical hazards; movement injuries; dusts and fibres; stress and tension in the workplace. While there is increasing recognition of the need to reduce single-task jobs and repetitive assembly line work both in terms of CSR and of productivity returns, this too is dependent upon the national standards and industry sector. Increasingly, too, other forms of workplace hazard such as stress and difficulties in setting a boundary between work and home are emerging for managers to deal with.

Respecting and guaranteeing employee rights relates to economic, environmental and social conditions, and sometimes firms may make trade-offs between these dimensions. For example, better environmental practices or labour conditions may be traded off against higher wages. There are also synergies between these dimensions of the responsible organisation. For example, making sure employees do not work excessive hours may also result in higher productivity and levels of performance generally. Similarly, implementing sustainable design principles, such as day-lighting, can result in high levels of employee engagement and productivity. Many companies now realise that investing in employee physical and mental health and safety is in the long-term interest of the company as well as the employee and their family. Hence family friendly conditions such as childcare, job-sharing and reimbursing various up-skilling and retraining initiatives are increasingly common, as are workplace gymnasiums, exercise routines and ergonomic office furniture.

Measurement is an important aspect of employee health and safety. Common indices include a lost time injury rate and the number of chemicals for which full toxicity data are available. Quality performance measures may also include the number of defective parts produced and measures of productivity.

SETTING STANDARDS

A wide range of national standards, regulations and codes of practice and conduct exist to deal with these hazards – these vary considerably from country to country. Commonly, national strategies focus on both short-term and long-term strategies. Typical priorities include reducing the impact of risk at work, improving the capacity of organisations to manage employee health and safety, preventing occupational disease more effectively and reducing risks and hazards through safe design. Industries most likely to be targeted by government strategies are agriculture, forestry and fishing; building and construction; health and community services; manufacturing, transport and storage. In Australia, for example, these industries have been shown to be most frequently associated with workplace incidents and workers compensation claims.

The United Nations has also been involved in the setting and harmonising of international standards in several key areas. These include the transport of dangerous goods and the classifying of risks associated with chemicals. For example, the Globally Harmonised System of Classification and Labelling of Chemicals (GHS) is an internationally agreed system for the classification and hazard communication of chemicals, developed by representatives from more than 30 countries and a number of non-government organisations.

Challenges remain for both small and medium enterprises (SMEs) and major multinational enterprises in terms of ensuring optimum workplace conditions. On the one hand, the issue for SMEs is that the payoff from investing in significant improvements in employee working conditions may lag behind the investment. Major multinationals, on the other hand, face the problem of ensuring employee health and safety along the supply chain. This has been a particular challenge for CSR in the toy, footwear and apparel industries, since much of the manufacturing is done in developing countries where the company may not have direct control over its supply chain factories. For example, there are claims of excessive work hours and poor working conditions in factories that supply for various multinational corporations in the footwear industry such as Nike and Adidas-Salomon in China and Indonesia. One answer appears to be strengthening the supplier management cycle, which

employee health and safety

includes supplier guidance, audits and training. A number of such companies now report results from their factory audits and provide other data, such as the number of training sessions given to its suppliers on how to achieve compliance with the company's health, safety and labour standards or codes. As described in the entry on Codes of Conduct, companies are now either developing their own codes or collaborating with the development of industry generic codes.

See also: *Codes of Conduct, Corporate Social Responsibility, Corporate Sustainability, Intragenerational Equity, Resource-Based View*

REFERENCES

Hatchuel, A. (2002) 'Sources of Intensity in Work Organizations', in P. Docherty, J. Forslin and A.B. Shani (eds), *Creating Sustainable Work Systems*. London and New York: Routledge, pp. 40–51.

···· Environmental Discourses ····

CLASSIFYING ENVIRONMENTAL DISCOURSES

Environmental discourses refer to the different ways we understand and describe the relationship between human society and the natural environment. Depending on the particular discourse we ascribe to, we have different expectations of how organisations, including business, government and NGOs, should deal with nature and what should be classified as responsible action. Changing environmental discourses over time reflect shifts in these expectations (Dryzek, 2005), and the historical dominance of a particular discourse has direct implications for what we understand at that time as corporate responsibility and sustainability. The drive to corporate sustainability and reinterpretations of CSR to include more emphasis on environmental practices has largely emerged in association with a shift away from the dominance of a discourse based on concepts of unlimited industrial growth towards more reformist interpretations such as sustainable development or ecological modernisation. Examples of the different trends in environmental discourse are set

Table 2   Examples of environmental discourses

Environmental discourses	
Reformist	**Radical**
Sustainable development	Deep ecology
Ecological modernisation	Ecofeminism
Risk society	Ecological democracy

Source: Adapted from Dryzek, 1995: 15. By permission of
Oxford University Press. Adapted with permission

out in Table 2. Reformist approaches accept the capitalist mode of industrial development and attempt to conceive strategies that might temper its impacts on intergenerational and intragenerational equity, while radical approaches look to reshaping society.

RADICAL DISCOURSES

Radical discourses include those approaches such as deep ecology, eco-feminism and ecological democracy. Proponents (e.g. Naess, 1989) eschew so-called anthropocentric forms of knowledge, including those concerned with addressing environmental problems such as climate change, as incapable of recognising the intrinsic value that is held by all life forms. Eco-feminist writers such as Merchant (1980) argue that nature, women and indigenous peoples are subordinated by men and men's interpretation of science and technology, and argue for a new approach to nature that is more intuitive and empathetic as well as less dominating. Proponents of ecological democracy (e.g. Dryzek, 2005) argue for new discursive designs that would promote more authentic forms of democracy where the boundaries between human social systems and ecological systems could be more rigorously and openly debated. The key principle underpinning ecological democracy is social learning – the need for organisations, groups and individuals to learn and reflect on their own limitations in dealing with the multiple uncertainties associated with ecological systems that are compounded as they interact with human, political, social and economic systems.

Alternative radical perspectives represented by environmental philosophies such as deep ecology may appear to have had little impact on the corporate world, yet they represent the shift across society to a more critical perspective on industrial development that underpins less overtly exploitative corporate behaviour towards nature.

environmental discourses

87

REFORMIST DISCOURSES

Reformist discourses that have been most taken up in management and organisational studies and literature are sustainable development, ecological modernisation and risk society. We have described sustainable development elsewhere in this book and in the entries on intergenerational and intragenerational equity. We will spotlight below the key points of ecological modernisation and risk society as two examples of influential and overlapping discourses impacting on contemporary corporate behaviour and thus influencing corporate practice.

Ecological modernisation

Mol (2006) suggests that ecological modernisation theory can be thought of in terms of clusters or themes of social and institutional transformations and practices:

1. Techno-scientific systems increasingly engaged with addressing environmental problems.
2. Growing use made of the market as a means of bringing about ecological restructuring and reform.
3. Diminishing role for the nation-state as non-state, decentralised actors assume traditional administrative, regulatory, managerial and mediating functions of the nation-states. These new and often more informal sub-political arrangements have the potential to challenge established systems of legitimacy and authority (Beck, 1992).
4. Emergent supra-national institutions also undermine the nation-state's traditional role in environmental reform.
5. Social movements and NGOs increasingly involved in partnerships with public and private decision-making institutions regarding environmental reforms.

Ecological modernisation theory is the subject of much debate in the literature. It has been accused as serving as a greenwash, deployed to represent those dominant stakeholders in the capitalist system whose activities and interests have facilitated the ecological crisis (York and Rosa, 2003). As such, it is frequently contrasted with the 'treadmill of production' (e.g. Schnaiberg et al., 2002) perspective that links capitalist systems of production to an inevitable ecological decline.

Scholars distinguish between weak and strong versions of ecological modernisation based on the comparative emphasis on techno-scientific change and innovation in lessening environmental impact. 'Strong' versions emphasise more radical and internationally focused changes in economies and policies to progress global sustainable development (Christoff, 1996). Other writers argue that the socio-political and economic innovations underpinning ecological modernisation can only proceed on the basis of critical self-awareness involving public scrutiny and democratic control (Dryzek, 2005).

RISK SOCIETY

The theory of a 'risk society' is largely associated with the well-known European sociologist Ulrich Beck. It refers to post-industrial society and attempts to explain emerging trends that are impacting on all the traditional forms of authority and influence such as the state, the church and business. The key argument is that new forms of politics are emerging within the nation-state as the state in its traditional form cannot deal with the high levels of uncertainty and risk associated with technological development. New and more informal means of governance emerge and are associated with local action and some international governance, and therefore there is less influence at the level of the nation state.

On this account, sub-political arrangements, operating externally to traditional political forms, are fostering a new reflexive capacity in society and are a driving force in ecological modernisation (Beck, 1992). The sub-political arena is decentralised, knowledge-intensive and populated by diverse actors who operate outside the formal system of politics but are drawn together by a common, often targeted goal. Expertise and knowledge are highly politicised aspects of this arena.

Sub-politics refers to an emergent, distributed and reflexive sphere of action that transcends and challenges the formal political system. It is characterised by high levels of uncertainty and rapid change in the knowledge base, compounded by change in the institutions of market, state and civil society and the relationships between them. Risk society approaches have been classified as a reflexive, strong form of ecological modernisation. On this account, post-industrial society develops its own critique so that techno-scientific expertise is increasingly called upon to alleviate the negative environmental impacts and replenish the environmental resources diminished as a result of industrialisation. A reflexive version of ecological modernisation can explain institutional change that impacts in favour of more responsible corporate behaviour as organisations are prompted to assess and address their negative impacts on

environmental discourses

89

society and on the environment. The implications for business are complex but basically involve corporations being required to form new partnerships and networks that will act as a new form of governance replacing the state.

See also: Business Networks, Intergenerational Equity, Intragenerational Equity, Social Partnerships, Sustainable Development

REFERENCES

Beck, U. (1992) *The Risk Society* (M. Ritter, Trans.). London: Sage.

Christoff, P. (1996) 'Ecological Modernization, Ecological Modernities', *Environmental Politics*, 5 (3): 476–500.

Dryzek, J. (2005) *The Politics of the Earth*, 2nd edn. Oxford: Oxford University Press.

Merchant, C. (1980) *The Death of Nature*. New York: Harper and Row.

Mol, A.P.J. (2006) 'Environment and Modernity in Transitional China: Frontiers of Ecological Modernization', *Development and Change*, 37: 29–56.

Naess, A. (1989) *Ecology, Community and Lifestyle*. Cambridge: Cambridge University Press.

Schnaiberg, A., Pellow, D. and Weinberg, A. (2002) 'The Treadmill of Production and the Environmental State', in F. Buttel and A.P.J. Mol (eds), *The Environmental State Under Pressure*. Oxford: Elsevier Science, pp. 15–32.

York, R. and Rosa, E.A. (2003) 'Key Challenges to Ecological Modernization Theory', *Organization & Environment*, 16: 273–288.

Environmental Policy Tools

TRADITIONAL APPROACHES TO ENVIRONMENTAL POLICY

Environmental laws and policies can be designed to limit the extent to which organisations can externalise the costs associated with the environmental consequences of their actions. That is, they are meant to reduce or prevent firms externalising the environmental costs of production and consumption onto the rest of society rather than bearing the costs themselves.

Stronger forms of environmental law only emerged in the late 1960s and 1970s – spurred on by increasing public awareness of emerging environmental problems such as toxic chemicals and the impact of industrial processes on local communities. In the USA, the passing of the National Environmental Policy Act (NEPA) in 1969 marked the beginning of a regulatory regime that continues today. Much environmental law since this iconic legislation falls into a general category of laws known as 'command and control'. Such laws typically involve three elements: the identification of a type of environmentally harmful activity; the imposition of specific conditions or standards on that activity; and the prohibition of forms of the activity that fail to comply with the imposed conditions or standards.

By the 1980s, major limitations to command and control had begun to emerge. They included the growing problem of dealing with non-point sources of pollution, such as pesticide run-off from agriculture, or greenhouse gas (GHG) emissions. In addition, many laws addressed 'end-of-pipe' pollution problems rather than pollution prevention. Through the 1980s and 1990s, environmental policy shifted away from command and control laws and regulations towards more market-based and voluntary approaches. The idea behind this shift was that instead of passing complex laws that were difficult to enforce, companies would be induced to improve their environmental performance through various incentive-based policy tools. The three key tools, representing the shift away from command and control, are: market-based or economic policies; voluntary programmes; and mandatory information disclosures.

MARKET-BASED POLICY TOOLS

Market-based policies are policy instruments that provide incentives for polluters to reduce their emissions. They are either price based or rights based. Price-based tools depend on charges being paid for the use of resources such as water, timber or oils. For instance, fees may be charged for emitting a certain unit of pollution in order to force firms to internalise their environmental costs. Supporters of price-based tools argue that higher charges for natural resources would ensure a more sustainable form of development. Based on the principle of 'polluter pays', pollution taxes require firms to pay a fee that is determined by the units of pollution they discharge. Obviously the greater the cost per unit of pollutant, the greater the incentive to reduce emissions. An example of this might be a carbon tax such as exists in varying degrees in a number of European countries. This is effectively a tax on carbon dioxide emissions and thus acts as a tax on fossil fuels. Such taxes may be placed on the use of oil, coal, natural gas, liquefied petroleum gas, petrol, and aviation fuel used in domestic travel. Although there can be complications such as varying the tax rate according to sector, the carbon tax is appealing because its revenues in developed countries are potentially huge and can be used to replace other taxes or input into various other environmental protection schemes. Aside from the extensive restructuring required in deciding what taxes to sacrifice in lieu of the carbon tax, there are disadvantages. Importantly, the environmental outcome is not guaranteed as there are no fixed limits set to the use of carbon.

Rights-based policies depend on governments creating property rights that will allow firms legally to emit certain types of pollutants or emissions such as various gases, like sulphur dioxide, that are by-products from industrial manufacturing. Rights-based policies include forms of pollution taxes where the company is given the right to pollute a certain amount, emission fees and tradeable emissions permits. Tradeable permits depend upon governments allocating each firm a certain number of permits to emit certain substances and then establishing markets where firms can buy or sell the permits. The various carbon trading schemes such as those called 'cap and trade' are an example. Cap and trade schemes work by governments setting a limit for a particular pollutant such as GHGs that can be emitted in a specific region over a specific time by specific industries. Firms are then either allocated or will bid at auction for allowances of the pollutant. A market forms around the fact that allowances can be bought or sold. Supporters of cap and trade schemes argue that these take advantage of the effectiveness of markets in fostering innovation and efficiency outcomes.

Problems from the over-allocation of permits have arisen with current cap and trade schemes, such as the market distortion that has occurred with the European Union Emission Trading Scheme, the largest GHG emissions trading scheme created in conjunction with the Kyoto Protocol. Companies who do not meet the emissions standards of such schemes that are set by a range of variables, including the amount of emissions, manufacturing sector, etc. can theoretically purchase 'credits' from those who have cut their emissions by a certain amount, depending on the scheme. There are also other options available for companies determining how to work within such schemes. They may arrange emission offsets by agreeing to contribute to environmental goods by planting trees; they can increase pollution at one place but decrease it at another (bubble policies); or they can store credits for later use (Epstein, 2008).

There has been much criticism of the market-based approach by environmentalists (e.g. Beder, 2006) on the basis that it legitimises pollution and is vulnerable to manipulation by vested interests. This has occurred in attempts to establish a carbon trading reduction scheme in countries such as Australia, where the issue has become heavily politicised.

VOLUNTARY ENVIRONMENTAL PROGRAMMES

The third type of environmental policy tool that has emerged over the last decade to replace or to complement command and control schemes is the voluntary environmental programme (see also entries on Codes of Conduct and Voluntary Regulation). These programmes are sets of practices concerning firm environmental behaviour that organisations of a particular sector, size or location can sign up to and will then agree to behave according to the set practices. Examples include Responsible Care established by the chemicals industry. Such schemes may not necessarily require firms to achieve set standards but may involve a partnership arrangement with a government organisation which requires them to implement various awareness raising or training schemes designed by the government. Governments may induce firms into such 'strategic' partnerships through incentives such as providing free environmental audits.

MANDATORY INFORMATION DISCLOSURE SCHEMES

Mandatory information disclosure schemes depend on firms being required to systematically measure and disclose information about their environmental behaviour (see entry on Corporate Responsibility Reporting). The idea is that publicity will force firms to change their behaviour because it gives various stakeholders, such as consumers, suppliers, investors, and NGOs, government information, and armed with this they can put pressure on the firm. One of the best known of these schemes is the Toxic Release Inventory in the USA, which appears to have had a major impact on firm behaviour. However, these schemes also have their drawbacks, and the leverage they give to certain stakeholders may not always be to the benefit of wider society.

See also: Codes of Conduct, Corporate Responsibility Reporting, Voluntary Regulation

REFERENCES

Beder, S. (2006) *Environmental Principles and Policies*. Sydney: UNSW Press.
Epstein, M. (2008) *Making Sustainability Work*. Sheffield: Greenleaf.

Ethical Consumerism

MARKETS AND ETHICAL DRIVERS

Ethical consumers consider a range of ethical issues in their consumer behavioural choices. The market for ethically orientated products has increased steadily over the past decade, although relative to the volume of markets as a whole the ethically related market is still small. Considered to be composed of three components, animal welfare, human rights and the environment, ethical consumerism describes purchasing that is concerned more with ethical implications than brand names or cost issues. Overall, environmental issues are ranked above human rights and animal rights/welfare issues for their perceived ethical importance. Research has shown that consumers are influenced more if the company is associated with negative environmental behaviour than if it is involved in proactive environmental initiatives. Findings also suggest that ethical drivers vary considerably across markets (Wheale and Hinton, 2007).

Many issues and patterns of behaviour might influence this decision making. Issues may include product safety, environmental impacts, consumer privacy, employee welfare, discrimination, fair pricing, community action and charitable donations. Voluntary simplification, where consumers make choices influenced by concerns for the extent and nature of consumption, is an emergent pattern of behaviour linked to ethical consumerism.

Most policy recommendations on consumption make the assumption that consumers are rational individuals operating autonomously and continuously making choices that are informed by time or money considerations. The reality is much more complex, as illustrated by the diverse ways in which consumers have reacted to different types of green marketing.

key concepts in corporate social responsibility

94

Crane (2001) argues that ethical considerations provide unsolicited products and services that can prompt purchasing at four different levels: the qualities of the product itself; the marketing process; the corporation and its reputation; and the country that the product is associated with. In addition, products can be ethically augmented in positive and negative directions. The ethical product is clearly a complex concept and one that Crane suggests is better represented as bundles of attributes. For example, the product groups will have different levels of importance to the ethical consumer, with each product group being considered on the basis of its bundle of ethical attributes. The 'food product goods' group is the most strongly associated with ethical issues, while the 'brown goods' group (electric goods such as stereos and TVs) is shown to be least associated with these issues.

Eco-labelling is used by companies to exploit these emergent market segments. Organic food certification is the most common form of eco-labelling, and appears to be growing at a rapid rate in many countries.

THE ROLE OF BOYCOTTS AND FOOD ACTIVISM

Boycotts have been the most visible face of ethical consumerism. The European boycott of Shell over its plan to dump the *Brent Spar* oil platform at sea; the US boycott of Texaco over alleged racial remarks by senior management; and the US boycott of Mitsubishi over alleged sexual harassment in the workplace have drawn attention to the power of consumers in influencing more responsible corporate behaviour. However, the boycotts themselves may be pushed along and organised by a variety of social interests, and some critics argue that the outcomes of boycotts are not necessarily the most socially or environmentally responsible.

Boycotts have, until quite recently, been seen as the most powerful means of exerting consumer voice. For instance, Survival International initiated a boycott on DeBeers, the world's largest miner and marketer of diamonds, as a response to their removal of Kalahari Bushmen from ancestral lands to mine a diamond deposit in Gope. The campaign made Gope a problematic asset for DeBeers, resulting in them selling their deposit in May 2007. In December 2009, human rights activists launched another major international boycott in response to DeBeer operating in another area of Botswana, resulting in the eviction of local people and again exerting considerable consumer pressure on the company (http://current.com/items/89433230_diamond-boycott-campaign-restarted.htm).

But the rise of food activism and eco-labelling associated with Fair Trade has seen political activity focus on non-consumption rather than on consumption as with the boycott. Fair Trade, a product certification system designed to allow people to identify products that meet agreed environmental, labour and developmental standards, offers a political challenge to the established markets. It audits transactions between companies in developed countries offering Fair Trade certified products and their international suppliers, in order to guarantee that the farmers and farm workers producing the Fair Trade Certified goods are paid a fair above-market price. In addition, annual inspections ensure that strict socio-economic development criteria are being met in the production process. In coffee alone over the past five years, Fair Trade has returned to producers more than $70 million above what they would have received from the conventional coffee market. Fair Trade currently covers coffee, tea, chocolate, bananas, mangos, grapes, sugar and rice, with new products coming out regularly. This form of certification only applies in developing countries. It is discussed further in the entry on Fair Trade.

Most firms now recognise that there are profitable niches for products that may be regarded as ethical. The use of ethical responsibility as a source of corporate differentiation with potential added value is regarded as a marketing strategy, and this differentiation can relate to a whole range of social preferences and ethical issues, including the environment, Fair Trade, animal rights/welfare and employee welfare. Ethical stance is a powerful differentiator for companies to consider as part of their strategy, although there remains a large consumer group who do not consider ethics in purchasing decisions. Price remains a major barrier to the wide take-up of ethical products. Studies have shown that customers are not tolerant of the lower quality and higher prices of green products (De Pelsmacker et al., 2005). An important point, however, is that the markets for environmental products in particular are widening. Consumables such as household detergents as well as larger items are now on the marketing agenda. Overall, ethical consumerism seems to have most impact as a marketing force when it is targeted at the personal or household, rather than the planetary or societal level.

IMPACTS OF ETHICAL CONSUMERISM

The impact of ethical consumerism is unclear. While it is a growing phenomenon, and particularly manifest in the phenomenon of boycotting perceived corporate irresponsibility, there is still a major gap between consumer attitude or intention and consumer behaviour or actual purchasing. Although there has been a considerable increase in some markets loosely described as 'ethical', such as free-range eggs or organic foods in general, price, quality, convenience and brand familiarity are often still the most important factors affecting the buying decision (De Pelsmacker et al., 2005).

Consumers appear to find it hard to change their patterns of consumption and there is a big difference between a willingness to embrace recycling, for instance, and actually changing the extent and type of purchasing. The credible opinion now is that population is not the problem, no more than technology is the answer. It may help reduce the problem, but only if consumption is held constant. Achieving sustainable consumption is the challenge. More optimistically, recent research suggests that consumers may support ethical choices, such as only manufacturing or selling products that are relatively environmentally or socially responsible, that are made by government, manufacturers or retailers.

See also: Business Ethics, Green Marketing, Greenwash, Social and Societal Marketing

REFERENCES

BRASS Policy Briefing (2008) 'Climate Change, Consumers and the Future of Brands'. Available at www.brass.cf.ac.uk/uploads/CLIMATEPBD.pdf, accessed 12 July 2009.
Crane, A. (2001) 'Unpacking the Ethical Product', *Journal of Business Ethics*, 30: 361–373.
De Pelsmacker, M., Driesen, L. and Rayp, G. (2005) 'Do Consumers Care about Ethics? Willingness to Pay for Fair-Trade Coffee', *The Journal of Consumer Affairs*, 39 (2): 363–387.
Wheale, P. and Hinton, D. (2007) 'Ethical Consumers in Search of Markets,' *Business Strategy and the Environment*, 16 (4): 302–315.

Fair Trade

WHAT IS FAIR TRADE?

Fair Trade is an organised social movement and market-based approach that looks to promote the development of marginalised actors in the production process – the small farmers and plantation workers of the developing countries. The movement advocates paying a higher price to producers to improve social and environmental standards as a means of addressing a situation where only a very small fraction of the final value of a product goes to the producer in the developing country. Subsidies paid to farmers in developed countries and vertically integrated companies such as big supermarkets and fast-food restaurants who grow, harvest, transport and market their own bananas, coffee or other products are other reasons why the farm worker or small farm owner in the developed world becomes so much at the mercy of and exploited by the global market chain.

Cooperatives are formed by bringing small farmers or producers together to sell their products directly into the market, thereby avoiding the costs that go to middlemen. By committing to the Fair Trade Label, companies that buy the products agree to pay sustainable prices and comply with the internationally agreed Fair Trade standards (see www.Fair Trade.net/standards.html). Companies trading Fair Trade products must:

- pay a price to producers that aims to cover the costs of sustainable production: the Fair Trade Minimum Price. This price acts as a floor price that protects small producers from sudden swings in the market, such as has notoriously occurred in the coffee market. Hence the small farmers working within the Fair Trade networks are ensured of some income security.
- pay an additional sum that producers can invest in improving social, economic or environmental conditions in the community: the Fair Trade Premium. The Fair Trade Premium is spent as directed by democratic decision making on the part of the producer organisations and is frequently directed towards education or health care benefit schemes.
- partially pay in advance, when producers ask for it. Producers can access up to 60 per cent of their final Fair Trade contract value to help them get the product to market.
- sign contracts that allow for long-term planning and sustainable production practices.

Other benefits offered to producers include access to export markets, facilitated through the Fair Trade network, being organised into democratic organisations that can assist in building skills and other aspects of producer capacity, and The Organic Price Differential, an incentive paid to producers of some Fair Trade products such as cocoa and coffee to cover the additional costs of certified organic production and to encourage the use of environmentally friendly practices.

Basically, this means that the participants in Fair Trade networks agree to pay a fair trade differential if the world market price for a commodity is less than the price established as the fair trade minimum. In addition to the generic standards, companies trading in certain products such as bananas or coffee must abide by special standards for that product. The two main types of product standards are standards for small-scale producers and standards for hired labour.

Fair Trade certification and auditing is conducted by independent third-party organisations, although there is some push to make this a more participatory process, where the producers themselves contribute to the assessment. Certification is given for a certain period, up to three years, and auditing also takes place within that time. As well, manufacturers who package the Fair Trade products are required to ensure the traceability of ingredients within that packaging.

Hence the three components of the Fair Trade system are: trading networks comprising producer groups, traders, licensed retailers and consumers; the marketing of Fair Trade labelled products through licensed mainstream retailers; and the politicisation of consumer activity through Fair Trade campaigns (Wilkinson, 2007). Organisations such as Oxfam may be involved both through retailing activities and through their campaigns on behalf of Fair Trade, although of recent years it has tended to focus more on its advocacy role.

The focus of the Fair Trade system is primarily on exports from developing countries to developed countries, including handicrafts, coffee, cocoa, sugar, tea, and foodstuffs such as bananas. For many, the Fair Trade coffee market exemplifies the movement. Coffee remains the highest selling Fair Trade product. In Australia, for instance, in 2008, coffee made up 73 per cent of all retail sales, and was sourced from 16 different countries in Asia, Asia-Pacific, Africa and Latin America.

HISTORY

Fair Trade has been in operation since the 1960s but seems to have really gained in strength over the last ten years and now is one of the fastest growing food segments of the US and European markets. It has gained in momentum as a result of the obvious dire effects on small producers of crashes in the price of cocoa and coffee during the 1980s and 1990s.

Although criticised by some as not offering a radical alternative to global capitalism, there is an undoubted take-up by consumers of the concept. It differs from similar movements such as organics, animal welfare and other aspects of ethical consumerism because it focuses on traditional issues of inequality rather than on establishing new codes of conduct or new systems of rights and duties (Wilkinson, 2007).

While fast growing, Fair Trade remains a small market segment, with a large majority of the estimated 400 million small farmers in the world not involved in its activities. Perhaps its greatest contribution, according to a number of commentators, lies in its capacity building, upskilling small producer groups in their marketing capabilities and linking into other social movements concerned with worker rights, organic foods and a range of global inequities. As well as building the confidence and skills of farmers, other indirect benefits are said to include support for environmental and cultural conservation projects.

One of the marks of the success of Fair Trade is the recent announcement by Cadburys' that its signature chocolate bar will be Fair Trade. Hence, Fair Trade demonstrates the emergence of new forms of collective action and is an example of activism that is focussed on the market rather than on the state or even on individual organisations.

CASE EXAMPLES

The Oromia Coffee Farmers Cooperative Union (OCFCU) is the largest Fair Trade certified organisation in Ethiopia. Ethiopia has 1.2 million coffee growers, and coffee accounts for more than 50 per cent of its export earnings. The OCFCU was formed in 1999 when almost 25,000 farmers representing 35 small cooperatives came together in order to export their coffee directly to the overseas markets. Since then the Fair Trade Premium has funded the building of three primary schools and provided ongoing resources for school projects.

In the New Guinea Highlands, the Fair Trade Premium associated with coffee-growing cooperatives has been allocated to the improvement of roads, making it easier for the farmers to get their goods to market.

CONACADO (the National Confederation of Dominican Cocoa Producers) is a group of 9,500 small-scale cocoa farmers in the Dominican Republic. Most CONACADO cocoa is certified organic and is grown under the shade canopy of fruit-producing trees. Benefits to the local community derived from the Fair Trade system include a low-cost plant nursery that enables farmers to grow their own food, various technology upgrades to enable them to grow better quality cocoa, and various education and health initiatives such as health clinics and infrastructure improvements.

See also: *Ethical Consumerism, Green Marketing, Sustainable Development*

REFERENCES

Associated Case Studies on Africa and Latin America, Case Studies by Nabs Suma (Africa) and Sarah Lyon (Latin America)', November. Available at www.rimisp.org/FCKeditor/UserFiles/File/documentos/docs/pdf/WDR/Paper%2011_Farnworth%20and%20Goodman.pdf, accessed 9 April 2010.
Wilkinson, J. (2007) 'Fair Trade: Dynamics and Dilemmas of a Market Oriented Global Social Movement', *Journal of Consumer Policy*, 30: 219–239.

Globalisation

THE TERM 'GLOBALISATION'

'Globalisation' has been defined in many ways that are often contradictory (Sutcliffe, 2004), yet is still used pervasively to describe the contemporary state of capitalist development and its influence on the world economy. There is significant debate around the positive and negative features of globalisation. A key concept around which the debate turns is the influence of world market forces (Glyn, 2004). This influence is manifest both in the way countries are shifting towards market-driven economies and in the pattern of global integration occurring through trade, investment and migration activities. Glyn acknowledges that national economies have become increasingly open 'with the exception of migration, the extent of international economic integration ... now exceed[ing] levels seen in the first wave of globalization prior to the First World War' (2004: 7). He also reminds both the supporters and detractors of the globalisation process that the extent and speed of the process are often exaggerated because of faulty metrics.

GLOBALISATION AND INEQUALITY

Both Glyn (2004) and Sutcliffe (2004) comment on the impact of globalisation on welfare and inequality. Glyn questions the impact of globalisation on the level and distribution of welfare world-wide. He differentiates between optimistic and pessimistic scenarios. The optimistic scenario suggests that globalisation leads to convergence between developed and developing nations (North and South) through increased labour productivity that would reduce disparities in income and lead to the elimination of poverty, clean technologies and accompanying productivity increases. The pessimistic view is that heightened competition will lead to a 'race to the bottom' in relation to working conditions, welfare provision and environmental degradation. Glyn adds that this negative scenario might be 'aided and abetted by the spread of corporate governance structures which are increasingly constrained to give overwhelming priority to shareholder value' (2004: 7–8). Both of these scenarios are challenged by debates around the definition of terms.

DEFINING 'INEQUALITY'

Sutcliffe (2004) raises the challenges associated with measuring changes in levels of world inequality. He identifies three ways of measuring inequality. The first is to look at income per head and population to calculate average income differences between large groupings of countries, e.g. the North–South divide. Another version of this same approach aims to take account of intra-country as well as inter-country distribution 'in effect considering the whole world as if it were one country', often referred to as 'global distribution' (2004: 16). The second approach considers world inequality from a perspective of welfare, not just income. This approach includes indicators such as life expectancy, education and so on. A third approach is similar to the first, but does not measure distribution on the basis of a single integral statistic of inequality; rather, it measures differences between the incomes of defined groups using ratios (usually percentages), e.g. measuring the income of the top 5 per cent with the lowest 5 per cent.

The availability of purchasing power parity (PPP) estimates of gross domestic product (GDP) and national income appears to provide more accurate comparisons between countries at any particular time because they measure the value of production at a common set of domestic prices rather than assuming, as is done by using exchange rates as a measure, that all national consumption is imported (Sutcliffe, 2004). National income is calculated differently when using the two measures; this impacts significantly on estimates of inequality. The PPP-based estimates, not surprisingly, appear to produce lower estimates. However, Sutcliffe notes that there can be problems also with this PPP-based approach when comparing countries with very different consumption patterns. In addition, the complexity and time required to produce PPP data can be problematic, resulting in simpler and more easily available exchange rates often being used to calculate comparative inequality across nations.

DEFINING 'GLOBALISATION'

Sutcliffe (2004) also asks whether it is possible to see any relationship between world inequality and the varied, broad and fluctuating nature of globalisation. He notes that the period since 1980 has been seen as one of very strong globalisation. However, this begs the question as to whether the chosen definition of globalisation includes only those occurrences concerning liberalisation and integration, or whether other 'happenings' have been considered. These other factors might include the hindrance of trade liberalisation by discriminatory protection in many developed countries (especially in the agricultural sector), and the decrease in aid as a percentage of GDP of donor countries (0.2 per cent in 2010), in essence impeding capital flows that might lessen inequality.

Sutcliffe concludes that the political orientation of the world discourse on global inequality veers heavily towards 'poverty' rather than 'distribution'. It is more politically acceptable to focus on policies for growth amongst the poor than on a redistribution of income. In this vein, he notes that although extreme poverty has been regarded as pathological and worth eliminating globally, extreme wealth has only been seen as pathological from the perspective of the environmental debate around economic growth. Sutcliffe appears to support O'Rourke's (2001) conclusions that the relationship between globalisation and inequality 'varies according to the initial endowment of countries, policies pursued and many other factors' (2004: 35), individual case studies often being more instructive than a broad analysis of general patterns.

GLOBALISATION AND ENVIRONMENTAL INEQUALITY

Polanyi (1957 [1944]) described a double movement within capitalism wherein the market expanded along with forms of social protection for populations and the environment (quoted in Boyce, 2004). Boyce identifies an unevenness in such development processes, observing that globalisation has developed most rapidly in capital and product markets, less in labour markets (due to mobility issues), but very little in the social sphere of governance, particularly in relation to the environment. However, there have been some global and regional efforts to integrate governance with markets around the environment. Examples include the 1987 Montreal Protocol curtailing the use of chemicals that deplete the ozone layer, and the European Union's (European Union, 2007) REACH regulations (Registration, Evaluation, Authorisation and Restriction of Chemical Substances) which deal with chemicals and their safe use and became law in 2007. REACH regulations not only require industry to manage the risks from chemicals and to provide safety information on the substances, but also call for the progressive substitution of the most dangerous chemicals should suitable substitutes be identified.

Boyce (2004) draws attention to the possibility of environmental polarisation. The impact of pollution and natural resource depletion often occur in specific localities, thus incurring 'environmental cost shifting'. He identifies possible reasons why governance fails to remedy market failures in the form of environmental externalities, i.e. the losers may belong to future generations, they may lack adequate information on 'the extent or sources of environmental burdens', or they may lack sufficient power to alter the behaviour of 'the winners'. He concludes that the future environmental impacts of globalisation will depend largely 'on how the new opportunities created by the globalization of markets and governance alter balances of power, both within countries and amongst them ... globalization could accelerate worldwide environmental degradation and deepen environmental inequalities ... [it could give] impetus to countervailing forces that could bring about a greener and less divided world' (2004: 124).

GLOBALISATION AND THE UN

The experience of an increasing diversity and complexity of agendas for global economic development has required a greater coordination of UN agendas by the UN Administrative Committee on Coordination (ACC) (which became the Chief Executive Board (CEB) in 2000). A significant part of its brief is now the achievement of policy coherence within and across nations in response to globalisation challenges.

However, Ruggie reminds us that 'the most distinctive institutional feature of the UN system is that it is not designed as a matrix ... but as a set of deeply rooted columns connected only by thin and tenuous rows ... This is an important fact to bear in mind when assessing the UN system's approach to the challenges of globalization' (2003: 303). Often the traditional UN role of championing inequality has been in tension with the UN commitment to promote and regulate global market forces. For example, the successful but different development paths of many East Asian economies have been treated as aberrations rather than promoted as models, 'despite the fact that their growth was both faster and more equitable than elsewhere' (2003: 304).

In the 1990s, Bretton Woods Institutions, including the World Bank and the International Monetary Fund (IMF), 'vigorously pushed capital market liberalization onto the developing countries with little regard for the absence of its institutional requisites' (Ruggie, 2003: 304). Today there is broader recognition of the increasing disparities between the world's richest and poorest nations by the IMF, together with the need for policies to support the opportunities offered by globalisation and to redress its negative impacts. Ruggie notes that this new consensus within the UN acknowledges the importance of governance, the rule of law and health and education as crucial to economic development. The consensus also recognises the consequences of impediments to the economic development of poorer nations in the form of trade barriers in developed nations, particularly their agricultural products, the inadequacy of development assistance, and the need for increasing debt relief, as well as the foreign investment that embodies skills and technologies. These directions are incorporated in the Millenium Development Goals of the UN that set targets for reducing world poverty to be achieved by 2015.

GLOBALISATION AND CSR

As described in the entry on Business Networks, the UN's Global Compact (GC) is an attempt to increase the balance between global standards that promote market expansion and social objectives concerning labour standards and environmental protection (UN, 2008). Corporations who join the GC are required to report annually by submitting a Communication on Progress (COP) concerning the implementation of the initiative's ten principles covering human rights, workplace standards, the environment, and anti-corruption. It is a network-based initiative, having the Global Compact Office and six

UN agencies at its core. It exemplifies the UN's approach to bridging the gap between policies of market liberalisation and those to decrease global inequities.

See also: Business Networks, Corporate Citizenship, Fair Trade, Intergenerational Equity, Postcolonialism

REFERENCES

Boyce, J.K. (2004) 'Green and Brown? Globalization and the Environment', *Oxford Review of Economic Policy*, 20 (1): 105–128.

European Union (2007) 'REACH: What is REACH'. Available at http://ec.europa.eu/environment/chemicals/reach/reach_intro.htm, accessed 2 April 2010.

Glyn, A. (2004) 'The Assessment: How Far Has Globalization Gone?', *Oxford Review of Economic Policy*, 20 (1): 1–14.

O'Rourke, K.H. (2001) 'Globalization and Inequality: Historical Trends', NBER Working paper 8339. Available at http://www.nber.org/papers/w8339

Polyani, K. (1957 [1944]) *The Great Transformation: The Political and Economic Origins of our Time*. Boston, MA: Beacon Press.

Ruggie, J.G. (2003) 'The United Nations and Globalization: Patterns and Limits of Institutional Adaptation', *Global Governance*, 9: 301–321.

Sutcliffe, B. (2004) 'World Inequality and Globalization', *Oxford Review of Economic Policy*, 20 (1): 15–37.

UN (2008) 'What is the Global Compact'. Available at www.unglobalcompact.org/, accessed 2 April 2010.

.... Governance ....

WHAT IS GOVERNANCE?

Corporate governance refers to the mechanisms and frameworks necessary for corporate decision making. From the perspective of CSR, however, 'governance' refers to managing competing corporate interests for the wider good of society, for the organisation and for the planet as a whole. Recent corporate scandals and the global financial crisis (as discussed in the entry on Corporate Accountability) have highlighted the connection between legitimacy, trust and good governance. Like governance more generally, corporate governance integrates the three elements of effectiveness, legitimacy and security. These general governance principles are fundamentally about how a firm is run and in whose interests.

A key concern for governance is the difference between management's perspective and that of the majority of its shareholders. This is what is termed 'the agency problem', or the separation of management and ownership, referred to earlier in this book in the entry on Agency Theory. Although there is some dispute over who should override whom, both executive and non-executive directors have roles in ensuring effective governance. For example, the Cadbury Committee (1992) viewed the role of non-executive directors as one of monitoring the executive directors, and some research shows that numbers of outside directors add value.

Studies of governance tend to focus on board performance and the presence of audit committees. But increasingly in a global and privatised world, business ethics is a matter of ensuring that governance addresses the considerations of numerous stakeholders and incorporates understandings from multiple disciplines. Corporate governance is also linked to strategy that is formulated according to international governance mechanisms, such as the numbers of international environmental governance arrangements. These range from formal regimes to combat climate change and ozone depletion to more informal and private regimes for tropical logging and the ISO 14000 environmental management standards. For instance, Shell has changed its corporate environmental decision making in response to the growing institutional pressures relating to corporate environmental governance.

GOVERNANCE, CSR AND SUSTAINABILITY

Despite the recent financial crisis, there is evidence that many senior managers continue to perceive good governance, CSR and corporate sustainability as fundamental to the long-term successful operations of any organisation. In the recent 13th Annual Global CEO survey by PricewaterhouseCoopers (2010), for example, more CEOs reported raising climate change investment during the crisis than reducing it and more than two-thirds thought such strategies would confer reputational advantages. Although there is little research that links these concepts, there is some convergence between the concepts at the level of the

governance

accountability requirements of corporations. Beltratti (2005) defines corporate governance as referring to the mechanisms that direct and monitor firm effectiveness, while CSR refers mainly to the consequences of the firm's functions for various stakeholders. Each can be associated with the creation and maintenance of market value. However, this is a highly contested point in the literature and very dependent upon how each of these terms is defined. Kolk (2008) argues that accountability in governance terms relates more to staff-related, ethical aspects, while sustainability accounting reporting has broadened from the environment to encompass social and financial issues. Her research indicates that multinationals, particularly in Europe and Japan, now incorporate governance mechanisms such as board supervision and external verification into the management of their CSR.

Corporate governance is concerned with the clarification of a corporate perspective on the purpose of companies, on who owns them, who should manage them, and how. It is a multi-faceted concept and a highly complex arrangement, unlike a simple functional business area (Clarke, 2004). For example, in terms of the natural environment, corporate governance refers to the way in which corporations manage their environmental impacts, risks, opportunities and performance, and their corporate accountability for their environmental impact. Business ethics, not just environmental considerations, transcend every aspect of corporate governance because they determine how the organisation will act in all areas of operation.

NEW MODELS OF CORPORATE GOVERNANCE

Management is now turning to new models of corporate governance which are inclusive of accountability to the natural environment and to the wider society. The financial crisis that commenced in 2007 has further compounded this challenge. Corporate governance is now interpreted more holistically, according to models that address firm accountability to a range of stakeholders that goes beyond shareholders, managers and boards of directors. The flagship legislation that heralded a change was the US Sarbanes-Oxley Act, as discussed in the entry on Corporate Accountability.

Academic researchers have focused on ethics as an important component of culture, values and decision making in their examination of corporate governance. As discussed elsewhere in this book, stakeholders are now more than ever pressuring organisations to take responsibility for the natural environment. The rise of socially responsible investment and the increase in sustainability and corporate responsibility reporting suggest that the viewpoint that corporations exist to satisfy a few key stakeholder groups is less influential. This has resulted in a 'corporate governance reform' in which the issues that management must be concerned with have been reconsidered as well as the stakeholders to whom firms are accountable.

To some writers, CSR is an extension to the model of corporate governance, based on the responsibilities that are owed to all the firm's stakeholders. Nevertheless, managers are struggling to balance issues such as to what and to whom should the company be accountable. Even taking the narrow version of shareholder responsibility as the key tenet of corporate governance raises difficulties of how we institutionalise this premise (Heath and Norman, 2004) and also raises real challenges for the broader models of corporate governance that attempt to incorporate broader understandings of CSR.

PARTNERSHIPS AND GOVERNANCE

Numerous scholars and commentators now regard partnership as an aspect of good governance and define governance as a network or partnership-based function. But there is still little research-based information on how partnership contributes to good governance. Partnership is most commonly seen to deliver on the effectiveness element through providing extra resources such as skills and other forms of labour, although it may also promote inclusiveness, which is one of the values-based aspects of partnership. It can reduce barriers to institutional change such as conflict, ambiguity and ignorance. In this view, partnership contributes to governance effectiveness. The partnership structure is also crucial to governance outcomes, such as legitimacy.

The organisational problem relates to the tension between flexibility and control on the one hand and between creativity and accountability on the other. For example, overarching forms of control and coordination appear to limit creative solutions developed across organisational boundaries. Governance models often grow from a rigid focus on standardised operational and governance systems and reflect management's determination to limit conflict, disorder and uncertainty. On the other hand, highly flexible governance frameworks appear to stimulate creative problem solving across different jurisdictional levels, scales and stakeholders.

The setting of targets is an important factor in establishing these frameworks. Drawing from empirical research, Bressers and Brujin (2005) have shown that covenants and agreements with unclear targets are associated with significant transaction costs, and that voluntary agreements are most successful when embedded in linked policy approaches so that the business sector is delivered a coherent approach by government. In other words, target setting for sustainability outcomes from partnerships needs to be made relevant in the wider context of sustainability policy setting if it is to be seen as a legitimate aspect of governance.

To implement governance systems that support CSR objectives, the challenge is to balance self-organised, individually crafted governance arrangements with clear frameworks of control in order to alleviate the problems noted with a diffusion of power, vague goal setting and a lack of clarity in sustainability or CSR objectives. Other sustainability and CSR challenges that might be addressed through good governance include high costs, low levels of motivation and tensions that derive from different frameworks of responsibility and accountability between public and private sectors.

See also: Agency Theory, Business Ethics, Corporate Accountability, Corporate Social Responsibility, Social Partnerships

REFERENCES

Beltratti, A. (2005) 'The Complementarity between Corporate Governance and Corporate Social Responsibility', *The Geneva Papers*, 30: 373–386.

Bressers, H. and Brujin, T. (2005) 'Conditions for the Success of Negotiated Agreements: Partnerships for Environmental Improvement in the Netherlands', *Business Strategy and the Environment*, 14: 241–254.

Cadbury Committee (1992) *Report on Committee on Financial Aspects of Corporate Governance*. Available at www.icaew.com/index.cfm/route/116205/icaew_ga/pdf, accessed 10 October 2009.

Clarke, T. (2004) *Theories of Corporate Governance*. London and New York: Routledge.

Heath, J. and Norman, W. (2004) 'Stakeholder Theory, Corporate Governance and Public Management: What Can the History of State-run Enterprises Teach us in the Post-Enron era?', *Journal of Business Ethics*, 53: 247–265.

Kolk, A. (2008) 'Sustainability, Accountability and Corporate Governance: Exploring Multinationals' Reporting Practices', *Business Strategy and the Environment*, 17 (1): 1.

PricewaterhouseCoopers (2010) 13th Annual Global CEO Survey, available at http://www.pwc.com/gx/en/ceo-survey/download.shtml, accessed 13 July 2010.

key concepts in corporate
social responsibility

Green Marketing

BACKGROUND

A historical perspective is useful to critique the robustness of this concept. The release of the Brundtland Report (WCED, 1987) stimulated significant activity in the area of 'green marketing', defined as initiatives taken by an organisation to design, promote, price and deliver products and services that are not harmful to the environment. The increasing growth of consumer awareness at the time was heralded by apparently reputable surveys evidenced by consumer boycotts of products such as CFC-driven aerosols. Research undertaken by Gutfield (1991) suggested that eight out of ten American consumers were claiming to be environmentalists. In the same year France's Institut Agronomique (INRA) reported a survey within the European Community that suggested UK citizens were the most concerned about environmental issues, demonstrating a sense of urgency concerning the need to redress environmental degradation. In 1992, 82 per cent of UK citizens were recorded as regarding the environment as an immediate and urgent problem (INRA, 1992). In response to shifts in consumer preferences, researchers reported that 92 per cent of European multinationals were claiming to be changing their products and 85 per cent their production systems. In the USA, green products increased from 11.4 per cent of new household products in 1989–90 to 13.4 per cent in 1991 (Vandermerwe and Oliff, 1990). Green TV ads also grew by 367 per cent and green print ads by 430 per cent in that period (Ottman, 1993). Elkington and Hailes (1988) produced *The Green Consumer Guide* to evaluate the swathe of initiatives around new product launches and campaigns as well as academic commentary concerning green marketing.

CORPORATE APPROACHES

Organisations approached green marketing in a variety of ways. One approach was to develop energy efficient products and services that conserved other natural resources. They also promoted their products and services by emphasising the commitment of their organisation to the principles of environmental sustainability. Customers were given options to accept a pricing structure that allowed for environmental sustainability

green marketing

111

practices, and firms also began to identify and reduce the footprint emanating from their packaging and distribution as well as the broad logistic infrastructure. Such strategic approaches to operations were often grouped into the three Rs – reusing, recycling and reducing (Grove et al., 1996).

In the service sector, success stories such as that of the Body Shop demonstrated commercially viable outcomes from the green market. McDonald's removed tens of millions of pounds in weight from its waste stream in packaging and saved costs. Hotels conserved heating and made appeals to customers to choose to save on what might be perceived as excessive laundry services, introducing low-water use shower heads, reduced paper usage, reduced use of toxic pollutants, and reusable containers as forms of green activities. As a means of conceptualising and evaluating greening initiatives, Grove et al. (1996) produced a greening of services matrix and advocated its adoption. They also began to recognise the challenge of evaluating new greening initiatives and taking account of unforeseen outcomes, such as the increased use of bleach and other pollutants in the move from using disposable nappies. The aspiration was that green marketing would develop into a system of comparative and shared benchmarking, as broader quality systems had.

GREEN MARKETING AS FALSE MARKETING?

After 1990, market research reflected less confidence in the consistent growth in green consumer practices, with many green brands evidently being discontinued. There have been many perspectives as to why this occurred. Peattie and Crane (2005) suggest that green marketing might have accentuated existing customer cynicism and distrust. They adapted King's (1985) taxonomy of 'false marketing practices' to explain the 'waxing and waning' of green marketing in the late 1980s and 1990s. Failed marketing practices that they identified included *green spinning*, which was used as a company reaction to the public criticism of 'dirty' practices such as those associated with 'spills' of contamination produced by the oil, chemicals and automotive industries. This approach has often been dismissed as public relations that falsely presented organisations' claims to care for or value environmental resources. *Green selling* was often perceived negatively as a bolt-on approach to existing products, incorporating green themes and unproven claims into marketing strategies. *Green harvesting* generated scepticism amongst customers in that it often used economies in energy and material to achieve short-term and immediate efficiencies and cost savings (without passing them on to the customer), whilst failing to make a strategic investment in initiatives that would have a greater green impact and benefits. *Enviropreneur marketing* occurred in both boutique enterprises and mainstream corporate green brands that often introduced new market products without undertaking effective market research. It proceeded from a production rather than a consumer orientation, and often failed to understand quality, price and impact issues as part of the business model, e.g. failing to recognise the link between brightness in the laundering of paper quality and a reliance on polluting ingredients. Finally, *compliance marketing* refers to companies that meet minimal regulatory standards and yet promote themselves as innovators and champions of the green cause.

Peattie and Crane (2005) conclude that the principles of 'real marketing', also suggested by King (1985), inform the way forward for marketing sustainability. These principles include a more intensive understanding of customer wants, needs, beliefs and values, whilst balancing this information with the needs of other stakeholders; adopting and communicating a more open-ended approach to consumer benefit; promoting and leveraging from a holistic approach to a company sustainability culture (not an easy challenge); and developing new mindsets around innovation that look beyond product and production technology, such as the introduction of sustainable after-purchase services including the disposal of products.

MARKETING SUSTAINABILITY AS A CSR INITIATIVE?

Mendleson and Polonsky (1995) suggest that green marketing suffered from poor credibility, consumer cynicism and consumer confusion. It has been widely suggested that these responses might have arisen because of the lack of effective market research to identify consumer needs, values and perspectives, including the trade-offs associated with buying green. One approach to increasing credibility with consumers might be a more effective use of alliances and associations, for example, between business and environmental groups to achieve product endorsements, corporate sponsorships and the licensing of products. Already there has been a significant amount of activity of this nature, an oft-quoted good practice example being that between McDonald's and the Environmental Defense Fund through which their business practices are evaluated according to accepted ecological standards.

A related question is how marketers might determine the shifting characteristics of the ethical consumer. Carrigan and Attalla (2001) refer to evidence that consumers do not readily make purchasing decisions on the basis of knowledge about a firm's ethical or unethical behaviour. Weybrecht (2010) acknowledges that in the past green marketing might have been the villain because it was aimed at convincing customers that very ordinary products were green, rather than adopting a breakthrough approach to identifying relevant green products required by and acceptable to customers at certain stages of their awareness. Neither do marketers appear to have invested much effort in understanding the shifting values of consumers in relation to ethical values and trade-offs. Nevertheless, it is hard to deny Weybrecht's assertion that the future skills of marketers will be critical in helping customers evolve towards more sustainable lifestyles. This raises challenges around influencing and educating consumers, and the role of social and societal marketing, discussed in a later entry.

See also: *Ethical Consumerism, Greenwash, Social and Societal Marketing*

REFERENCES

Carrigan, M. and Attalla, A. (2001) 'The Myth of the Ethical Consumer – do Ethics Matter in Purchase Behaviour?', *Journal of Consumer Marketing*, 18 (7): 557–560.

Elkington, J. and Hailes, J. (1988) *The Green Consumer Guide*. London: Gollancz.

Grove, S.J., Fisk, R.P., Pickett, G.M. and Kangun, N. (1996) 'Going Green in the Service Sector: Social Responsibility Issues, Implications and Implementation', *European Journal of Marketing*, 30 (5): 56–66.

Gutfield, R. (1991) 'Eight out Ten Americans are Environmental, at Least they Say so', *Wall Street Journal*, 2 September, Section A: 1.

INRA (1992) 'Europeans and the Environment in 1992', report produced for the Commission of the European Communities Directorate General XV11 Energy, Brussels.

King, S. (1985) 'Has Marketing Failed, or Was it Never Really Tried?', *Journal of Marketing Management*, 1: 1–19.

Mendleson, N. and Polonsky, M.J. (1995) 'Using Strategic Alliances to Develop Credible Green Marketing', *Journal of Consumer Marketing*, 12 (2): 4–18.

Ottman, J.A. (1993) *Green Marketing: Challenges and Opportunities*. Chicago, IL: NTC Books.

Peattie, K. and Crane, A. (2005) 'Green Marketing: Legend, Myth, Farce or Prophesy?', *Qualitative Market Research: An International Journal*, 8 (4): 357–370.

Vandermerwe, S. and Oliff, M. (1990) 'Customers Drive Corporations Green', *Long Range Planning*, 23 (6): 10–16.

WCED (1987) *Our Common Future*. Oxford: Oxford University Press.

Weybrecht, G. (2010) *The Sustainable MBA*. Chichester: Wiley.

Greenwash

WHAT IS GREENWASH?

'Greenwash' can be thought of as a form of environmental public relations. It derives from the term 'whitewash' and refers to the phenomena of organisations trying to cover up environmentally and/or socially damaging activities. Sometimes the greenwash is just with rhetoric, and at other times with minor or superficial environmental reforms. It is most frequently applied to corporations, but governments, political candidates, trade associations and NGOs have also been accused of greenwashing. Greenwashing is clearly linked to the manipulation of image by the media and advertising industry.

The public backlash against greenwash has been particularly triggered by evidence that public relations exercises can be used to stall regulation, deceive governments and customers, and even build customer support on the basis of a company's environmentally responsible actions. Basically, greenwash is a deceptive use of green public relations. A well-known example is when Phillip Morris spent $100 million in 1999 to promote $75 million worth of charitable donations. Another well-known example is the use of green labels by the hotel industry, promoting a re-use of towels in the name of saving water and the environment, while the real strategy is to reduce operating costs. While it may be argued that this is just an example of the business case for corporate sustainability and CSR, the issue is intent – whether this activity reflects a wider commitment to sustainability or just a token gesture.

It seems that most of the problems arising in relation to greenwash can be associated with large corporations. There are several key reasons for this. First, most attention is directed at them. Second, multinationals have both the resources and the investment capacity to turn opportunities for seeking sustainable solutions into greenwash opportunities, largely by enlisting the services of public relations firms. The environmental aspects of this industry burgeoned in the 1980s in response to rising public concerns over the environmental and social impacts of corporate activity. According to Beder (2001), by the mid 1990s, US-based firms were spending about $1 billion year on public relations advice on how to green their own image and deal with environmental opposition.

Public relations firms have been known not only to build their corporate clients' environmental reputations unjustifiably, but also to attempt to destroy those of environmental activists or to discredit environmental causes. The misleadingly named US-based Global Climate Coalition formed in the late 1980s to actively counter suggestions that global warming was occurring as a result of human activity is a now notorious example of greenwash. The coalition, composed of fossil-fuel producers, energy providers, car companies and trade associations, spent millions to raise doubts on the veracity of climate change, influencing politicians and impeding the development of a consensus and the global community's ability to deal with the problem.

RECOGNISING GREENWASH

Assessing greenwashing has become a more complex task as numerous companies whose core business activities have negative environmental impacts are now promoting their environmental credentials and capabilities. BP, for instance, is one of the oil companies currently positioning themselves as part of the solution to energy shortages and climate change. This position is particularly chronic given the huge oil slick that threatened the US coastline in 2010. The complexity of large organisations operating with many different business divisions across multiple countries means that a company may indeed be contributing to the benefit of society and the environment while simultaneously damaging it. However, misleading consumers and employees about the environmental practices of the company is clearly an act of greenwashing. Examples include natural products that are preserved using chemicals. In recent North American research, of the more than 2,000 self-described environmentally friendly products examined in the study, only 25 were found to be indisputably legitimate (see http://sinsofgreenwashing.org/findings/). The rest were greenwashing. Toys and baby products, cosmetics and cleaning products are the three categories where green claims, and greenwashing, are most common.

The 'sins of greenwashing' checklist (Terrachoice Environmental Marketing, 2009) has been developed for consumers (see http://sinsofgreenwashing.org/):

1. *Hidden trade-off*, in which companies highlight one eco-friendly attribute, and ignore their product's other (potentially more significant)

environmental concerns. In the above North American study, 57 per cent of all environmental claims committed this sin.

2. *No proof*, which, just like it sounds, involves claims that can't be verified (the study found that 26 per cent of environmental claims fell into this category).
3. *Vagueness*, with terms like 'chemical-free' or 'non-toxic', which are both universally true, and universally false, depending on your interpretation; 11 per cent of environmental claims fell into this category.
4. *Irrelevance*, when companies make claims that, while true, are unhelpful (like 'CFC-free', when CFCs have been banned for almost thirty years). These represented 4 per cent of environmental claims.
5. *Lesser of two evils*, like 'green' herbicides, which ignores the fact that herbicides in any form aren't good for the environment. These were about 1 per cent of environmental claims.
6. *Fibbing*, which is the most obvious, in which companies blatantly lie (less than 1 per cent of companies made this mistake, but it does happen). These represented less than 1 per cent of environmental claims.

A seventh sin, 'worshipping false labels', refers to the fact that some marketers are mimicking third-party environmental certifications on their products to draw consumers. In the recent study, transgressions fell into three categories: a lack of proof, vague language or 'hidden trade-offs' – the practice of emphasising a product's green aspects while concealing others that are environmentally damaging. The problem with these examples of greenwashing is that the demand for legitimate green products can be diminished as consumers feel tricked or betrayed by false advertising or when they realise corporate double standards are operating. Even voluntary environmental programmes such as ISO 14000 have been accused of supporting greenwashing because of perceptions that they may have lenient standards and lack strict enforcement rules.

A public backlash against perceived greenwashing has resulted in some famous boycotts and anti-corporate campaigns. Perhaps as a result of the perceived resistance of many consumers to green marketing or ethical consumerism, and because companies are now alert to the public backlash against greenwashing, promoting CSR or good corporate citizenship is now being increasingly targeted at employees and other internal stakeholders rather than at consumers. For example, the senior vice president for corporate and external affairs at Alcan, the giant Canadian aluminium company, has stated that its environmental efforts are primarily targeted at its internal audience. Developing a commitment to the company is seen as the key benefit (Deutsch, 2005). Basically, companies are now recognising that the pervasive influence of the media and an ease of access to information via the Internet mean that claims about CSR or sustainability performance need to be more than just cosmetic.

Some examples of greenwash

- Packaging food products with environmentally friendly imagery without lowering the environmental impacts of production. The European McDonalds' initiative to shift its logo from yellow and red to yellow and green in 2009 is a prime example here – promoting an environmental stance in the abstract while making only limited, vague claims of actual environmental action.
- The American Coalition for Clean Coal Energy (ACCCE) spent $38 million in 2008 to promote coal as a green, clean and carbon-free energy source. Given the large carbon footprint with coal, this is a difficult case to argue. The ACCCE claimed its coal power plants were 70 per cent cleaner, but in what context? In reality, the industry cut its emissions of sulphur dioxide and nitrogen oxides but not its carbon dioxide emissions.
- The Bank of America is marketing an 'eco' Mastercard, which supposedly rewards customers with carbon offsets. In reality, only 0.5 per cent of the purchase price goes towards purchasing carbon offsets – with the remainder going to the bank.
- Ubisoft has announced that it will no longer supply paper manuals for all future PlayStation 3 and Xbox 360 titles. They argue that this is part of their bid to be more environmentally conscious, but it will inevitably reduce their production costs.

See also: *Ethical Consumerism, Green Marketing, Social Marketing*

REFERENCES

Beder, S. (2001) 'Greenwash', in J. Barry and E. Gene Frankland (eds), *International Encyclopedia of Environmental Politics*. London: Routledge. Available at www.herinst. org/sbeder/PR/greenwash.html, accessed 5 July 2009.

Deutsch, C. (2005) 'It's Getting Crowded on the Environmental Bandwagon', *The New York Times*. Available at www.nytimes.com/2005/12/22/business/22adco. html?_r=1, accessed 10 October 2009.

Terrachoice Environmental Marketing (2009) 'The Seven Sins of Greenwashing'. Available at http://sinsofgreenwashing.org/findings/, accessed 9 October 2009.

Human Rights

WHAT DO WE MEAN BY HUMAN RIGHTS?

'Human rights are widely considered to be those fundamental moral rights of the person that are necessary for a life with human dignity. Human rights are thus means to a greater social end' (Forsythe, 2006: 3). As an expression of morals and values, the notion of human rights has a long history, identifiable in all major religions and cultures. This can be traced through the development of natural law originating in Ancient Greece through to the European philosophers of the Enlightenment. A key outcome was the notion of a social contract between citizens and rulers that in turn influenced Bills of Rights in England and America, and the Declaration of the Rights of Man and the Citizen in France.

During the Second World War, the focus on human rights was regenerated in the form of the 'Four Freedoms'. These covered freedom of speech and of assembly, and freedom from fear and want, espoused by the Allies as underpinning their war goals. In the aftermath of Nazi atrocities, global agreements were reached on a tighter definition of human rights, embodied within the United Nations Charter. This led to the drafting of the Universal Declaration of Human Rights.

ARE HUMAN RIGHTS UNIVERSAL?

The Universal Declaration of Human Rights (UDHR) is a non-binding declaration adopted by the United Nations General Assembly in 1948, consisting of 30 articles which have been incorporated into international treaties, national constitutions and laws, as well as human rights instruments. Importantly, Article 1 reads 'All human beings are born free and equal in dignity and rights. They are endowed with reason and conscience and should act towards one another in a spirit of brotherhood'. The UDHR and the legal treaties identifying civil, political, cultural and economic rights, together with those specifically covering the rights of women, children, ethnic groups and religions, were intended to act globally as a safety net, with restrictions only being allowed in times of national emergency (Franck, 2001).

The adoption of the UDHR has not resulted in its unquestioning acceptance. Rather, there has been significant reaction to its apparent

human rights

119

employment to enforce values associated with globalisation and its orientation to individualism. For example, Kofi Annan's plea for nation-states to redefine their national interests in order to uniformly pursue the basic values underpinning the UN Charter (including democracy, pluralism, human rights and the rule of law) has been interpreted by some states as threatening cultural identity. In some instances the status of 'cultural exceptionalism' has been claimed for traditional indigenous societies and theocratic states.

Some Western intellectuals have expressed concern that 'human rights' rhetoric supports a notion of individual autonomy that could work against the maintenance of community values. For example, ex-Malaysian Prime Minister Mahathir bin Mohamad, Australia's former Prime Minister Malcolm Fraser and former German Chancellor Helmut Schmidt all commented on an apparent philosophical and cultural bias inherent in the drafting of the UDHR. They claimed that this outcome resulted in a lack of balance between the concepts of freedom and responsibility, thus incurring a possible danger of political instability. In other words, 'cultural exceptionalism' reflects the argument that ethical propositions cannot reflect universal, moral truths; rather, truths need to be assessed in the context of cultural boundaries.

Franck (2001) has put forward a case against 'cultural exceptional-ism', arguing that those purporting this doctrine do not necessarily represent the social groups on whose behalf they claim to speak. Rather, they often do so in order to protect their own power bases. A second line of argument is that human rights are grounded in a 'modern trans-cultural social economic and scientific development' (2001: 196–197) contributing to multi-layered and voluntary affiliations that can supple-ment rather than oppose 'tradition, territory and genetics'. These volun-tary affiliations might only work against traditional values to the extent that 'traditional communities are no longer able, alone, to resolve some of the most difficult problems facing humanity' (2001: 201) including environmental degradation and global warming. Franck advocates a coordinated front against 'cultural exceptionalism' in these circum-stances, drawing on military and fiscal resources from governments, NGOs and labour. He acknowledges that the process will not be easy because 'cultural exceptionalism' often constitutes a means by which developing countries will express their resentment against globalisation as a manifestation of Western and/or American hegemony (2001: 204).

HUMAN RIGHTS, GLOBAL ETHICAL CODES AND TRANSNATIONAL CORPORATIONS

In considering the need for global business ethics, Kung (1997) assumes 'that globalization is unavoidable, ambivalent, incalculable and can be controlled rationally.' He argues that given these assumptions, ethics has a critical and central role to play in the process of globalization, but in considering ethical behaviour it is important to consider not only human rights, but also human responsibilities.

In 2005 over 77,000 transnational corporations (TNCs) were operating with over 770,000 foreign affiliates, generating an estimated US$4.5 trillion in value added, employing over 62 million workers and exporting goods and services valued at more than US$4 trillion (UNCTAD, 2006). Yet World Bank data also show that the gap between rich and poor countries has grown 10 times during the past thirty years (Sethi, 2003), raising questions about the relationship between globalisation and world poverty. In response, there have been renewed attempts to use global codes of ethics to regulate the conduct of businesses operating transnationally, although there is still little agreement about the exact level of social responsibility held by corporations.

As discussed further in the entry on Codes of Conduct, a series of codes has been adopted to shift transnational companies towards an acceptance of human rights within ethical standards regarding both people and the physical environment. These have included the Sullivan Principles (Sullivan, 1977), initiated to stop legal segregation based upon race in South Africa by asking firms to endorse principles around integrating racial groups in workplace activities, developing black workers for skilled and managerial roles, and improving the quality of lives of black workers through better housing and other community facilities. Eventually these principles were seen to be failing to achieve change quickly enough and so were replaced by the goal of a complete divestment of companies from South Africa.

The Caux Round Table Principles for Business (1994) were written and endorsed by an international group of business leaders promoting a form of moral capitalism. These have been seen by some as composing a comparatively narrow code, with key areas missing, e.g. those around marketing, health and safety, and environmental harm. Yet, within the framework of 'stakeholder rights', the Caux document addressed human rights issues

human rights

121

concerning dignity, non-discriminatory treatment across gender, race, age and religion, and the equal treatment of workers. These principles extended to suppliers and contributed to reformist initiatives concerning human rights and democratic practices within local communities.

The OECD Guidelines for Multinational Enterprises (2008) developed in 1976 were revised in 2000 to provide a government-backed set of standards around good corporate conduct, requiring a respect for human rights consistent with the host government's international obligations and commitments. Although these were non-binding, they had the endorsement of member states and provided a benchmark for organisations.

Carasco and Singh (2008) suggest that in the new millenium there has been some progress in shifting the debate around CSR and human rights away from questions concerning whether corporations might be responsible for human rights and towards determining the extent to which they are responsible. To that end, the formation of the Global Compact in 2000 as a result of the partnership between the UN and the International Chamber of Commerce constitutes 'a voluntary international corporate citizenship network ... to advance responsible corporate citizenship and universal social and environmental principles to meet the challenges of globalization' (2008: 363). (The Global Compact is further discussed in the entry on Business Networks.)

CONCLUSION

Donaldson and Dunfee (1999) suggested a need for balance between the universal and the particular within ethical frameworks utilised by business. In other words, core human values (including human dignity, basic rights and good citizenship) should be respected by corporations, but there must also exist 'moral free space' in which local traditions can be acknowledged. Is progress towards that end being achieved? Some would see the 'Norms on the Responsibilities of Transnational Corporations and other Business Enterprises with Regard to Human Rights' (UN, 2003) as evidence of an advance towards that goal. The 'Norms' make clear that states are responsible for respecting and protecting human rights as recognised in national and international law, and this includes their responsibility to ensure that businesses respect human rights. Although there is no explicit enforcement mechanism, they do embrace UN declarations on Human Rights, Civil and Political

Rights and Economic, Social and Cultural Rights. Businesses are required to disseminate, act upon and report on these Norms, placing the responsibility for human rights directly with business. Although it has been acknowledged that the Norms do not clearly identify the extent of corporate obligations and the penalties associated with non-compliance, there is still support for the conclusion that 'The Norms have clearly put life back into the dying hope of establishing an effective and legally binding international mechanism for regulating the conduct of TNCs' (Carasco and Singh, 2008: 371).

See also: *Business Ethics, Business Networks, Codes of Conduct, Corporate Citizenship, Globalisation, NGOs, Stakeholder Theory, Sweatshops*

REFERENCES

Carasco, E.F. and Singh, J.B. (2008) 'Human Rights and Global Business Ethics Codes', *Business and Society Review*, 113 (3): 347–374.
Caux Round Table (1994) 'Principles for Business' Available at http://www.cauxroundtable.org/index.cfm?menuid=8
Donaldson, T. and Dunfee, T.W. (1999) 'When Ethics Travel: The Promise and Peril of Global Business Ethics', *California Management Review*, 41 (1): 45–63.
Forsythe, D.P. (2006) *Human Rights in International Relations*. Cambridge: Cambridge University Press.
Franck, T.M. (2001) 'Are Human Rights Universal?', *Foreign Affairs*, 80 (1): 191–204.
Kung, H. (1997) 'A Global Ethic in an Age of Globalization', *Business Ethics Quarterly*, 7 (3): 17–32.
OECD (2008) OECD *Guidelines for Multinational Enterprises*. France: OECD publishing. Available at www.oecd.org/daf/investment/guidelines
Sethi, S.P. (2003) *Setting Global Standards: Guidelines for Creating Codes of Conduct in Multinational Corporations*. Hoboken, NJ: Wiley.
Sullivan, L. (1977) 'The Sullivan Principles' Available at http://muweb.marshall.edu/revleonsullivan/indexf.htm
UN (2003) 'Economic, Social and Cultural Rights: Norms on the responsibilities of transnational corporations and other business enterprises with regard to human rights'. Available at http://www.unhchr.ch/huridocda/huridoca.nsf/(Symbol)/E.CN.4.Sub.2.2003.72.Rev.2.En
United Nations Conference on Trade and Development (UNCTAD) (2006) *World Investment Report, FDI from Developing and Transition Economies: Implications for Development*. New York and Geneva: United Nations.

human rights

Intergenerational Equity

WHAT IS MEANT BY INTERGENERATIONAL EQUITY?

Intergenerational equity is closely identified with protecting the rights of future generations to access natural and human-produced capital. It is a values-based concept and each of the range of environmental discourses, as discussed in the Environmental Discourses entry, has a particular perspective on what is fair for our current generation to consume and how much should be protected for the future. Are lower levels of biodiversity and other forms of ecological activity justifiable, for example, if associated with the development of higher levels of human capital in the form of skills and capabilities or built capital such as railway, roads, libraries and schools? These are the key questions of sustainable development as set out in the Rio Declaration (UNCED, 1992). They also have implications for the principle of *Intra*generational Equity, as further discussed in the entry on that topic.

Natural capital can be defined as the stock of natural resources, such as land, water and minerals, used for production. It can be either renewable or non-renewable. Renewable natural capital can be replaced by human action and ecological processes and includes fish and forestry, while non-renewable resources include minerals and fossil fuels and can only be replaced on a geological timescale. Many of the ideas in this book flow from the need to maintain at least reasonable stores of natural capital in comparison with other forms of capital. They include moving from eco-efficiency to eco-effectiveness, industrial ecology and closed-cycle production, lifecycle assessment and systems thinking.

IMPLICATIONS FOR CORPORATE DECISION MAKERS

Developments such as the Global Compact are moral appeals to corporations to guide their behaviour in relation to intergenerational and intragenerational equity. The principles underlying the latter relate to equity and justice and are set out in the entry devoted to that topic. The implication of intergenerational equity for business is that it needs to consider the distribution of its impacts on stakeholders across generations as well as current generations.

Risk management increasingly concerns the business impact on future as well as present generations in relation to environmental and human health. Strengthening the legislation to protect the rights and interests of future generations is now evident in developing and developed nations. A key challenge is how to measure natural capital – if it is to remain constant, i.e. how to measure it and compare it to other forms of capital, with major implications for corporate decision makers as they attempt to factor in environmental value.

ASSESSING NATURAL CAPITAL

Difficulty in assessing such value is exacerbated by the uncertainty surrounding many such decisions. Variability in the natural environment and the inherent interconnectedness of natural systems mean that impacts on future generations may be very difficult to assess. Biodiversity is the most obvious example of this problem. For instance, how to assess the impact of oil spills on biodiversity and thus the availability of natural capital for future generations is a growing problem for industry, government and the wider community. But there are also impacts on current generations that may not be equitably distributed. Oil spills such as from the *Exxon Valdez*, which ran aground on Bligh Reef in Prince William Sound, Alaska, in 1989 causing massive damage to more than 1,100 miles of coastline, and the massive 2010 BP oil spill in the Gulf of Mexico, have received extensive publicity. But there have also been many other large spills that have been less publicised because they occurred in developing nations. The impact of oil spills along the Niger Delta, for instance, is a major cause of social unrest and activist protests targeted at the multinationals associated with the oil industry working in that area. The by now heavily polluted Delta is home to much of the remaining mangrove swamp in Africa and a major breeding ground for fish stocks along the coast. Yet comparatively, these destructive activities have received little international attention.

THE PRECAUTIONARY PRINCIPLE

Uncertainty around assessing the impact of industrial activity on natural and social systems is the reason why the principles of intergenerational equity are inherently linked to that of the precautionary principle. The precautionary principle is another core principle of sustainable development enshrined in the Rio Declaration of 1992 (UNCED, 1992). (The Rio Declaration is also described in the Sustainable Development entry.)

The precautionary principle states that public and private decisions should be guided by: a careful evaluation to avoid, wherever practicable, serious or irreversible damage to the environment; and an assessment of the risk-weighted consequences of various options (Deville and Harding, 1997: 13). In other words, it is the principle of 'better safe than sorry' and as such is now an aspect of many international agreements. A recent example of how the precautionary principle has been drawn on in an attempt to institutionalise intergenerational equity is the Stockholm Convention on Persistent Organic Pollutants (POPs) (see http://chm.pops.int/default.aspx), which came into effect in 2004. This Convention identifies certain chemicals as potentially harmful to human health and the environment, allows for regulators to restrict or eliminate their use and reduces the onus on regulators to prove risk in relation to other chemicals in the future, even if uncertainty remains about their effects.

The particular relevance of the precautionary principle to CSR hinges on its implications for technological development. In relation to corporations, the precautionary principle aims to support intergenerational equity by ensuring that long-term costs do not exceed the short-term economic benefits of the activity. Basically, it means that companies should exercise caution when developing new products or processes by having the means to systematically analyse the long-term environmental effects or social impacts. For instance, the Stockholm Convention has major implications for chemicals companies.

The example of genetically modified organisms (GMOs) illustrates the implications for corporate research and development. GMOs bring the possibility of major benefits in food security but possible negative impacts on biodiversity and human health. The European Union reacted to this uncertainty by applying the precautionary principle, adopting a moratorium on GMO commercialisation between 1999 and 2004. In 2004, after five years with no new marketing authorisations, certain GMO foods or foods containing GMOs were permitted to be placed on the market. The marketing and growing of GMO seeds was also authorised, but not until a strict assessment process had taken place. Strict labelling conditions were also required.

The application of the precautionary principle to such technological developments has been criticised as being overly pessimistic and conservative. In practical terms, how it should be applied so that technology and scientific development can still occur to benefit humankind and the planet is dependent upon the underlying relationship between scientific uncertainty and the potential level of threat to current and future generations posed by the activity. Applying the principle is most critical when both the threat level and scientific uncertainty are high.

Rather than a stringent set of prohibitive requirements forestalling research and development, the precautionary principle should be thought of as facilitating a different way for governments and business to make decisions. In that sense, Peel (2005) argues it is encouraging higher levels of scrutiny for the evidence upon which such decisions are made and a more process-based approach to decision making to enable accountability and transparency. In the name of intergenerational equity, it represents a discourse of precaution that challenges the discourse of 'sound science', which requires regulators to demonstrate that products or processes are harmful before their use can be restricted (Maguire and Hardy, 2006).

See also: Environmental Discourses, Intragenerational Equity, Risk Management, Sustainable Development

REFERENCES

Deville, A. and Harding, R. (1997) *Applying the Precautionary Principle.* Annandale, NSW: The Federation Press.

Maguire, S. and Hardy, C. (2006) 'The Emergence of New Global Institutions: A Discursive Perspective', *Organization Studies*, 27 (1): 7–29.

Peel, J. (2005) *The Precautionary Principle in Practice.* Annandale, NSW: The Federation Press.

UNCED (United Nations Commission on Environment and Development) (1992) *Rio Declaration on Environment and Development.* New York: United Nations.

Intragenerational Equity

EQUITY AND SUSTAINABLE DEVELOPMENT

'Equity' is an important concept in sustainable development and has significant implications for government approaches to identifying and promoting citizen wellbeing at a state and global level. The concept of *intra*generational equity has received less attention in the literature on sustainable development and ecological economics than the concept of *inter*generational equity (Stymne and Jackson, 2000). This is possibly because intergenerational equity was embedded in the definition of sustainable development used by the Brundtland Commission (WCED, 1987). Nevertheless, the literature around the concept of intragenerational equity has grown, demonstrating important links between economic growth, income inequality, social wellbeing and environmental degradation and posing challenges to policy makers at both a state and national level concerning a nation's contribution to global environmental regimes (e.g. the United Nations Framework Convention on Climate Change, or UNFCCC).

EQUITY AND SOCIAL JUSTICE

A broad definition of equity considers fairness and impartiality towards concerned parties based on the principle of 'giving as much advantage, consideration, or latitude to one party as ... is given to another' (BusinessDictionary.com). In the context of sustainable development, the goal of intragenerational equity has been described as requiring 'justice' amongst the present population, based on the belief that people in communities at every level have the same basic needs. Environmental justice involving considerations of the distribution of environmental risks is now an integral consideration of environmental sustainability.

The concept of equity is derived from that of social justice, so it might be useful to consider briefly the five main Anglo-American interpretations of the concept of justice. The *utilitarian* approach, derived from consequentialist ethics, is concerned with outcomes which result in an ultimate good (welfare) for the greatest number of people. The *communitarian* approach is more concerned with the need to take into account the cultural context and values associated with the benefit in question (Miller, 1995). A third approach around *justice as liberal equality* was developed by Rawls on the basis that 'each person has an equal right to the most extensive basic liberties that are compatible with similar liberties for others ... and that social and economic inequalities [should be] arranged so that they are both (a) reasonably expected to be to everyone's advantage, and (b) attached to positions and offices open to all' (Weiss, 2006: 128). The fourth approach is the *Kantian categorical imperative* that justice is a means of meeting the needs of people,

key concepts in corporate social responsibility

acknowledging the moral equality of all human beings (Kant, 1964). Okereke (2006) suggests that the *Marxist approach to justice* is closely aligned to the Kantian approach in that it requires the distribution of social and economic benefits and responsibilities on the basis of 'from each according to his ability, to each according to his needs'. Many believe that this notion of justice is most relevant to the goal of sustainable development. The Brundtland Report explicitly argues a sustainability definition that meets the needs of the global population for food, clothing, shelter and work, on the basis that 'inequality is the planet's main environmental problem' (WCED, 1987: 6). By way of contrast, the *libertarian approach* views individual liberty and property rights as entitlements based on market allocation regardless of the degree of inequality or need that such allocation creates (Nozick, 1974: 238).

POVERTY, CHOICE AND ENVIRONMENTAL DEGRADATION

Beder (2000) contends that a major reason that inequity or poverty are major concerns in sustainability literature is that social inequities are a cause of environmental degradation and poverty can deprive people of choices concerning the activities that will have environmental impact. The Brundtland Report reinforces this view:

> Those who are poor and hungry will often destroy their immediate environment in order to survive: they will cut down forests; their livestock will overgraze grasslands; they will overuse marginal land; and in growing numbers they will crowd into congested cities. The cumulative effect of these changes is so far-reaching as to make poverty itself a major global scourge. (WCED, 1987: 72)

Inequity can manifest itself more acutely when high levels of affluence are a cause of increased damage to the environment, high levels of consumption contributing to the depletion of resources and the accumulation of waste (Beder, 2000). In contrast, the 'libertarian' approach to social justice might regard this situation as a legitimate social justice outcome and perhaps anticipate a subsequent market-based solution.

Governments have also been seen as stimulating inequity and thus contributing to environmental degradation by failing to provide adequate access to public transport, and by failing also to manage the development of cities as nuclei of political energy and innovation to promote rational and sustainable resource usage, at a national and global level (Moavenzadeh et al., 2002), as well as failing to address poverty issues through redistribution policies.

INEQUITY IN ENVIRONMENTAL VALUATION AND DECISION MAKING

Inequity in pricing the environment

Environmental economists argue that environmental degradation is a consequence of the market system failing to price environmental assets appropriately. This assumes that the solution might be a more appropriate pricing of environmental resources, ultimately reflected in GNP and GDP. Beder classifies this approach as a form of 'weak sustainability' practice, 'the process of pricing the environment to ensure that decisions take account of environmental degradation work[ing] against [both] intergenerational and intragenerational equity' (2000: 5). She maintains that difficulties arise in equitably pricing the environment through determining people's willingness to pay. Poorer people do not have as many options in choosing to pay for environment sustaining initiatives in a market-based situation. Economic instruments such as taxes on polluting behaviour or 'user pays' fees can also be an unfair burden on those with lower incomes, and thus further reinforce the poverty cycle.

Inequities in power and decision making at a state level

'Inequities in power [can also] lead to inequities in people's ability to influence decisions affecting their environment' (Beder, 2000: 4). Examples here include alleged 'environmental racism' in decision-making bodies in the USA and the exclusion of women and women's interests in environmental sustainable development working groups and decision-making bodies in Australia (Bullard interviewed in Multinational Monitor, 1992; Brown and Switzer, 1991, quoted in Beder, 2000). People with lower incomes or less influence in dominant political discourses also have fewer opportunities to communicate the value of environment to their socioeconomic and demographic groups and to policy makers and other influential decision makers.

Beder (2000) concludes that decision-making frameworks that integrate economic and environmental considerations have severe limitations. Cost–benefit analysis is still the major framework for evaluating private and public projects requiring monetary values to be ascribed to all relevant aspects of the decision, including environmental assets, benefits and costs. The use of a methodology that aggregates costs and benefits often ignores their distribution and related equity considerations. For example, valuing environmental costs using lost wages due to health problems will always lead to the conclusion that potentially health damaging industries are best located in low-wage areas. As Okereke concludes, 'environmental costs and benefits are so distributed such that those who already suffer other socio-economic disadvantage tend to bear the greatest burden' (2006: 725).

Inequity in multilateral environmental regimes

Okereke draws attention to intragenerational equity and concepts of justice in the international allocation of costs concerning global environmental degradation: '[t]he political North [being] seen, based on their commanding role in the international political economy, as having great leverage over the South' (2006: 726). Certain commentators have interpreted this reality from a postcolonial perspective, seeing multilateral environmental regimes using environmental protection as yet another mechanism to continue the existing pattern of colonial domination and inequalities that had underpinned the affluence and trade domination of the North (Guha and Martinez-Alier, 1997). The 2009 Copenhagen meeting of the UNFCCC recognised these disparities in the capabilities of developed and developing nations to redress environmental degradation. The 'Accord' agreement pledged US$ 30 billion to the developing world between 2010 and 2012, increasing this figure to US$100 billion per year by 2020 in order to assist poor countries adapt to climate change. The Accord also recognised the importance of the REDD+ scheme (reduce emissions from deforestation and degradation, plus conservation, the sustainable management of forests and the enhancement of forest carbon stocks). It called for the immediate establishment of a REDD+ mechanism to operationalise the scheme under which developed countries would pay developing countries to achieve its objectives. Part of the US$30 billion supporting mitigation of emissions is expected to finance REDD+. In addition, the USA, Australia, France, Japan, Norway and Britain pledged US$3.5 billion to REDD activities between 2010 and 2012.

INTRAGENERATIONAL EQUITY AND CSR?

The social justice frameworks described above suggest a need to consider the notion of intragenerational equity in decision making around

CSR policies and corporate citizenry behaviours, while at the same time acknowledging the tensions between morals and rights frameworks and the libertarian justice framework.

Are these necessarily polar approaches that business cannot reconcile?

Global institutions such as the World Business Council for Sustainable Development and the World Economic Forum have suggested a need for new mindsets around the role and responsibilities of business working in markets and with governments to resolve such issues as poverty and social exclusion, as these are seen as impediments to sustainable development and environmental improvement. Beder (2000) anticipated this agenda, noting that such initiatives would be constrained until 'new ways of decision making [were found], for example those that would enable the multifaceted values associated with the environment to be fully considered and heeded'. Merely extending market values to incorporate the environment into existing economic systems will not achieve the goals of intragenerational inequity (2000: 243).

See also: Business Ethics, Environmental Discourses, Intergenerational Equity, Postcolonialism, Sustainable Development

REFERENCES

Beder, S. (2000) 'Costing the Earth: Equity, Sustainable Development and Environmental Economics', *New Zealand Journal of Environmental Law*, 4: 227–243.

Guha, R. and Martinez-Alier, J. (1997) *Varieties of Environmentalism*. London: EarthScan.

Kant, I. (1964) *Groundwork of the Metaphysics of Morals* (trans. H. Patton). New York: Harper & Row.

Miller, D. (1995) *On Nationality*. Oxford: Oxford University Press.

Moavenzadeh, F., Hanaki, K. and Baccini, P. (2002) *Future Cities: Dynamics and Sustainability*. New York: Springer.

Multinational Monitor (1992) 'The politics of race and pollution: An interview with Robert Bullard', *Multinational Monitor*, 14 (6) available at http://multinationalmonitor.org/hyper/issues/1992/06/mm0692-01.html

Nozick, R. (1974) *Anarchy, State and Utopia*. New York: Basic Books.

Okereke, C. (2006) 'Global Environmental Sustainability: Intragenerational Equity and Conceptions of Justice in Multilateral Environmental Regimes', *Geoforum*, 37: 725–738.

Stymne, S. and Jackson, T. (2000) 'Intragenerational Equity and Sustainable Welfare: A Time Series Analysis for the UK and Sweden', *Ecological Economics*, 33: 219–236.

Weiss, J.W. (2006) *Business Ethics*, 4th edition. Mason, OH: Thomson South-Western.

World Commission on Environment and Development (WCED) (1987) *Report of the World Commission on Environment and Development: Our Common Future*. Available at www.un-documents.net/wced-ocf.htm, accessed 1 August 2009.

NGOs

WHAT IS AN NGO?

The term 'non-governmental organisation' (NGO) originated with the United Nations (UN) in an attempt to differentiate between intergovernmental specialised agencies and international private organisations, and to award respective representation rights (Willetts, 2002). Prior to 1945, institutions equivalent to NGOs had cooperated as international institutes, organisations or unions, gaining recognition on the basis of their status as private organisations. When the Economic and Social Council (ECOSOC) was established under the UN Charter in 1945, it clarified its relationship with these newly entitled NGOs, the term being adopted quickly and widely in the community. Under Article 71 (UN, 1945), 'Non-governmental organizations could have suitable arrangements for consultation'. Today, the NGO Branch of the Department of Economic and Social Affairs coordinates the communication or consultation of NGOs with ECOSOC.

To gain recognition by the UN as NGOs, private bodies are required to be 'independent from government control, not seeking to challenge governments either as a political party or by a narrow focus on human rights, non-profit-making and non-criminal' (Willetts, 2002: 1). NGOs include small grass-roots organisations through to large professional organisations. They are difficult to categorise as they will often change their characteristics and scope of activities. A common point of differentiation is that between *operational NGOs* and *campaigning NGOs*. Operational NGOs will usually have to mobilise resources to undertake their mission and can require complex organisational designs for fundraising. Campaigning NGOs will often require a smaller fundraising function, aiming primarily to attract community support for their cause.

NGOs have developed diverse global organisational structures, both strongly centralised and loosely federated. They might be based in a single country but have branches internationally, or they might be locally based groups operating at the national or global level through coalitions of more or less similarly thinking entities. Umbrella NGOs embrace organisations that are focussed on agreed issues but have different areas of focus. NGOs might also form loose issue-based networks or even ad hoc caucuses with the purpose of lobbying (Willetts, 2002).

NGOs are often differentiated from social movements, with the latter frequently being regarded as more radical. Willetts (2002) suggests that NGOs are components of social movements. However, Bendaña emphasises their differences, suggesting that while NGOs and social movements share the common goal of changing social policies, social movements have an 'organising dynamic' that is quite different to the networking carried out by NGOs who are in the main committed 'to policy advocacy, service delivery and monitoring' (2006: 7). Social movements often have underlying critiques or political philosophies concerning the operations of the capitalist system, e.g. a shared view condemning the effects of neo-liberal globalisation on vulnerable socio-economic groups and regions. NGOs are more accountable to their funding bodies whose supporters may not share a common philosophical or ideological orientation.

THE RISE OF NGOS

Spar and La Mure suggest that although NGOs are perceived as modern or even postmodern phenomena, in fact they have operated as 'figure[s] of the global economy for over four hundred years, starting with the Rosicrucian Order, an Egyptian educational organization founded in the sixteenth century' (2003: 79). NGOs have traditionally organised around ideas and a commitment to principles concerning societal issues that were perceived as being ignored domestically or internationally, or, although sponsored by other institutions, were seen as requiring additional support. For example, the Pennsylvania Society for Promoting the Abolition of Slavery, founded by the Quakers in 1775, was followed by the establishment of the British Society for Effecting the Abolition of the Slave Trade a decade later (Spar and La Mure, 2003). Such activities quickly transitioned into mainstream politics. Equivalent approaches today campaigned by NGOs include child labour, female circumcision in Kenya and the rights of women.

More recently, pressure from NGOs has shifted from being directed at governments to targeting multinational corporations: '[A]s Corporations have gained prominence in the global economy, they have become more and more the direct target of activism – of boycotts, consumer protests and shareholder rebellion' (Spar and La Mure, 2003: 80).

THE ROLE OF NGOS IN THE POLITICAL PROCESS

Independence from governments

Although NGOs are constituted to be free from government influence, the reality is often different. Sometimes governments will create NGOs to work with them whilst defining the financial, political and ideological parameters of the partnership. Bendaña has noted that the US distinction between humanitarian aid and its military and political agenda has sometimes been blurred. He cites Colin Powell, the US Secretary of State, as having said

'just as surely as our diplomats and military, American NGOs are out there serving and sacrificing on the front lines of freedom. NGOs are such a force multiplier for us, such an important part of our combat team'. (Bendaña, 2006: 2)

In other instances, social movements and NGOs have reacted negatively to government pressure. One example is the NGO response to the World Bank's Poverty Reduction Strategy Papers introduced in 1999. The World Bank requested civil society organisations (CSOs) to carry out consultations and help develop a 'national ownership' of overseas poverty reduction programmes. Some social movements and associated NGOs adopted a hard line against international financial institutions, drawing attention to the fact that the poverty reduction programmes were failing to address other factors influencing poverty levels, such as corruption and cut-backs in social services. Many NGOs maintained their critical stance to the politics of structural adjustment programmes that were predetermined in Washington (Bendaña, 2006: 3).

Bendaña still perceives significant NGO activity as supporting the overarching 'development' agenda that continues the domination of the South by the North, wherein 'Northern prescriptions and methodologies ... [for capacity building are] ... very often funded by donor governmental agencies' (2006: 12). He suggests that when finance ministers in the

ngos

135

South accept IMF formulas for poverty alleviation and growth, NGOs in the North and South 'develop coping strategies to assist civil societies to accept the macroeconomic impositions, and not to change them' (2006: 12).

Different institutional impacts: EU versus US

Doh and Guay (2006) suggest that the influence of NGOs also needs to be understood in the context of the role of political institutions and their approach to NGO involvement in policy making. Social protest movements have had a long history in Europe and a positive track record in exerting influence in the EU policy-making forums. They have leveraged significantly from the expansion of the EU's policy-making powers. Doh and Guay contrast this situation with that in the USA where 'interest groups have no formal or traditional standing in the public policy process' (2006: 50), noting that the Constitution has been framed to limit their influence despite the pluralism embedded in US politics that encourages their formation.

BUSINESS AS NGOS

Some non-profit-making federations of companies, e.g. the International Chamber of Commerce, have been given NGO status by the UN. Willetts (2002) notes that until the 1990s, certain companies were called upon mainly for their technical expertise, whereas forums such as the 1992 Rio Earth Summit engaged business more in the work of ECOSOC concerning global environmental politics. As a result, commercially-based NGOs have been formed around specific issues concerning environmentally friendly business, e.g. the World Business Council for Sustainable Development.

NGOs have used meetings of the World Economic Forum (WEF) to pressure business to widen its social responsibilities. For instance, in 1999 at Davos, businesses were invited to enter a Global Compact with the UN endorsing core principles concerning human rights, labour standards and protection of the environment.

BUSINESS RESPONSE TO CAMPAIGNING NGOS

Businesses have responded differently to the activities of campaigning NGOs. Some multinationals have supported NGO activities, e.g. by providing resources to disadvantaged communities. Others have aimed to support NGOs to redress negative externalities of their business; for example, petroleum, trucking and chemical companies have funded foundations for clean air, and tobacco firms have funded NGOs that support consumer freedom (Bendaña, 2006).

Campaigning NGOs have influenced corporate strategies and behaviours to stop directly or indirectly supporting deleterious political, social and environmental outcomes. As an example, the Free Burma Coalition (FBC) arose in response to the civil rights record of the Burmese military, seeking to dissuade foreign investors in Burma. FBC activities included consumer boycotts, protests, shareholder activism and federal and state lawsuits (Spar and La Mure, 2003). Other NGO tactics have included labour activism to stop child labour in Indonesia and opposition to political violence in Sierra Leone. NGOs have been heavily focused on the role of corporations, realising that '[i]f economic influence can be translated into political pull then the best way to change a country's laws and practices may well be through the corporations that invest there' (2006: 81). Consumer and broader public pressure has then been brought to bear on the situation.

NGOS AND CSR

NGOs will often try to pressure corporations into appropriate action through the threat of financial harm caused by their campaigning activities. However, two key issues can arise. First, whether NGO pressure on businesses (often to withdraw investment) improves social and economic conditions in the host country. A second question is whether acts of capitulation or resistance to NGO pressure might benefit or harm corporate interests. The evidence is conflicting. Some commentators claim to have demonstrated empirically boycotts' negative impact on shareholder wealth (Epstein and Schnietz, 2002). Others have assessed a positive impact (Koku et al., 1997). Spar and La Mure (2003) conclude from their case studies that firms with high brand recognition in highly competitive industries, e.g. Nike and Merck, are more likely to capitulate to NGO pressure. An organisation with low brand presence, such as Unocal, which operates in oil exploration and production, appeared to perceive itself as better placed to resist the NGO pressure to pull out of Burma.

Although corporate responses to NGO pressure have been significantly different, Spar and La Mure (2003) suggest that this pressure might only make a slight difference to profit maximisation outcomes. Nevertheless, they also acknowledge that NGO pressure has forced firms to factor variables into their decision-making processes that they might have chosen to ignore previously. They note as well that the commitment of managers to CSR has played an important part in decision making, though this is lessened when corporate citizenry behaviours come at a high cost.

Despite the diversity of corporate responses to NGO pressure, Spar and La Mure conclude that NGOs 'are increasingly focussing their powers of persuasion on firms and that firms, in turn, have become increasingly responsive' (2003: 94). This is not to understate the importance of an NGO focus on collaborative partnerships to address social and environmental issues. For example, since its establishment in China in 2003, the Global Environment Institute's projects have involved a collaboration between academic researchers, local governments, local communities, industry and other local and international NGOs, demonstrating the benefits of contextual and interdisciplinary research that takes account of community needs. Projects include the commercialisation of small natural gas heat and power technologies in urban areas and integrated approaches to renewable energy, agriculture and ecotourism in rural areas.

See also: Community Relations, Corporate Citizenship, Globalisation, Social Capital, Social Entrepreneurship, Social Partnerships

REFERENCES

Bendaña, A. (2006) 'NGOs and Social Movements: A North/South Divide?', *Civil Society and Social Movements*. Programme Paper Number 22. Geneva: United Nations Research Institute for Social Development.

Doh, J.P. and Guay, T.R. (2006) 'Corporate Social Responsibility, Public Policy, and NGO Activism in Europe and the United States: An Institutional Stakeholder Perspective', *Journal of Management Studies*, 43 (1): 47–73.

Epstein, M. and Schnietz, K. (2002) 'Measuring the Cost of Environmental and Labour Protests to Globalization: An Event Study of the Failed 1999 Seattle WTO Talks', *The International Trade Journal*, 16 (2): 19.

Koku, P., Akhigbe, A. and Springer, T. (1997) 'The Impact of Financial Boycotts and Threats of Boycott', *Journal of Business Research*, 40: 15–20.

Spar, D.L. and La Mure, L.T. (2003) 'The Power of Activism: Assessing the Impact of NGOs on Global Business', *California Management Review*, 45 (3): 78–101.

UN (1945) 'United Nations Charter, Chapter 10: the Economic and Social Council'. Available at http://www.un-documents.net/ch-10.htm

Willetts, P. (2002) 'What is a Non-Governmental Organization? An article for UNESCO Encyclopaedia of Life Support systems'. Available at www.staff.city.ac.uk/p.willetts/CS-NTWKS/NGO-ART.HTM, accessed 2 May 2010.

key concepts in corporate
social responsibility

Performance Evaluation and Measurement

WHAT IS CSR PERFORMANCE EVALUATION AND MEASUREMENT?

'CSR evaluation and measurement' means assessing how the firm's impacts on its stakeholders lead to value creation or destruction. The implication is that creating value for its shareholders does not destroy value for other stakeholders. In contemporary understandings of business, as noted elsewhere in this book, the natural environment is accepted as a stakeholder. In this more holistic understanding of CSR, assessing stakeholder impacts means understanding the product or service lifecycle and how it impacts in social, environmental and economic terms along the value chain from suppliers to customers and end-users (Laszlo, 2008: 130–141).

WHY IS CSR PERFORMANCE EVALUATION AND MEASUREMENT IMPORTANT?

CSR benefits to the firm that have been discussed in recent research include: positive effects on company image and reputation; positive effects on employee attraction, engagement and retention; cost savings; revenue increases from a higher market share; CSR or sustainability related risk management (Weber, 2008). As discussed in the Business Case for CSR entry, however, there is considerable debate concerning these claims and much rests on the ability of companies to be able to measure and track the potential CSR impacts and associated business benefits, particularly given the materiality concerns of shareholders.

HOW TO DEVELOP CSR METRICS

Epstein (2008) suggests a model for corporate sustainability that is very relevant to CSR in terms of establishing suitable performance metrics. The model links inputs, processes, outputs and outcomes in a cause–effect set of relationships and feedback loops. Measurement occurs in each category of the model and drives performance in the next. For

Table 3   Measurement and performance metrics

Inputs	Processes	Outputs	Outcomes
Funds for employee training	Diversity of workforce	Noise levels in community	Income from green products
Market size	Percentage of suppliers certified to green standards	Donations of products/services	Increased sales from improved reputation
Pollution standards	Average years of experience for senior executive	Number of local business opportunities generated	Workers' compensation costs

Source: Adapted from Epstein, 2008: 169–174

CSR, each category has metrics for social, environmental and economic dimensions. Examples of these metrics are set out in Table 3.

Indicators to enable these measurements can be lagging (recording the effects of past actions) or leading (predictors of future performance), and both should be included in the array of CSR metrics. Epstein (2008) gives the example of work-related injury as being a lagging indicator of health and safety programme efficiency, but also a leading indicator of employee satisfaction.

To achieve the benefits from CSR measurement, it is particularly important that the firm establish a range of indicators that will enable the measurement of both monetary and non-monetary outcomes as these can then feed back into the inputs and processes elements in order to improve future performance. Non-monetary outcomes can be measured using both quantitative (e.g. reputation indices) and qualitative measures (e.g. stakeholder attitudes). Weber (2008) posits that the potential CSR positive outcomes suggested in the literature can translate into five key performance indicators for CSR:

- monetary brand value
- customer attraction and retention
- reputation
- employer attractiveness
- employee motivation and retention.

ASSURANCE

An independent verification is important if the performance evaluation and measurement is to be perceived as legitimate across the stakeholder groups. As described in the entry on Corporate Accountability, the AA1000 framework provides a standard for the assessment of performance measurements as set out in corporate reports. It does this by assessing reports against three assurance principles: materiality, completeness and responsiveness. As an emerging area of speciality, most companies using this framework do so in conjunction with the Global Reporting Initiative (GRI) and the Global Compact, both described in the entry on Business Networks. The major accounting firms evaluate the measurement and evaluation procedures within reports.

The performance evaluation and measurement of non-financial data presents many ambiguities. Establishing social performance measures and gathering data are particularly difficult. The challenge is to establish proxy variables that can be associated or correlated with the particular CSR initiative or area of corporate impact that is of interest. But the outcomes of CSR initiatives may not be well understood and may also change over time. Tracking initiatives designed to improve employee health and safety through measuring site incidents, for example, may be difficult as other factors may influence outcomes as well. In another example, using the number of lawsuits filed by environmental groups as a measure of community relations may be problematic because it may be influenced by other factors, such as the groups' access to finances.

However, this topic area of social and environmental evaluation and performance remains the subject of considerable current research, and while the challenges are daunting they are not insurmountable. Identifying and collecting multiple proxies for a single social or environmental outcome, for instance, is suggested as one way to get around some of these problems (Borck et al., 2008).

CASE STUDY

Westpac Banking Corporation

Westpac Banking Corporation is one of the world's leading banks as assessed by several external performance measures, such as the Dow Jones Sustainability Index. Westpac's *Customer Brandwidth, Annual Review and Sustainability Report 2009* emphasises the relationship between CSR, corporate sustainability and shareholder value. It utilises the GRI Financial Sector as its guiding framework. Westpac's website states that the 'report and Group's underlying policies, systems and processes have been independently tested applying the AA1000 Assurance Standard'.

The Westpac 2009 report lists the firm's sustainability objectives as:

- Going mainstream – sustainable products
- People and places – local social leadership and responsible banking
- Treading lightly – environmental footprint
- Climate change – carbon and water
- Speaking out – in support of sustainable business practice
- Solid foundations – governance and risk.

The report then sets out the Scorecard measuring the firm's progress against these objectives, as the examples in Table 4 show.

Table 4   Performance evaluation at Westpac Banking Corporation

Sustainability objectives	Outcome for firm
Going mainstream – sustainable products (e.g. develop additional wealth offerings based on sustainability principles)	Customer-centric design workshops were held to inform the development of new products. A strategic review of emerging and future customer product needs arising from the impact of the global financial crisis was also undertaken. A number of new products are in development as a result.
People and places – local social leadership and responsible banking (e.g. maintain a group-wide employee engagement score of 78 per cent)	Employee engagement increased to 81 per cent across the group. Now equal to the Towers Perrin-ISR Global High Performing Companies norm. This included an engagement score of 82 per cent for St George.
Treading lightly – environmental footprint (e.g. reduce Scope 1 and 2 emissions by 5 per cent)	Like-for-like emissions decreased by 5 per cent against the 2008 baseline. Emissions from the newly merged St. George portfolio also decreased by 7 per cent over the reporting period.
Climate change – carbon and water (e.g. complete institutional and business banking carbon risk training)	More than 300 employees from institutional and business banking divisions completed a half-day session on carbon risk, including client case studies during 2008/09. Training sessions were also undertaken with The Westpac Group and Institutional Banking Executive Teams in September 2009. This has been supported by ongoing information sessions and client engagement tools.
Speaking out – in support of sustainable business practice	Continue to advocate for robust emissions trading schemes in Australia and New Zealand. We have been involved in ongoing policy dialogue with the Australian and New Zealand governments including contributing to Parliamentary Committee inquiries in both countries.

key concepts in corporate social responsibility

Table 4 *(Continued)*

Sustainability objectives	Outcome for firm
Solid foundations – governance and risk (e.g. further integrate financial and non-financial reporting)	External stakeholder consultation completed and discussions held with the Board Sustainability Committee. This year's Annual Review combines financial, strategy and sustainability information in a single report.

Source: Westpac Group, 2009.

See also: *Business Case for CSR, Business Networks, Corporate Accountability, Corporate Responsibility Reporting*

REFERENCES

Borck, J., Coglianese, G. and Nash, J. (2008) 'Evaluating the Social Effects of Performance-based Environmental Programs', *Corporate Social Responsibility Initiative Working Paper No 48*. Cambridge, MA: John F. Kennedy School of Government, Harvard University.

Epstein, M. (2008) *Making Sustainability Work*. Sheffield, UK and Stanford, CA: Greenleaf.

Laszlo, C. (2008) *Sustainable Value: How the World's Leading Companies are Doing Well by Doing Good*. Sheffield, UK and Stanford, CA: Greenleaf.

Weber, M. (2008) 'The Business Case for Corporate Social Responsibility: A Company-level Measurement Approach for CSR', *European Management Journal*, 26 (4): 247–261.

Westpac Group (2009) *Customer Brandwidth, Annual Review and Sustainability Report, 2009*. Available www.westpac.com.au/docs/pdf/aw/ic/annualreview-2009.pdf, accessed 19 April 2010.

philanthropy

Philanthropy

143

WHAT IS PHILANTHROPY?

Scholars suggest that the word 'philanthropy' was used 2,500 years ago by the writer Aeschylus in the myth 'Prometheus Bound'. The evolution of humanity from primitive people to rational humanity is explained by the act of Prometheus, who gave to these primitive creatures (who were in fear and danger of destruction by the god Zeus) two life gifts, 'fire and optimism', to improve the material and spiritual dimensions of their lives, thus creating humanity. Prometheus bestowed these gifts as a function of his 'philanthropos tropos' or humanity-loving character. Thus, the term 'philanthropia' began to define the act of loving the characteristics of what defined humanity or the essence of civilisation (McCully, 2008). The term also has political connotations. It underpins certain democratic ideals and values that embody the aspiration towards an educated humanity that acts and produces for the good of humanity.

The philanthropic tradition thrived in colonial society in America, with many of the English colonies identifying themselves as Commonwealths, i.e. political communities founded with the intention that members contribute voluntarily to the public good. In the quest for American independence, Thomas Paine noted in 1776 in *Common Sense* that the revolution was fighting for universal values and principles for all lovers of mankind, exhorting and practising private initiatives for public good. However, over time, such classical philanthropic traditions have been eroded by various political ideologies and movements and also by the processes of industrialisation and, more recently, globalisation. Nevertheless, the tradition of private endeavour supporting public good still continues and is particularly common in education, medicine, science, the welfare sector, environmental protection and other humanitarian causes.

EVOLUTION OF THE LEGAL STATUS OF CORPORATE PHILANTHROPY

The determination of a corporation's freedom to pursue corporate philanthropy is often seen as emanating from the 1953 Supreme Court of New Jersey ruling in the case of *A.P. Smith* versus *Barlow*. The ruling went against shareholders who challenged a corporation's power to make reasonable charitable contributions, in this instance, concerning a donation of $1,500 to Princeton University. This outcome clarified the freedom of corporations to make gifts that did not necessarily provide a direct and immediate economic benefit to the corporation. This outcome resulted in many US companies establishing in-house foundations, e.g. Levi Strauss and Dayton Hudson. Some companies donated up to 5 per cent of their pre-tax income to philanthropic causes, often selecting causes that were not associated with their core business, e.g. the Exxon Education Foundation (Smith, 1994).

DRIVERS OF CORPORATE PHILANTHROPY

Smith (1994) notes that the *Exxon Valdez* oil spill in 1989 demonstrated possible risks in adopting philanthropic approaches that were distinct from core business. For example, the philanthropic activities of Exxon did not include activities that developed stakeholder relationships with environmental groups. This contrasted with its competitor ARCO's stakeholder relationships. Its strategic alliances developed as part of the corporate philanthropy paradigm, eliciting stakeholder support that was available to protect ARCO's reputation in times of crisis.

Smith (1994) credits Reynold Levy of AT&T with developing a new model for philanthropic initiatives in the mid-1980s, in which business units supported philanthropic activities from a strategic perspective that included sharing and developing management and technological expertise, and human resources, e.g. through volunteer programmes. This arrangement had a two-way benefit, i.e. besides an obvious donor benefit there was also a benefit to the corporation through innovation, employee and broader stakeholder engagement, public relations, corporate government affairs and so on.

Seifert et al. (2004) argue that despite American companies having a long history of corporate philanthropy, the drivers of corporate philanthropy have been ambiguous concerning the extent to which companies were committed to sharing profits with broader social causes, and the associated rationale around a competitive advantage to firms in so doing. In reality, philanthropy budgets as a percentage of profit in US companies have declined; 'even in good years companies are increasing their giving less than the increase in profits' (Smith, 1994: 113). Siefert et al. have investigated correlations between financial indicators and corporate philanthropy, focusing on the relationship 'between having and giving', and the relationship 'between giving and getting'. They conclude that giving relative to income does in fact depend on the availability of what they call financial 'slack resources', thus 'doing well enables doing good'. However, in line with other research findings they concluded that there was little definitive evidence of 'doing good to do well'. In other words, 'it appears that society benefits while firm owners do not lose, when firms contribute to charitable causes' (2004: 154).

Duncan (2004) has contributed to the debate concerning motives behind philanthropic activity from the perspective of public economics. From the charitable contributions literature, he identified 'two distinct yet equally believable models: the public goods model in which donors give motivated by what their gifts accomplish, and the private consumption model in which donors give motivated by how giving makes them feel' (2004: 2159). *Public good philanthropy* assumes that philanthropists receive utility by the achievement of their objectives, with all givers achieving benefit from each other's donations. The recipients of such charity will use the donations to relieve their situation. *Private consumption philanthropy* is unrelated to the giving of others, donors only being interested in the 'warm glow' from their individual donation regardless of the outcome. Duncan develops a third model of philanthropic motivation that he calls *impact philanthropy*. Impact philanthropists are motivated to give in order to make a difference personally. Their philanthropy is related to the gifts of other impact philanthropists but in a manner opposite to that assumed for public good philanthropists: 'rather than free-riding off the gifts of others, or being unaffected by them, giving by others can reduce an impact philanthropist's charitable fulfilment – an impact philanthropist cannot enjoy saving children if other philanthropists save them first' (2004: 2160). Although Duncan recognises the multiple rather than singular motives of philanthropists, he also argues that impact philanthropy can lead to some 'unphilanthropic' behaviour. He gives the example that 'a fundraising policy that targets a donor's gift at a specific part of a production process will maximise the donor's perceived impact, but may not maximise the total supply of the charitable good' (2004: 2177). For example, donors might want to directly fund a child to gain an education, but not the administrators, even though administration is a bottleneck to the impact of a charitable gift.

PHILANTHROPY AS AN ELEMENT OF CSR

Carroll (1991) concludes that 'corporate philanthropy has long been regarded as a corporate social responsibility and thus a measure of a firm's corporate social performance'. Significantly, Porter and Kramer (2002) have argued for a shift towards context-focused philanthropy in those areas most important to an organisation's industry and strategy as an aid to competitive advantage. They suggested this more strategic approach might require: a consideration of the competitive context in each of the company's geographic locations; ascertaining the strategic fit with the existing philanthropic portfolio, e.g with the values and behaviour concerning communal obligation, goodwill building or strategic giving; selecting the most effective recipients that can complement business philanthropy by leveraging organisational assets and expertise, attracting other funders and improving performance; seeking opportunities for collective action within a cluster and with other partners, thus creating social capital that is relevant to social change outcomes; and finally rigorously evaluating the results. Porter and Kramer's (2002) framework was developed in their later work exploring the links between competitive advantage and strategic CSR.

This framework, together with analysis undertaken by Seifert et al. (2004) and Duncan (2004), aids an understanding of the extent to which contemporary corporate philanthropy is becoming more or less consistent with the roots of philanthropy, as embodied in the Promethean notion of 'philanthropia' or the act of loving the characteristics of what defines humanity.

See also: *Business Case for CSR, Business Ethics, Corporate Citizenship, Corporate Social Responsibility, Employee Engagement, Performance Evaluation and Measurement*

REFERENCES

Carroll, A.B. (1991) 'The Pyramid of Corporate Social Responsibility: Towards the Moral Management of Organizational Stakeholders', *Business Horizons*, 34 (4): 39–48.

Duncan, B. (2004) 'A Theory of Impact Philosophy', *Journal of Public Economics*, 88: 2159–2180.

McCully, G. (2008) *Philanthropy Reconsidered*. Boston, MA: A Catalogue for Philanthropy.

Paine, T. (2007 [1776]) *Common Sense*. Minneapolis, MN: Filiquarian Publishing.

Porter, M.E. and Kramer, M.R. (2002) 'The Competitive Advantage of Corporate Philanthropy', *Harvard Business Review*, December.

Seifert, B., Morris, S.A. and Bartkus, B.R. (2004) 'Having, Giving and Getting: Slack Resources, Corporate Philanthropy, and Firm Financial Performance', *Business and Society*, 43 (2): 135–161.

Smith, C. (1994) 'The New Corporate Philanthropy', *Harvard Business Review*, May/June: 105–116.

philanthropy

Pollution and Waste Management

WHAT IS POLLUTION?

Pollution can be defined as the undesirable physical, chemical or biological changes in earth, land or water that negatively impact on the health of the ecosystem. Earlier understandings of pollution only understood negative impacts as they related to human health. More recent understandings, however, recognise the dependence of human health on the wider ecosystem and the intrinsic value of the natural world and hence take a more holistic approach to pollution, considering the wider impacts that go beyond human survival or wellbeing.

Pollution includes sewage, energy, garbage and toxic wastes as well as greenhouse gases (GHGs) and other forms of emissions. It is often classified as either point source or non-point source pollution. Pollution coming from a single identifiable source such as a discharge from a factory is termed point source, whereas pollution from fertilisers or other forms of crop maintenance is labelled non-point source.

Both the nature and impact of pollution depend on a host of factors. These include:

- sources of pollutants
- processes by which the pollution is transported (for example, run-off or spray drift)
- potential build-up of pollutants due to long-term or repeated exposure.

(CSIRO, 2008: www.csiro.au/org/PollutionOverview.html)

IMPACTS OF POLLUTION

Clearly, one of the major concerns of the age is the ongoing increase in pollution that is leading to climate change and global warming.

The Intergovernmental Panel on Climate Change has found that it is very likely that most of the observed global warming since the mid-twentieth century has been due to human activity causing increases in GHGs. Although the Earth has experienced other periods of global warming previously, the linear warming trend over the past fifty years of 0.13 °C per decade is much more rapid than the rate of warming between ice ages and warm interglacial periods of around 0.001 °C per decade (see www.csiro.au/resources/). It appears ongoing changes in the climate, including increased rain in some areas, drought in others and some sea level rise are now unavoidable.

Some researchers claim that more than a billion deaths per year can be attributed to pollution of one type or another. Millions each year, the majority of whom are children, die from gastrointestinal diseases caused by drinking contaminated water. In the developed world, where such diseases may be less prevalent, there are increasing concerns about the pollutants associated with some plastics that may disrupt the production of certain hormones. High percentages of lead may cause ongoing neurological effects and be difficult to trace.

Of all forms of pollution, researchers have found that hazardous or toxic wastes arouse most publicity and provide the most difficult problems for policymakers. Studies show that there are major differences between how scientists and the public assess the risks associated with pollution. Risks that are borne involuntarily or are difficult to quantify are often perceived as more threatening by the public (Preuss and Benn, 2007).

Hazardous wastes are now a major issue in some developing countries. Illegal trading in e-waste, for example, has resulted in children and other local workers being employed to dismantle used products that contain concentrations of toxic substances. In countries where there are few economic or other resources to address public health issues, or where there are weak governance systems, such trade highlights the negative aspects of globalisation. Effectively, it is a case of the environmental injustice of richer countries externalising their risks to poorer parts of the world. By 'externalities' we mean passing on to society the environmental or social costs or risks associated with the production of goods or services. Another linked issue is that underprivileged members of the community have a greater chance of living near highly polluting sites or hazardous waste and are therefore bearing a higher proportion of the risks associated with these externalities. These issues are also referred to in the entry on Intragenerational Equity.

The Blacksmith's Institute World's Worst Polluted Places Report (2009: 19) lists the following as the areas in the world most affected by pollution and in need of a clean-up, and highlights the underpinning issues of environmental justice:

- Phasing out leaded gasoline – Global
- Disarming and destroying chemical weapons – Global
- Reducing indoor air pollution – Accra, Ghana
- Managing mine tailings to protect a scarce water supply – Candelaria, Chile
- Mitigating nuclear contamination – Chernobyl Affected Zone, Eastern Europe
- Improving urban air quality – Delhi, India
- Removing lead waste – Haina, Dominican Republic
- Preventing mercury exposure – Kalimantan, Indonesia
- Mitigating lead exposures – Rudnaya River Valley, Russia
- Disposing of DDT – Old Korogwe, Tanzania
- Transforming an urban waterway – Shanghai, China
- Removing arsenic – West Bengal, India

ADDRESSING POLLUTION AND MANAGING WASTE

The overall trend in pollution management reflects a shift from viewing pollution as an end-of-pipe problem to an issue of prevention and mini-misation, a trend supported by research showing that waste prevention as compared to other means of reducing pollution is more likely to lead to financial gain (King and Lennox, 2002). It is now well recognised that to reduce the impact of pollution on the Earth's climate, it is crucial that business adapt to climate change by reducing GHG emissions through energy efficiency measures and investing in renewable energy. Alternatives to electricity that can be utilised include sustainably produced biofuels, hydrogen and natural gas. One of the key problems of climate change is that agricultural systems are a major source of GHGs. According to a major Australian scientific research institute (CSIRO), the world will need to triple its food production by 2025, while at the same time cutting its GHGs by at least one-quarter of current levels, perhaps even one-half. Greatly increasing agricultural productivity is one obvious solution, but it is not clear how this can be done without a further acceleration of the gas concentration and therefore a temperature increase.

Like other pollutants, GHGs can be thought of as wastes from indus-trial production, and managing pollution is closely related to waste management. A number of approaches have been developed to address pollution and manage industrial waste. Key drivers for business to engage in these schemes are seen to include the potential for more efficient resource use, improved quality, a higher reputation, increased innovation and new niche markets. (Some of these drivers are also discussed in the entries on Systems Approaches and Sustainable Development.) Many commentators would argue that sustainable development is not possible unless patterns of production and consumption are informed by lifecycle thinking.

Cleaner production

Cleaner production refers to the prevention of pollution such as toxic byproducts or various emissions occurring as a result of manufacturing. Cleaner production is essentially a range of management processes, tools and strategies that aim to prevent pollution.

In an example of this approach, *Cadbury's Guide to Low Carbon Dairy Farming* (see http://www.cadbury.co.uk/cadburyandchocolate/ OurCommitments/Documents/Cadbury-Carbon-Footprint-Guide.pdf) aims to make cuts in an emissions-intensive sector (agriculture is responsible for 7 per cent of the UK's GHG emissions). It also attempts to extend pollution prevention into the supply chain. The milk that goes into a Cadbury's chocolate bar is responsible for 60 per cent of its GHG emissions, according to the carbon audit carried out by the Carbon Trust. In a pilot programme, Cadbury has advised farmers in several counties in Britain on sustainable farm management practices. Such practices can increase milk yields and reduce GHG production, improving herd health, reducing the fibre levels, and increasing the starch level in cow feed (see www.climatechangecorp.com/).

Life cycle analysis

Lifecycle analysis is well established as a means of considering the environmental impacts that may flow from each stage of the life of a product or service, from cradle to grave. It is increasingly used as a method for assessing the social impact of products on a range of stakeholders including workers, the local community, society, consumers and value chain actors. A holistic approach to lifecycle analysis for a particular product, such as a T-shirt, would take into account the GHGs produced during manufacture, including the extraction of the raw materials used for production, the manufacturing process, marketing and disposal. It would also estimate social impacts such as worker hours, health and safety and other such issues along the life of the T-shirt (Andrews, 2009).

Industrial ecology

Industrial ecology is a relatively new field that attempts to address pollution and waste from a perspective that models industrial systems upon ecological systems (Ehrenfeld, 2004). In other words, it uses the metaphor of sustainable ecosystems to provide new understandings of how organisations might interrelate and provide a more sustainable system of production and consumption. The field draws together management studies with the study of matter and energy flows.

See also: *Environmental Policy Tools, Intergenerational Equity, Pollution and Waste Management, Sustainable Development, Systems Approaches*

REFERENCES

Andrews, E., (2009) *Guidelines for Social Life Cycle Assessment of Products*. Geneva: UNEP, SETC, Lifecycle Initiative.

Blacksmith Institute/Green Zone (2009) '*The Blacksmith's Institute World's Worst Polluted Places Report 2009*'. Available at www.worstpolluted.org/, accessed 12 April 2010.

Ehrenfeld, J. (2004) 'Industrial Ecology: A New Field or Only a Metaphor?', *Journal of Cleaner Production*, 12 (8–10): 825–831.

King, A. and Lennox, M. (2002) 'Exploring the Locus of Profitable Pollution Reduction', *Management Science*, 48 (2): 289–299.

Preuss, L. and Benn, S. (2007) 'Hazardous Waste', *Encyclopedia of Business Ethics and Society*. Thousand Oaks, CA: Sage. Available at www.sage-ereference.com/ethics/Article_n392.html, accessed 11 April 2010.

Postcolonialism

A CRITIQUE OF MODERNIST THEORIES OF DEVELOPMENT

'Postcolonialism' is a description of discourses concerned mainly with cultural issues around societies that have been colonised. It is an emancipatory discourse in the same tradition as multiculturalism and feminism, fitting within a postmodernist tradition of critique. Specifically, it offers a critical perspective on a modernist approach to development in the developing world. It critiques modernism as a meta-theoretical view of socio-technological progress driven by Western capitalist philosophies, values, economic strategies, initiatives and knowledge. As Bannerjee notes,

> the benefits delivered by the grand design of progress and modernity are, at best, equivocal. Despite phenomenal advances in science, technology, medicine and agricultural production, the promise that 'development' would eradicate world poverty remains unfulfilled in several parts of the globe, especially in the Third World. (2003: 143)

In considering the relationship between the concepts of postcolonialism and CSR, it is useful to understand the former's critique of modernism and postmodernism; its theoretical origins in the exploration of the relationship between the Occident (Western world) and the Orient (Eastern or non-Western world) with a focus on the nature of power manifest in colonialism; the nature of development and underdevelopment as a critique of modernisation theory; and the application of a model of 'postcolonialism' for critiquing both global sustainable development across the developed and less-developed world as well as the role of corporations in the development process.

THEORETICAL FOUNDATIONS

Knowledge as power in the perpetration of colonial relations

Edward Said (1978), a founding theorist of postcolonialism, explored and critiqued the Western notion of 'orientalism'. Said provided an understanding of the relationship between power and knowledge through a critique of Western descriptions of non-Euro-American 'others'. He argued that Western colonial domination had been rationalised and justified through 'ontological and epistemological distinction' (1978: 2) between the Occident and the Orient. This contrast was represented as 'hierarchical binaries … e.g. civilized/savage, developed/undeveloped, modern/archaic, nation/tribe, scientific/superstitious, and so on' (Banerjee and Prasad, 2008: 92). Through these dichotomies the Occident was represented by terms denoting civilisation, e.g. 'modern' and 'developed', whilst the Orient was represented as inferior to the West through descriptors such as 'undeveloped' and 'archaic', the inference being that the Orient needed an Occidental direction and influence to become civilised and developed. Said further suggested that the continuing power and influence of colonialism through terms of trade in a post-independence period was based on the ability of the West to investigate and produce knowledge on other societies and use it as a form of continuing power to be deployed against them, serving the coloniser's interests.

Historicism: a coherent unity

Said notes that one of the epistemological foundations and critical legacies of Orientalism is historicism as reflected in the writings of Hegel, Marx, Ranke and others, which maintains that the history of humankind can be understood in any given period as 'one human history uniting humanity ... possessing a complex but coherent unity' (1985: 101). Such an appraisal was developed from a European or Western perspective. Thus an important feature of postcolonialism is its assertion that modernism feeds the rationale and knowledge that supports colonial domination. Said's *Culture and Imperialism* (1994) introduces discourse analysis and postcolonial theory as tools for rethinking forms of knowledge that help establish the social identities of postcolonial systems. More recently, Banerjee and Prasad (2008) conclude that a postcolonial perspective challenges the 'unquestioned sovereignty' of Western economic, political and cultural capital in the growth and development processes.

The 'development' discourse

The postcolonial school of thought has been seen as problematising issues arising from colonial domination through a retrospective reflection on the impact of colonial relations on post-independence states (Banerjee, 2003). Said (1994) noted that the legacy of imperialism and its domination of territories by force and through political, economic, social and cultural approaches not only constituted the acquisition and accumulation of land, but also included the assumption that colonised people actually sought domination and the associated forms of knowledge that underpinned domination. Clegg (1989) comments on how practices, embodied in global economic institutions (e.g. the IMF, World Bank and WTO) reproduce the knowledge of the Western imperial and colonial traditions in newly independent territories, converting into natural rules or norms. Banerjee (2003) identifies the price associated with this ideology and practice including global warming, ozone depletion, a loss of biodiversity, soil erosion, and air and water pollution, suggesting that although these are global problems, they have significantly more harmful results for the rural poor in developing countries, many of whom directly depend on agricultural production for their livelihood.

Banerjee (2003) supports Foucault's (1980) suggestion to study techniques of domination other than 'sites of power' when considering the new era of colonial domination. This disciplinary power 'transmits itself through a complex system of institutions, regulations, text, policies and practices signifying not relations of sovereignty but relations of domination' (2003: 147). Banerjee illustrates how this power discourse can label and disenfranchise less-developed nations by contrasting their development potential with Western standards and culturally defined patterns of development and 'modernisation', whilst ignoring their unique characteristics and opportunities for alternative and culturally sensitive development paths (an attitude known as 'ethnocentrism'). For example, he noted that the US President Truman's 1949 inaugural address for a global programme of development, to make available to 'underdeveloped areas' the technological and industrial advances of the West, by its very nature made over 2 billion people 'underdeveloped' by holding up a 'mirror that define[d] their identity, which is really that of a heterogeneous and diverse majority, simply in the terms of an homogenizing and narrow minority' (Esteva, 1992: 7). In other words that development proceeded by identifying problems perceived through a Western mindset around progress which denied differences in culture (Escobar, 1995). This 'grand model of "progress" ... validat[ed] the assimilative imperatives of development under the banner of national interest' (1995: 56). The notion of development became synonymous with that of economic growth, ignoring the social and cultural consequences of Western-based economic growth imperatives and the power– knowledge nexus defining the development challenge.

Most importantly, Banerjee (2003) suggests that the concept of 'sustainable development' also warrants critical analysis using techniques espoused by postcolonial theory. He perceives the Brundtland definition of 'sustainable development' as a 'slogan' that attempts to reconcile economic growth, environmental protection, social justice and human development within 'the framework of social equity and the equitable distribution and utilization of resources' (2003: 152). Harvey also notes that the concept of sustainable development is promoted by 'situating it against the background of sustaining a particular set of social relations by way of a set of ecological projects' (1996: 148).

Therefore it could be argued that in the same way that the development discourse attempts to reconcile competing interests, the sustainable development discourse also tries to reconcile economic, environmental, social, intergenerational and regional equity agendas. Such tensions between developed and developing nations became very apparent at the Copenhagen meeting of the UNFCCC in December 2009. These tensions cannot be ignored when considering CSR initiatives to address poverty, social exclusion and other development challenges.

POSTCOLONIALISM AND CSR

CSR has been identified frequently as a contributor to international development by international organisations and national development agencies. However, Newell and Frynas question the assumption that CSR initiatives can meet the needs of the poor and the marginalised, asking 'is there a danger that by basing development policies around a business case, we fail to tackle or worse deepen the multiple forms of inequality or social exclusion?' (2007: 669). This tension is articulated by their distinction between CSR as a *business tool* and CSR as a *development tool*, contrasting business models that focus on the market opportunities available through servicing the world's poor (Prahalad and Hart, 2002) with alternative corporate strategies 'aligned with the pressing need to tackle poverty and social exclusion across the majority world' (Newell and Frynas, 2007: 670).

Other postcolonial critiques of CSR suggest that the 'business tool' model of CSR will be the dominating influence on what has been labelled 'sustainable development'. Banerjee concludes that the

> (post)modern form of corporate social responsibility produces a truth effect that is not dissimilar to Milton Friedman's (1962) concept of corporate social responsibility involving the maximization of shareholder value, despite the rhetoric of 'stakeholders' and 'corporate citizenship'. (2003: 163)

In other words, Banerjee claims there is no evidence of a shift in fundamental economic theory supporting sustainable development. From his perspective, organisational practices associated with CSR still incorporate colonial and neo-imperialistic perspectives of the colonised 'other', producing only a 'greener' version of the corporate objective of meeting shareholder value creation, with little concern for broader agendas such as the redress of poverty and social exclusion.

See also: *Business at the Bottom of the Pyramid, Civil Society, Fair Trade, Globalisation, Intergenerational Equity, Stakeholder Theory, Sustainable Development, Sweatshops*

REFERENCES

Banerjee, S.B. (2003) 'Who Sustains Whose Development? Sustainable Development and the Reinvention of Nature', *Organization Studies*, 24 (1): 143–180.

Banerjee, S.B. and Prasad, A. (2008) 'Introduction to the Special Issue on "Critical Reflections on Management and Organizations: A Postcolonial Perspective"', *Critical Perspectives on International Business*, 4 (2/3): 90–98.

Clegg, S. (1989) *Frameworks of Power*. London: Sage.

Escobar, A. (1995) *Encountering Development: The Making and Unmaking of the Third World 1945–1992*. Princeton, NJ: Princeton University Press.

Esteva, G. (1992) 'Development', in W. Sachs (ed.), *The Development Dictionary.* London: Zed Books, pp. 6–25.

Foucault, M. (1980) *Power/Knowledge: Selected Interviews and Other Writings*. New York: Pantheon.

Friedman, M. (1962) *Capitalism and Freedom*. Chicago, MA: Chicago University Press.

Harvey, D. (1996) *Justice, Nature and the Geography of Difference*. Oxford: Blackwell.

Newell, P. and Frynas, J.G. (2007) 'Beyond CSR? Business, Poverty and Social Justice: An Introduction', *Third World Quarterly*, 28 (4): 669–681.

Prahalad, C.K. and Hart, S.L. (2002) 'The Fortune at the Bottom of the Pyramid', *Strategy + Business*, 26: 2–14.

Said, E.W. (1978) *Orientalism*. New York: Vintage Books.

Said, E.W. (1985) 'Orientalism Reconsidered', *Cultural Critique*, 1 (Autumn): 89–107.

Said, E.W. (1994) *Culture and Imperialism*. New York: Vintage.

Product Stewardship

DEFINING PRODUCT STEWARDSHIP

Product Stewardship is an approach that recognises that manufacturers, importers, governments and consumers have a shared responsibility for the environmental impacts of a product throughout its full life cycle. Product Stewardship schemes establish a means for relevant parties in the product chain to share responsibility for the products they produce, handle, purchase, use and discard (Environment Protection Heritage Council, 2009).

Product stewardship takes a lifecycle rather than an end-of-life approach. The linked concept of extended producer responsibility refers to policy requirements or incentives that encourage or require companies to accept responsibility for the final disposal of their products. Extended producer responsibility and product stewardship schemes are in the process of being developed by many countries to address a perceived market failure in relation to waste management. Market failure refers to circumstances in which markets do not allocate resources to achieve the best returns for the community. The build-up of wastes in association with industrial development is an example of such a failure, and attempts to curtail this failure are increasingly being seen as a necessary element within an organisation's wider CSR profile.

Internationally, product stewardship approaches have been used principally for packaging waste, electronic and electrical equipment, batteries, bottles, paint cans, automobiles, waste oil, tyres, refrigerants and other products. As management approaches, product stewardship and producer responsibility are dependent upon lifecycle analysis. For example, The Natural Step's Sustainability Life Cycle Assessment (SLCA) approach, based on the The Natural Step Framework and described in the entry on Systems Approaches, helps organisations to analyse the sustainability of their products.

POLICY-MAKING MEASURES

Policy making to encourage this environmental dimension of CSR and corporate sustainability is well advanced in some European countries, with follow-on implications for other countries because of trade agreements. Administrative arrangements to implement the schemes vary, but may include voluntary partnerships between government and industry, government regulation or voluntary initiatives by industry, perhaps facilitated by industry associations. Policy measures may include take-back requirements, deposit refunds, product leases, performance targets and advance disposal and recycling fees. Others include tradeable recycling or landfill diversion credits, education and awareness initiatives and product labelling. But for such schemes to be successful there needs to be a significant buy-in from participating firms, such as manufacturers, retailers and other parties throughout the supply chain.

Extended producer responsibility legislation like the European Union's (EU) End-of-Life Vehicles (ELV) Directive aims to make vehicle dismantling and recycling more environmentally friendly. It sets clear quantified targets for the reuse, recycling and recovery of vehicles and their components, and requires manufacturers to begin to ensure the safe handling of their products' materials after the customer use phase, so encouraging a design for new vehicles that incorporates recyclability concerns. The ELV Directive has stimulated the formation of automobile industry collaborations that will link the supplier organisation with those organisations responsible for the end-of-life aspects of the lifecycle.

Take-back and re-use/recycling initiatives are also being introduced in the information and communication technology industry via product stewardship. As described in the entry on Systems Approaches, Design for the Environment is a means of addressing product stewardship so that producer responsibility can be implemented in a cost-effective way. For example, Hewlett Packard (HP) implements environmental considerations throughout the lifecycle of each product through a core design strategy, 'Designed for Recyclability, Designed for Environment'. HP supports the shift towards modular designs so as to facilitate easier disassembly and recycling. Additionally, products are now assembled using 'snap-on' features, removing glues and adhesives from the production process. It now uses moulded pulp (which is also recyclable post use) to produce packaging or protective casings for its products (Chelliah et al., 2008).

PRODUCT SERVICE SYSTEMS

Adding product value through increasing the service component, while diminishing material through output, is now a matter of international and national policymaking, and many industry sectors have already started on such a journey. As the ultimate form of product stewardship and extended producer responsibility, product service systems involve provision of a service to customers through producers maintaining ownership of products and the products being a part of the service – a different procurement model to the traditional buy-and-own approach. Different arrangements may apply, such as a product lease, purchase and service or service sharing. 'Call-a-bike', 'energy management services' and long-term service agreements with take-back provisions such as now offered by information technology companies are examples.

But product service approaches such as lease maintenance and take-back strategies do not necessarily result in dematerialisation. While they may extend the use life of products, they may create additional transportation, packaging or energy consumption for the individualised delivery of services, causing extra environmental impact. Furthermore, other authors have noted a possible 'rebound effect', where more efficiencies in product service systems are outweighed by overall increases in consumption.

The Sustainable Product Service System (S-PSS) has been suggested by management systems scholars such as Ness (2008) and Xing et al. (2009) as a further step up the improvement ladder. The sustainability advantages of S-PSS over product stewardship are that the provider manages a fleet of products for the customer, leading to increased utilisation and a reduction in fleet and efficiencies, resulting in a greater likelihood of product take-back, less resource use (materials, energy, water), fewer emissions and less waste due to products being kept in a closed loop. Business advantages such as the ease of technological updating by a provider and a closer relationship between customer and service provider can also act as incentives for firms to engage in such schemes.

Product service strategies enabled by such creative approaches to the supply chain include 'intelligent materials handling' (Braungart et al., 2007). In this model, materials are owned by a materials bank which leases them to companies, who in turn will make them into products that are then leased to customers. At the end of the product life, the materials are then returned to the materials bank. As the bank actually takes ownership of the information, Braungart et al. (2007) argue that such a scheme can enable the progressive development of shared knowledge around better and more effective materials.

CASE EXAMPLE: INTERFACE

The leading carpet manufacturer, Interface, is a well-known example of a firm that is attempting to shift its business model towards the integration of environmental and social responsibility. Product stewardship is a key aspect of the firm's strategy. The firm's website states that the elimination of waste, by which it means anything that does not provide value to the customer, is a priority. Waste in this definition includes remnants and scrap, but also overuse of materials and inventory losses. An example of how it applies product stewardship principles to this objective is its modular carpet tiles that customers can return in a used or damaged state for recycling. The firm claims to be the first carpet manufacturer to implement a process whereby carpet fibre can be cleanly separated from its backing, allowing for more effective materials recycling. The separated carpet fibre is in such a state that it can be incorporated with virgin raw material to make new carpet. Energy use is also tracked, and the company claims that their recycled products are lowering the benchmark for embodied energy use for the industry. Overall, Interface claims that the cumulative avoided costs from waste elimination activities since 1995 have been calculated to be over $433 million.

See also: Environmental Policy Tools, Pollution and Waste Management, Stewardship, Systems Approaches, Voluntary Regulation

REFERENCES

Braungart, M., McDonough, W. and Bollinger, A. (2007) 'Cradle-to-cradle Design: Creating Healthy Emissions – a Strategy for Eco-effective Product and System Design', *Journal of Cleaner Production*, 15 (13–14): 1337–1348.

Chelliah, J., Benn, S. and Low, S. (2008) 'HP Australia: Strategies in Response to Global Sustainability', *The Management Case Study Journal*, 8 (2): 38–47.

Environment Protection Heritage Council (2009) *Product Stewardship*. Available at www.ephc.gov.au/taxonomy/term/45, accessed 17 April 2010.

Ness, D. (2008) 'Sustainable Product Service Systems: Potential to Deliver Business and Social Benefits with Less Resource Used', in Wang, H.-F. (ed.), *Web-based Green Products Life Cycle Management Systems*. New York: Information Science Reference, pp. 232–249.

Xing, K., Ness, D., Benn, S. and Qian, W. (2009) 'A Framework for Sustainable Product Service Systems: With Particular Reference to ICT Industries', 7th ANZAM *Operations, Supply Chain and Services Management Symposium* 2009. Theme: Integration through Innovation. 8–10 June, Adelaide, South Australia.

resource-based view

Resource-Based View

ORIGINS OF THE RESOURCE-BASED VIEW (RBV) OF THE FIRM

Wernerfelt (1984) has been credited with the first coherent theory of the resource-based firm, drawing from an earlier economic theory that conceptualised firms as broad sets of resources. He looked at the strategic options of firms from the perspective of their resources rather than in terms of their products, arguing that specifying a resource profile for a firm allowed it 'to find the optimal product-market activities' (1984: 171). He also argued it was possible to create resource position barriers for competitors by identifying unique resource mixing through the use of a resource–product matrix. His examples of 'resources' included 'brand names, in-house knowledge of technology, employment of skilled personnel, trade contacts, machinery, efficient procedures, capital, etc.' (1984: 172). His resource-based approach recognised the need for dynamic capability in resource usage, acknowledging that in competing for market position firms may start out with homogeneous resources, but will become increasingly heterogeneous in their resource usage in order to maintain and grow their market position.

CONTRIBUTION TO COMPETITIVE ADVANTAGE

Prahalad and Hamel (1990) further related the resource-based view (RBV) to the notion of organisational competencies. They stated that although in the short term a company's competitiveness was largely determined by the pricing and quality of their products and services, in the long term 'competitiveness derives from an ability to build, at lower cost and more speedily than competitors, the core competencies that spawn unanticipated products' (1990: 81). They referred to this concept as 'competing for the future', noting management's responsibility to bring together socio-technical competencies to meet emerging and shifting market needs.

Barney (1991) commented on RBV's relevance to strategy planning, identifying that rare and valuable resources that are inimitable and non-substitutable can sustain competitive advantage. He clearly positioned his RBV relative to the strategic positioning theories of competitive advantage rather than to other possible theoretical frameworks, including neo-classical microeconomics (concerning the supply inelasticity of resource-based factors of production) or evolutionary economics (how firms vary routines to achieve the most efficient ones to gain competitive advantage). This choice influenced the direction of theoretical discourse around the topic. Consequently, there has been significant consensus on locating RBV within the competitive positioning and strategic management arena.

However, Priem and Butler (2001) have questioned the extent to which RBV theory is likely to enrich the theory of competitive advantage.

They suggested that the fundamental premise of RBV was not testable in that 'Simply advising practitioners to obtain rare and valuable resources in order to achieve competitive advantage, and, further, that those resources should be hard to imitate and non-substitutable for sustainable advantage, does not meet the operational validity criterion' (2001: 31). However, they concluded that RBV could achieve theory status in the area of competitive advantage and thus more clearly inform managerial practice by integrating its ideas more rigorously within an environmental demand model.

FACILITATING CHANGE THROUGH FOSTERING DYNAMIC CAPABILITY

Another approach to RBV concerns its contribution to an understanding of the organisational capacity for change (OCC), underpinning a firm's responsiveness to challenges and opportunities in the business environment. A key feature of RBV theory is that it recognises the value of a firm's dynamic capabilities, based on unique, emergent and innovative resource building and bundling in response to environmental shifts. The literature suggests that this approach is facilitated by a culture of change readiness, often fostered by leadership that earns trust through sense-making collective goals and providing resourcing appropriate to high change environments. So what might be the characteristics of a culture that promotes change readiness and employee wellbeing?

Judge and Elenkov (2005) compare the OCC and the 'readiness' for change constructs, suggesting that the former describes the organisational change challenge while the latter addresses the individual's readiness for change. Bolton (2004) also argues for an understanding of the dynamic interaction between the two dimensions of organisation and employee. Employing a resource-based view of an organisation's resilience to change that includes the contribution of resilient employees and other stakeholders, she provides a model to appraise the readiness for change of a culture through considering coping capability in constant and turbulent change environments. The model draws from the work of Lazarus and Folkman (1984), who demonstrated that the process of coping with new stressors (change) involved two stages. Initially, a change challenge is appraised as new and either positive or negative, thus affecting the emotional response towards the new event. A secondary appraisal assesses coping capabilities and available resources to meet the challenge or threat. In other words, the change challenge is appraised and then the culture and resources are evaluated as being more or less sufficient in meeting change challenges by employees and other stakeholders. Figure 4 reflects how an employee or other stakeholders might appraise change challenges and the OCC through evaluating a firm's capacity to accrue and apply the resources to achieve long lasting and integrated commercial, social and environmental outcomes perceived as appropriate to the sector and organisation. This model appears relevant to the behaviour of executive leadership, governance bodies, individual employees and other stakeholders.

In today's complex environment it might also be appropriate to consider change readiness cultures within the framework of risk management, given the increasing focus of governance on the management of material non-financial risk. However, Barney (1991) also reminds us that such a culture is as difficult to produce as it might be to imitate.

RBV, CSR AND PEOPLE MANAGEMENT

The advent of RBV within the strategy literature has led to strategic human resource management being given a place at the strategy table (Wright et al., 2001). Wright et al. purport three areas of people management systems that support the RBV for competitive advantage: the human capital pool; employee relationships and behaviours (including psychological contracts and organisational citizenship); and people management practices.

Figure 4 illustrates Priem and Butler's (2001) claim that RBV might become more responsive to current environmental challenges, by alluding to certain people management issues associated with triple bottom line accounting, perhaps not yet recognised in the human resource (HR) literature. Those areas highlighted include:

- accountability within firms for negative externalities associated with ineffective management of people in heavy change environments that can incur cost to the broader community around health, skill depletion and welfare (reflected, for example, in recent changes to certain occupational health and safety legislation in the UK to address the management of stress in firms)
- new forms of leadership to deal with complexity and people management in increasingly fast-paced and changing contexts
- developing new mindsets and skills about people management supporting the process of building social capital, a dynamic capability often not traditionally recognised by HR (Wright et al., 2001: 714)

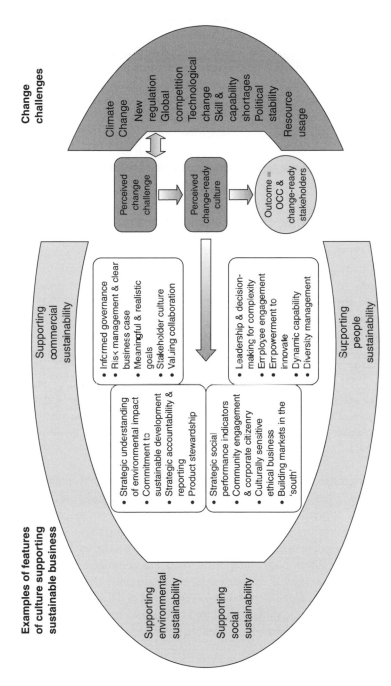

Change challenges

- Climate Change
- New regulation
- Global competition
- Technological change
- Skill & capability shortages
- Political stability
- Resource usage

Perceived change challenge → Perceived change-ready culture → Outcome = OCC & change-ready stakeholders

Examples of features of culture supporting sustainable business

Supporting commercial sustainability

- Informed governance
- Risk management & clear business case
- Meaningful & realistic goals
- Stakeholder culture
- Valuing collaboration

Supporting people sustainability

- Leadership & decision-making for complexity
- Employee engagement
- Empowerment to innovate
- Dynamic capability
- Diversity management

Supporting environmental sustainability

- Strategic understanding of environmental impact
- Commitment to sustainable development
- Strategic accountability & reporting
- Product stewardship

Supporting social sustainability

- Strategic social performance indicators
- Community engagement & corporate citizenry
- Culturally sensitive ethical business
- Building markets in the 'south'

Figure 4   *Resource-based approach to developing a sustainable business culture*

- diversity management (a key CSR function in an increasingly global marketplace) as an area of risk for sustainable business practice. Many organisational cultures are building on a compliance approach, associated with non-discrimination through Equal Employment Opportunity (EEO), and directing this towards one of inclusion that leverages and benefits from diverse skills and insights in the workplace to better meet stakeholder needs, e.g. meeting customer and community needs through representative and collaborative partnerships.

These approaches require new mindsets, values and definitions of success in people management and culture building.

RBV, CSR AND ENVIRONMENT

Hart (1995) suggests that RBV theory still employs a narrow perspective on managerial theory around its economic, political and social dimensions, excluding the natural environment. Yet the irreversible damage to the planet's basic ecological systems posed by population growth and resource usage suggests the need for a paradigm shift in strategic management thinking. Hart believes new features would include waste minimisation, green product design and technology cooperation with the developing world:

> In other words, it is likely that strategy and competitive advantage in the coming years will be rooted in capabilities that facilitate environmentally sustainable economic activity – a natural resource-based view of the firm. (1995: 991)

Hart also suggests a competitive advantage would be increased by: pollution prevention as a key resource of continuous improvement and cost reduction; product stewardship that minimises the lifecycle costs of products around stakeholder integration; and sustainable development strategies that minimise the negative externalities of business growth on the environment and support any future positioning of the firm. His comments have been prescient given the scale of the current global community debate around the use of renewable versus depletable energy resources. These perspectives that require paradigmatic shifts in thinking about resource usage to achieve sustainable business outcomes have been incorporated into Figure 4.

See also: *Corporate Sustainability, Employee Engagement, Risk Management, Social Capital, Stakeholder Theory, Sustainable Development, Triple Bottom Line*

REFERENCES

Barney, J.B. (1991) 'Firm Resources and Sustained Competitive Advantage', *Journal of Management*, 17 (1): 99–120.

Bolton, D. (2004) 'Change, Coping and Context in the Resilient Organisation', *Mt Eliza Business Review*, Winter/Spring: 57–66.

Hart, S.L. (1995) 'A Natural-Resource-based View of the World', *Academy of Management Review*, 20 (4): 986–1014.

Judge, W.Q. and Elenkov, D. (2005) 'Organizational Capacity for Change and Environmental Performance: An Empirical Assessment of Bulgarian Firms', *Journal of Business Research*, 58: 893–901.

Lazarus, R. and Folkman, S. (1984) *Stress, Appraisal and Coping*. New York: Springer.

Prahalad, C.K. and Hamel, G. (1990) 'The Core Competence of the Corporation', *Harvard Business Review*, May-June: 79–91.

Priem, R.L. and Butler, J.E. (2001) 'Is the Resource-based "View" a Useful Perspective for Strategic Management Research?', *Academy of Management Review*, 26 (1): 22–40.

Wernerfelt, B. (1984) 'A Resource-based View of the Firm', *Strategic Management Journal*, 5: 171–180.

Wright, P.M., Dunford, B.B. and Snell, S.A. (2001) 'Human Resources and the Resource Based View of the Firm', *Journal of Management*, 27: 701–721.

Responsible Leadership

There are many definitions of leadership but almost all centre on the concept of influence – on the ability of an individual or a group to influence the behaviour of others. Even scholars who debate the motivations for CSR decisions and what constitutes appropriate leadership behaviours agree that leadership is key to formulating and implementing CSR initiatives (Waldman and Siegel, 2008). Yet despite the enormous interest for many years in defining leadership, there has been relatively little research on what is meant by leadership in the context of responsible corporate behaviour. As Maak and Pless (2006) put it, responsible leadership is underpinned by both ethics and effectiveness, but what does this mean for the personal qualities of the leader? What styles or skills should he or she have? What should be the relationship between the leader and their followers? What roles must he or she fulfil? In this entry we summarise current understandings in relation to these questions.

LEADER CHARACTERISTICS

Trustworthiness, integrity, honesty, tolerance and flexibility are typically suggested as the personal qualities of the responsible, ethical leader. In the context of CSR and corporate sustainability, research on leadership style has tended to focus on the behaviours, mindsets and actions of the heroic or charismatic leader as a means of driving the organisation towards the achievement of transformative change (e.g. Egri and Herman, 2000; Benn and Dunphy, 2009). The leader as charismatic visionary is associated with 'big picture' thinking, and linked to values-based approaches to leadership. Particular psychological strengths, self-leadership characteristics such as enthusiasm and motivation, visioning and empathy, and the ability to make deep changes within themselves are some of the wide range of attributes associated in the literature with charismatic or transformational leadership towards CSR.

The charismatic model has recently been challenged by Waldman et al. (2006), who found that it was chief executive officer (CEO) intellectual stimulation rather than CEO charismatic leadership that may encourage a firm to engage in 'strategic' CSR. Other scholars have argued that the emphasis on the charismatic model and 'great man' theory may hinder responsible leadership because it limits our focus to a certain set of traits, marginalising our consideration of serving or caring versions of leadership. On this account, leadership is all about relationships. In other words 'responsible leadership is all about building and sustaining trustful relationships to all relevant stakeholders by being servant, steward, architect, change agent, coach and story teller' and 'leadership authority comes with relationship work, service, care and commitment' (Maak and Pless, 2006: 50).

Relevant skills appear to be of two main types: critical cognitive skills and stakeholder engagement skills. As noted in the entry on Corporate Responsibility Reporting, high levels of uncertainty surround many CSR and sustainability issues, such as how to measure and compare the social, economic and environmental costs and benefits. Critical cognitive skills are required to evaluate information and assess an appropriate corporate strategy concerning issues such as the impact of a potential global carbon economy underpinned by carbon taxes and carbon trading schemes.

Hoffman and Bazerman (2007) argue that leaders' cognitive and organisational bias, such as overconfidence, the tendency to discount the future, and an over-reliance on compliance, may be restricting organisations shifting towards more responsible and sustainable behaviour.

Skills of stakeholder engagement are also required to provide effective leadership given the diversity of stakeholders associated with economic, social and environmental sustainability objectives. Stakeholder relationship management is a leadership skill also linked to spiritual practices, such as demonstrating fair treatment, recognising the contributions of others, and engaging in reflective practice (Reave, 2005).

LEADER ROLES

Being an effective CEO or organisational leader demands a varied role repertoire and the flexibility to move in and out of different roles as the needs of a situation change. Effective leaders need to be able to understand the issues (in the role of analyser), inspire others (in the role of vision setter) and help them focus their energy (in the role of motivator) (Benn and Dunphy, 2009). For example, to implement transformational change associated with redesigning the organisation around CSR or sustainability principles, the CEO and other corporate figures must be able to face the realities of what the organisation is and what it needs to change and then inspire and motivate followers so as to implement this analysis. Ray Anderson, chairman of the carpet manufacturer Interface Inc., demonstrates such leadership qualities. Through his leadership and with the advice of designers who can envision business models based on the creativity of Nature, Interface has saved $255 million in the last decade by implementing innovative manufacturing processes aimed at eliminating hazardous wastes (Debold, 2005).

In line with the demands of dealing with these uncertainties, there is some evidence that leaders who are influencing their firms towards a more holistic approach play roles that are enabling rather than directive, encouraging a learning approach that incorporates such activities as decentralization, diversity, connections, shared focus, constraints and feedback. This line of research suggests that enabling rather than determining or guiding leadership can deal more effectively with the challenges facing contemporary organisations (Marion and Uhl-Bien, 2001). Leadership capabilities on this complexity model are those that encourage novelty, and make sense of emerging events for others (Plowman et al., 2007).

responsible leadership

Such an approach would appear particularly relevant given the multiple ambiguities and complexities associated with increasing environmental and social responsibility. These are leaders working with the characteristic features of complex adaptive systems. Such leaders embrace uncertainty, and encourage innovation and connections between people.

Another and linked approach is distributed leadership. This approach is gaining support in the literature given increasing recognition that no one person, no matter how charismatic, can deliver the effective leadership of today's large, complex organisations around emergent issues such as sustainability and holistic understandings of corporate responsibility. The dynamic, interactive nature of shared leadership and its associated relationship characteristics, such as collective learning and mutual empowerment, contributes to its appropriateness where leaders face the highly complex task of balancing the demands of many diverse and competing stakeholders, as with CSR strategies (Mehra et al., 2006).

See also: Complexity Theory, Corporate Responsibility Reporting, Corporate Social Responsibility, Corporate Sustainability, Systems Approaches

REFERENCES

Benn, S. and Dunphy, D. (2009) 'Leadership for Sustainability', in R. Staib (ed.), *Business Management and Environmental Stewardship.* Basingstoke: Palgrave Macmillan, pp. 56–75.

Debold, E. (2005) 'New Operating Reality', *Executive Excellence*, 22 (11): 8.

Egri, C.P. and Herman, S. (2000) 'Leadership in the North American Environmental Sector: Values, Leadership Styles, and Contexts of Environmental Leaders and their Organizations', *Academy of Management Review*, 43 (4): 571–604.

Hoffman, A.J. and Bazerman, M.H. (2007) 'Changing Practice on Sustainability: Understanding and Overcoming the Organizational and Psychological Barriers to Action', in S. Sharma, M. Starik and B. Husted (eds), *Organizations and the Sustainability Mosaic: Crafting Long-term Ecological and Societal Solutions.* Northampton, MA: Edward Elgar, pp. 84–105.

Maak, T. and Pless, N. (2006) 'Responsible Leadership: A Relational Approach', in T. Maak and N. Pless (eds), *Responsible Leadership.* London and New York: Routledge.

Marion, R. and Uhl-Bien, M. (2001) 'Leadership in Complex Organizations', *Leadership Quarterly*, 12: 389–418.

Mehra, A., Smith, B., Dixon, A. and Robertson, B. (2006) 'Distributed Leadership in Teams: The Network of Leadership Perceptions and Team Performance', *Leadership Quarterly*, 17: 232–245.

Plowman, D., Thomas, S., Beck, T., Baker, L., Kulkarni, M. and Travis, D. (2007) 'The Role of Leadership in Emergent, Self-organization', *Leadership Quarterly*: 341–356.

Reave, L. (2005) 'Towards a Paradigm of Spiritual Leadership', *Leadership Quarterly*, 16: 655–687.

Waldman, D. and Siegel, D.(2008) 'Defining the Socially Responsible Leader', *The Leadership Quarterly*, 19 (1): 117–131.

Waldman, D., Siegel, D. and Javidan, M. (2006) 'Components of Transformational Leadership and Corporate Social Responsibility', *Journal of Management Studies*, 43: 1703–1725.

Risk Management

WHAT IS RISK?

Risk management is an essential feature of effective direction setting, decision-making and accountability. A better understanding of the nature of risk in today's organisations is critical to decision-making given the complex and dynamic dimension of CSR and corporate sustainability.

Kytle and Ruggie (2005) argue that risk can be understood in terms of a company's threats, vulnerabilities, controls and countermeasures. Risk arises 'when a vulnerability exists within an organization's operating systems in the absence of effective controls and countermeasures' (2005: 4).

Francis and Armstrong focus on the relationship between risk and decision-making, suggesting that risk constitutes

a threat posed by the failure of corporate decisions: the exposure to such issues as economic or financial loss or gain, physical injury, or delay as a consequence of pursuing or not pursuing a particular course of action. (2003: 376)

They suggest that managing such risks requires

the application of policies and procedures to the tasks of identifying, analysing and assessing risks, determining the degree of exposure to risk that organisations can accommodate, and taking appropriate steps to avoid litigation, loss of reputation or injury. (2003: 376)

risk management

SOCIAL RISK AND RISK MANAGEMENT

The increasing complexity associated with globalisation has witnessed growing numbers of social interactions in the global economy that increase the risk to organisations. Such 'dynamic system(s) effectively have more levers and pressure points than previously, many of them critical to smooth operations and playing a role in the optimisation of the whole. These pressure points on business, most notably those pressures by civil society and stakeholders more broadly, constitute *social risk*' (Kytle and Ruggie, 2005: 6). Kylie and Ruggie explain further that when 'empowered stakeholders' pressure a company about a social issue they are threatening 'earning drivers' such as brand and reputation. While economic, technological and political risks are routinely recognised, modelled and managed in organisations, it is only recently that forms of social and environmental risk such as those associated with human rights and environmental standards have been acknowledged in corporate decision-making processes.

Scrutiny by civil society can constitute significant or ambiguous threats to corporations. Examples have included responses to: the environmental impact of oil spills such as the *Exxon Valdez*; activity by pharmaceutical companies to prevent 'generic' brands of life-saving drugs being made available in poor countries; and the employment of sweatshop labour often being used as a cost-cutting measure. In these situations, corporations need to observe local laws that can be in tension with their strategic intent and values. Such tensions are apparent at the time of writing concerning BP's level of responsibility for oil leaks in the Gulf of Mexico and their impact on the fragile coastline of Louisiana and the wetlands of the Mississippi Delta. At the beginning of September 2010 clean up costs were in the order of US$8 billion, raising issues around the extent of BP's responsibility for a range of externalities including the lost livelihoods of affected residents. Kytle and Ruggie (2005) identify an area of social risk for global corporations emanating from their greater capacity to meet community needs than that of governments. This can be a source of criticism if they do not respond to local emergencies. A good example is the pressure put on Coca-Cola to use its marketing and logistics capabilities to increase awareness of AIDS and deliver medical supplies to hospitals in Africa.

STRATEGY AND RISK

Scholars began to have a significant interest in risk management as an aspect of strategic management in the 1980s. In differentiating between systematic and unsystematic (or business) risk, Husted (2005) suggests that investors have paid more attention to systematic risk in stocks through identifying shifts in market value, whereas unsystematic risks, concerned with business risk at the firm level, have received less attention from investors and more from management. 'Strategic adaptation by skilful, rigorous and continuous management of unsystematic (business) risk lies at the very heart of strategic management' (2005: 175).

The strategic management of business risk in contemporary global business is increasingly challenged by economic, environmental and social pressures requiring new forms of governance and accountability. As Lacy and Pickard have noted, globalisation has presented industry with significant opportunities and also those risks associated with 'climate change, energy security, pollution, poverty and water scarcity' (2008: 139). These risks introduce pressures on a firm's strategic management of its supply chain, manufacturing operations and stakeholder groups requiring new forms of risk management. As a result, Kytle and Ruggie suggest that social, economic, political and technical risk need to be 'mainstreamed into the entire organization's value proposition and strategic risk management paradigm' (2005: 8).

ETHICS AND RISK

Francis and Armstrong (2003) argue that an essential feature of a risk management strategy is a commitment to ethics in an organisation. They refer to Francis's (2000) ethical principles that might guide organisational values, i.e. treating stakeholders with dignity, equitably, prudently, honestly, openly, with goodwill, and in a manner that avoids suffering.

They argue that risk management should address the threats posed by unethical decisions related to the treatment of an organisation's stakeholders through leadership values, culture, systems and procedures that elicit and reward compliance with ethical behaviours. Francis and Armstrong purport a 'beneficial symbiosis' based on 'a synthesis between legal compliance and ethical compliance through aspirational self-regulation' (2003: 383). They argue that there is less risk associated with an organisational culture in which ethical behaviour is not regulated but is understood to be in an organisation's best interests.

CSR AND RISK MANAGEMENT

Kytle and Ruggie (2005) conclude that CSR programmes should be included in a risk management framework because they provide principles and insights into stakeholder management whilst supplying critical information on social and environmental issues that inform a corporate risk agenda. This approach can mitigate such risks. Husted (2005) reinforces this view but purports a more measurable approach to CSR as a risk management tool.

Husted also reminds us that corporate investments are traditionally evaluated by calculating the net present value (NPV) of their cash flows. This approach can result in the rejection of important CSR projects that do not produce a positive cash flow because 'the NPV approach fails to take into account the value of strategic flexibility that certain investments create' (2005: 176). By way of contrast to NPV, he notes the increasing use of options (investments, resources and capabilities that can help decision makers select a favourable outcome) the decision makers can use as risk management tools in managing downside risk. He contrasts financial options with real options that are concerned with operating assets rather than financial assets, i.e. they allow firms to undertake activities or acquire resources that provide strategic flexibility. He suggests that CSR constitutes a real option in that it can provide direct benefits or strategic flexibility based on the creation of new products and services, or it can provide less tangible benefits such as fostering goodwill and creating valuable human capital. Husted argues that from a strategic point of view the value of the CSR option is like other real options in that 'If the value of a CSR option is greater than its price, ... [the firm] should acquire the option; otherwise, it should not' (2005: 179). Thus he suggests that real options theory supports a more strategic view of the concept of CSR in contrast to what he perceives as sporadic treatment of the relationship between CSR and risk management, and CSR and financial performance in the business and society literature.

Story and Trevor (2006) have argued that the key question is not whether companies should be socially responsible and manage these associated risks, but rather how they should manage decision-making to incorporate and align financial, commercial and socially related risk. They noted that many organisations were now using risk management techniques and audits to demonstrate CSR activities within the accreditation frameworks for management standards, advocating a more holistic approach to CSR in existing international standards. The new international standard, ISO 26000: Guidance on Social Responsibility, is intended to provide 'harmonized globally relevant guidance based on international consensus amongst expert representatives of the main stakeholder groups and so encourage the implementation of best practice in social responsibility world-wide' (IOS, 2009). It draws on existing public and private sector social responsibility initiatives and UN and OECD declarations and conventions.

See also: Business Case for CSR, Civil Society, Complexity Theory, Corporate Citizenship, Corporate Social Responsibility, Globalisation, Sweatshops

REFERENCES

Francis, R.D. (2000) *Ethics and Corporate Governance: An Australian Handbook.* Sydney: University of NSW Press.

Francis, R.D. and Armstrong, A. (2003) 'Ethics as a Risk Management Strategy: The Australian Experience', *Journal of Business Ethics*, 45: 75–385.

Husted, B.W. (2005) 'Risk Management, Real Options, and Corporate Social Responsibility', *Journal of Business Ethics*, 60: 175–183.

International Organization for Standardization (2009) 'Future ISO 26000 Standard on Social Responsibility Published as Draft International Standard'. Available at www.iso.org/iso/pressrelease.htm?refid=Ref1245, accessed 21 March 2010.

Kytle, B. and Ruggie, J.G. (2005) 'Corporate Social Responsibility as Risk Management', *Working Paper no. 10 of the Corporate Social Responsibility Initiative.* Cambridge, MA: John F. Kennedy School of Government, Harvard University.

Lacy, P. and Pickard, S. (2008) 'Managing Risk and Opportunity', *Journal of Corporate Citizenship*, 30: 139–146.

Story, P. and Trevor, T. (2006) 'Corporate Social Responsibility and Risk Management', *Journal of Corporate Citizenship*, 22: 39–51.

Social and Societal Marketing

BACKGROUND

Tensions have developed between advocates of 'the dominant model' of marketing and those who have questioned the social responsibilities embedded in the marketing function. Crane and Desmond (2002) note that the dominant model of marketing (espoused as marketing science and emanating from the Harvard Business School of economic thought) was based on the belief that the marketing process is technical, and as such is concerned only with the act of purchasing and exchange at the customer interface, and not with moral or ethical considerations about whether this exchange is in the customer's or society's longer term interests. They also identify Kotler as having been a key contributor to this debate, attempting with others to embed social, moral and ethical concerns into the marketing function. Contributions have developed in two schools, those of social marketing and societal marketing.

SOCIAL MARKETING

A historical perspective on social marketing provides useful insights into its impact on current business practices. The notion of social marketing developed in the 1950s from observations that social campaigns were more successful if they adopted the tactics of a product campaign. Social advertising was being increasingly used in the USA at this time to promote the business of non-profit organisations. Kotler and Zaltmane enhanced this notion to become that of social marketing, defined as

> the design, implementation and control of programs calculated to influence the acceptability of social ideas and involving considerations of product, planning, pricing, communication, distribution and marketing research. (1971: 5)

Kotler and Zaltmane emphasised that when comparing social marketing to standard commercial marketing, the product design of ideas is more challenging. For example, in marketing safer driving or healthier eating no one product is available, and various products have to contribute to the achievement of the social goal. A single level of expertise in promotion cannot be employed; rather, varying types of expertise need to be coordinated. Communication and distribution are particularly challenging as people need to know how to act on their decisions. This might involve a series of outlets and service providers that require coordination within public policy frameworks and bureaucracies, e.g. in health-related services. In relation to price, the marketer can rely less on an individual being able to undertake the cost–benefit analysis, thus an approach might attempt to maximise the benefits relative to cost, or reduce the costs relative to benefits. However, despite these challenges, Kotler and Zaltmane concluded that social marketing offered 'a useful framework for effective social planning at a time when social issues were becoming more relevant and critical' (1971: 12).

Today, social marketing has become mainstream in the marketing of social causes and in fundraising for not-for-profits. Australia readily embraced social marketing initiatives in the 1980s and particularly in the health sector, e.g. the 'Quit' campaign of the Victoria Cancer Council, the 'Slip! Slop! Slap!' slogan of 'Sunsmart' (both in 1988), and more recently 'Homecomings', a WorkSafe campaign (2006) that has been adopted nationally. In 2007, the UK government announced 'Choosing Health: Making Healthy Choices Easier', as part of its policy to use a social marketing approach to encourage positive health behaviour.

SOCIETAL MARKETING

Kotler (1972) has subsequently called for marketers to add another dimension to their professional responsibilities, which he determined as concern for 'long-run consumer welfare', noting the increasing number of negative externalities of consumer choices such as health problems, pollution, congestion, waste disposal problems and so on.

'Societal marketing thus promised a fundamental reconstruction of marketing, suggesting the possibility of a more ethical marketing approach, which embraced rather than excluded public concerns' (Crane and Desmond, 2002: 549). Kotler's societal marketing concept (SMC) suggested that marketing should embed the values and ethics of social responsibility into commercial marketing strategies. He categorised the types of products that might be relevant to societal marketing. *Deficient products*, which offered neither short- nor long-term benefits, were excluded. *Salutary products*, which had low immediate appeal but high long-term consumer benefit, and *pleasing products*, which gave immediate satisfaction but could cause harm in the long term, would be modified to move them towards the category of *desirable products*, which provide both immediate satisfaction and long-term benefit. By 2000, Kotler was advocating that societal marketing should move beyond the goal of long-term consumer wellbeing towards the goal of society's wellbeing. At this stage the SMC can be seen as being broadly aligned with CSR principles, taking into account both the current and longer-term interests of stakeholders that included sustainable development issues.

Although Kotler incorporated SMC into his mainstream marketing texts, writers such as Dixon (1992) have suggested that this approach is still a bolt-on to mainstream marketing approaches that continue to focus heavily on customer satisfaction and profitability. Crane and Desmond (2002) acknowledge that while the principles of SMC have had an impact on some aspects of marketing activity, they have not produced a new moral basis for marketing, nor found their way into business discourse (as have marketing terms such as 'green marketing', 'social marketing', 'ethical marketing', 'cause-related marketing' and broader business terms such as 'CSR', 'business ethics' or 'corporate citizenship'). They suggest that this is because SMC 'attempted to reconstruct the moral basis of marketing' (2002: 552) and in so doing left major theoretical and practical questions unanswered. For example, the assumption was made that a societal marketing approach would protect consumer welfare, without answering the question as to who should decide what is and isn't in the consumer's interests.

SIGNIFICANCE TO THE DEBATE ON SUSTAINABLE DEVELOPMENT AND CSR

Perhaps a key contribution of the social marketing movement has been to raise issues around the marketing of social messages and services in economic, social and political contexts in which the marketing task is not about promoting options in response to established values and behaviours, but requires the reshaping of attitudes and values through varied and aligned information and service packages. On the other hand, whereas the social marketing movement had a clear community mandate to operate, the history of the SMC demonstrates the danger of purporting moral certainty as a basis for business behaviour outside of such a mandate and without the associated theoretical clarity.

See also: Business Case for CSR, Green Marketing, Greenwash

REFERENCES

Crane, A. and Desmond, J. (2002) 'Social Marketing and Morality', *European Journal of Marketing*, 36 (5/6): 548–569.

Dixon, D.F. (1992) 'Consumer Sovereignty, Democracy, and the Marketing Concept: A Macromarketing Perspective', *Canadian Journal of Administrative Sciences*, 9 (2): 116–125.

Kotler, P. (1972) 'What Consumerism Means for Marketers', *Harvard Business Review*, 50 (May–June): 48–57.

Kotler, P. (2000) *Marketing Management: The Millenium Edition*, 10th edn (International). London: Prentice-Hall.

Kotler, P. and Zaltmane, G. (1971) 'Social Marketing: An Approach to Planned and Social Change', *Journal of Marketing*, 35: 3–12.

DEFINING SOCIAL CAPITAL

Woolcock suggests that there is a general consensus developing around the definition that 'social capital refers to the norms and networks that facilitate collective action' (2001: 8–9). Over the past decade there has been increasing cross-disciplinary interest in the term 'social capital'. In an attempt to develop a more rigorous appreciation of the term, Woolcock developed a model of the multi-dimensional *sources* of social capital. *Bonding social capital* refers to close intra-group relationships or horizontal connections within and between people, groups and communities, whereas *bridging social capital* is concerned with developing links between communities or groups. Vertical connections associated with social capital formation might include those, for example, between NGOs and formal institutions such as the World Bank, and with influential, powerful and concerned individuals who can provide information, ideas and resources. Woolcock classified these vertical institutional connections as *linking social capital*. Rydin and Holman (2004) have described this latter aspect of social capital formation as 'bracing social capital', which bonds and links micro- and macro-scale initiatives between sectors, e.g. between state, business and civil society, as would occur in discrete, policy-oriented projects. In other words, this type of social capital is created through binding and leveraging from communities and from capabilities in different sectors and on different scales in transient and outcome-oriented ways, including, for instance, community initiatives around sustainable development.

'SOCIAL CAPITAL' USED TO ANALYSE ECONOMIC AND BUSINESS DEVELOPMENT

Exploring the social and economic development of nation-states

Woolcock considers the notion of social capital might be of such significance in terms of economic analysis as to be regarded as an independent factor of production alongside the traditional factors of land, labour and physical capital. In this manner, social capital might complement the neo-classical concept of human capital with its focus on education and wellbeing 'in that literate and informed citizens are better able to organize, evaluate conflicting information, and express their views in constructive ways' (2001: 6).

Across disciplines, social capital has been seen as an analytical tool to better appreciate the role of political, social and economic institutions in the process of the economic development of nation states. Economists in the 1990s increasingly recognised that the characteristics of formal and informal institutions were critical to the level of economic performance. Political scientists began to appreciate the capacity of local civic associations as intermediaries for information exchange and for creating social trust, benefitting effective governance and economic development. Sociologists demonstrated how public institutions and the nature of state–society relations influenced whether a state acted in a manner that was either developmental or predatory (Woolcock, 2001).

Thus a shared appreciation of the analytical and normative value of the term 'social capital' has been developing, acknowledging its contribution to the analysis of economic development. The resurgence of interest in the social aspect of economic development, as manifest in social capital, has also been attributed in part to the visible impact of the socio-political dimensions of development, highlighted, for example, in the 'ostensible difficulties of creating market institutions in transitional economies' subsequent to the demise of communism (Lehtonen, 2004: 200).

Exploring the environmental – social interface of sustainable development

Lehtonen's interest in the notion of social capital has served to focus attention on what he calls the 'weakest pillar of the triple bottom line' (TBL) framework, i.e. social sustainability. He utilises the concept of social capital to explore the interface between the environmental and social dimensions of the TBL. He suggests two ways of analysing the social aspect of sustainability. The *capability approach* emphasises the improvement of social conditions from one generation to another, acknowledging the interactions between economic, social and environmental spheres of development. This approach adopts both an individualistic and a broader social point of view. The alternative *social capital approach* values stocks of social capital built through networks and infrastructure that can support sustainable development. Thus, social capital is a valuable tool in achieving a better understanding of the social-environmental interface which might inform both positional – and resource-based approaches to organisational strategy, highlighting the benefits of community alliances and capability development embodied in CSR, corporate social initiatives or corporate citizenry behaviours.

Contributing to organisational competitive advantage

The resource-based view of the firm (explained in greater depth in a separate entry) suggests that successful organisations develop unique and flexible resources that confer a competitive advantage. Nahapiet and Ghoshal (1998) have argued that the development of social capital is likely to contribute such an advantage in three dimensions. These are in the form of: *structural social capital* that manifests as appropriate combinations of networks; *relational social capital* that displays a sense of identity between individuals, groups and institutions based on a common understanding of norms and obligations, supported by high levels of trust; and shared *cognitive social capital* that is characterised by shared language and communication styles, processes and cultures. In exploring the resource-based view of the firm, Bolino et al. (2002) examined the relationship between desirable 'organisational citizenship behaviours' (OCBs) and the structural, relational and cognitive dimensions of social capital. They concluded that three key areas of behaviour, i.e. obedience and loyalty to the organisation and a willingness to participate in the organisation (from the perspective of social, advocacy and functional participatory behaviours), play an important part in the development of social capital in organisations. This organisational resource would appear to be particularly valuable in strategic multi-sectoral community initiatives.

IS SOCIAL CAPITAL A USEFUL TERM?

Social capital has been seen as an ambiguous, confusing and boundary-less concept by some. Healey et al. have described it as 'just a *portmanteau* term to bring social relations, culture and civil society back into focus' (1999: 21). In rejecting the term they have substituted the notion of 'institutional capacity'. However, others believe that while the term 'social capital' lacks rigour, it is not appropriate to jettison it.

Woolcock (2001) asks for more consistent and rigorous scholarly standards around this concept. He acknowledges its use in identifying a broad range of positive and negative social and economic outcomes. For example, it can describe the negative impact of high cohesion amongst criminal elements of society as well as describing effective strategic

social capital

alliances between firms, the positive behavioural dispositions of individuals in organisations (such as trust, reciprocity, social skills), and the many forms of social capital that constitute macro-institutional measures of the strength and effectiveness of relationships (manifest in, for example, contract enforceability, an adherence to the rule of law, and the existence of civil liberties). Woolcock suggests that greater clarity around the term might prevail if there existed a better understanding of what social capital *is* rather than what it *does*, an understanding of the institutional context making it a more relevant analytical tool. In other words, 'the vibrancy or paucity of social capital cannot be understood independently of its broader institutional environment' (2001: 12).

Thus the concept of social capital, with its focus on the norms and networks that facilitate social action, has been seen as an aid to a better understanding of the social dimension of sustainable development at an organisational and broader community level. It makes apparent the interactions between economic, environmental and social actors, communities and groups, focussing on dynamics within groups, across boundaries and with formal institutions to develop an innovative capability to address emerging agendas. These initiatives might include micro- and macro-scale projects between the state, business and civil society, leveraging from capabilities in different sectors and on different scales.

See also: Community Relations, Corporate Citizenship, Employee Engagement, NGOs, Resource-Based View, Social Partnerships, Sustainable Development

REFERENCES

Bolino, M.C., Turnley, W.H. and Bloodgood, J.M. (2002) 'Citizenship Behaviour and the Creation of Social Capital in Organizations', *Academy of Management Review*, 27 (4): 505–522.

Healey, P., de Magalhaes, C. and Madanipour, A. (1999) 'Institutional Capacity-building, Urban Planning and Urban Regeneration Projects', *Futura*, 18 (3): 117–137.

Lehtonen, M. (2004) 'The Environmental-Social Interface of Sustainable Development: Capabilities, Social Capital, Institutions', *Ecological Economics*, 49: 199–214.

Nahapiet, J. and Ghoshal, S. (1998) 'Social Capital, Intellectual Capital, and the Organizational Advantage', *Academy of Management Review*, 23: 242–266.

Rydin, Y. and Holman, N. (2004) 'Re-evaluating the Contribution of Social Capital in Achieving Sustainable Development', *Local Environment*, 9 (2): 117–133.

Woolcock, M. (2001) *The Place of Social Capital in Understanding Social and Economic Outcomes*. Cambridge, MA: Development Research Group, The World Bank and John F. Kennedy School of Government, Harvard University.

Social Entrepreneurship

WHAT IS SOCIAL ENTREPRENEURSHIP?

The theoretical basis of social entrepreneurship is still nascent with many definitions of social entrepreneurship operating in business and academia. Yet, common to all definitions is the claim that social entrepreneurship aims to create value around social objectives rather than creating wealth for individuals and shareholders. Certo and Miller (2008) suggest social value might include meeting the basic needs of social groups in need, e.g. food, water, shelter, education and medical services.

Austin et al. define social entrepreneurship from a broad perspective that 'refers to innovative activity with a social objective in either the for-profit sector, ... or in corporate social entrepreneurship ... or in the nonprofit sector, or across sectors, such as hybrid structural forms which mix for-profit with nonprofit approaches' (2006: 2). Their narrower definition 'typically refers to the phenomenon of applying business expertise and market-based skills in the nonprofit sector such as when nonprofit organizations develop innovative approaches to earning income' (2006: 2).

HOW IS IT DIFFERENT TO COMMERCIAL ENTREPRENEURSHIP?

Austin et al. (2006) have compared the characteristics of business and social entrepreneurship, developing a framework that facilitates a more systematic and effective understanding of the social entrepreneurial process. Through their comparative focus they highlight entrepreneurial action as constituting the recognition of an opportunity mustering commitment and support, capturing and managing resources, and maintaining commitment through appropriate recognition and reward systems. In other words, entrepreneurial action is 'the pursuit of opportunity beyond the tangible resources currently controlled' (Stevenson, 1983, quoted in Austin et al., 2006: 4). A second point of comparison between the commercial and social entrepreneurship models uses Salman's (1996) 'people, context, deal and opportunity' (PCDO) model that describes entrepreneurship as a dynamic fit between the people, the context, the deal, and the opportunity. The comparative application of these frameworks suggests that whilst many commonalities do exist

social entrepreneurship

183

between social and commercial entrepreneurship, there is strong evidence of differentiation in the following factors:

- Social purpose organisations arise when there is *social market failure*, i.e. the commercial market forces do not meet social needs.
- Although commercial entrepreneurship can benefit society through goods and job creation, the underlying *mission and purpose* of social entrepreneurship is to create social value for the public good in contrast to creating private gain through profitable operations.
- Generally, social entrepreneurship has to address very different problems in accessing and *mobilising human and capital resources* than does a commercial operation.
- It is more difficult for the social entrepreneur to *measure performance* based on social impact than it is for commercial enterprises to measure outcomes.

They also note that there are no pure forms of either commercial or social entrepreneurship, there being a continuum from the purely social to the purely economic.

SOCIAL ENTREPRENEURSHIP IN INCREASINGLY COMPETITIVE MARKETS

Not-for-profits (NFPs) are being increasingly affected by expanding societal needs, shifts in client groups, increased competition for donations and government grants, and also by the deregulation of service provision allowing the private sector into the traditional NFP service space. Such pressures have resulted in the need to adopt a more competitive approach, with this requiring effective strategic and operational thinking to provide innovative ways of creating superior value.

Weerawardena and Sullivan Mort (2006) consider the development of social entrepreneurship in the context of this environment. Although this environment highlights some commonalities in entrepreneurial roles in commercial and social enterprises, it has been claimed that social entrepreneurship might also be differentiated on the basis of leadership skills. Social entrepreneurs seek a stakeholder commitment to social values and related change in a unique, complex and shifting environment. This challenge requires 'catalytic leadership … both in terms of the area of social concern and in public policy related to that area of social concern' (2006: 22). The social entrepreneur also needs to be venturesome in acquiring and utilising resources more competitively.

However, there is also concern that social entrepreneurs should be careful not to undermine rights-based social services and possibly create discrete access for certain groups (Cook et al., 2002, quoted in Weerawardena and Sullivan Mort, 2006). The need to avoid such outcomes whilst achieving a social mission and operational efficiency is a complex strategic challenge for social entrepreneurs in an increasingly dynamic environment in which traditional boundaries between the profit and not-for-profit sectors are blurred, and with the new competitive market-place rewarding 'discipline, performance and organizational capacity rather than simply not-for-profit status and mission' (2006: 25). They conclude that dynamic capabilities required for social entrepreneurship might include the constantly interacting levels of innovation, proactivity and risk management necessary to be responsive to contextual forces comprising the business environment, the social mission and environmental sustainability.

SOCIAL ENTREPRENEURSHIP, SUSTAINABLE DEVELOPMENT AND CSR

Social entrepreneurship may be a valuable capability in implementing new forms of CSR. Seelos and Mair suggest that social entrepreneurship 'creates new models for the provision of products and services that cater directly to the social needs of underlying sustainable development goals' (2005: 243) in both public and private sectors. These social needs might be associated with inequity, poverty, social exclusion, alternative resource usage, carbon pollution, contaminated water and other challenges requiring environmental management. Certo and Miller (2008) argue that social entrepreneurs have an acute awareness of social needs and an ability to manage resources relevant to competitive value-adding projects. This capability extends to building social capital as appropriate in environments in which the public/private interface is becoming more ambiguous.

Although emergent theoretical frameworks are exploring similarities and differences between entrepreneurial approaches in the commercial and social domains, research is also concerned with the selection and appropriateness of certain organisational forms of social entrepreneurial ventures. Townsend and Hart (2008) indicate that social entrepreneurs appear to be organising under both for-profit and not-for-profit organisational forms to engage in 'essentially the same activities', with some organisations engaging in both and considered to have a 'double bottom line' (Dees, 1998, quoted in Townsend and Hart, 2008: 685).

These arguments concerning social entrepreneurship (and associated leadership qualities) sit alongside traditional debates as to whether or not shareholder-owned corporations should pursue CSR activities with social goals, and whether such pursuits reduce or improve profitability. It might be argued that the notion of social entrepreneurship has provided a new dimension to this debate by elaborating on the forms and conditions of entrepreneurship that create social value.

Friedman (1970) suggested that social entrepreneurship within the private sector disadvantaged shareholders. Baron (2007) has refuted this, arguing that shareholders are not disadvantaged if they are able to anticipate an organisation's CSR strategic intent in their investment decisions. In such cases, Baron argues that the risks associated with implementing CSR through social entrepreneurship, including those initiatives undertaken at a loss, are not borne by the shareholder but by the social entrepreneur/CEO who is responsible for such decisions and who is judged by the market in relation to financial outcomes. Shareholders are not put at risk because they are able to anticipate the CSR strategy of organisations, which in turn enables them to make their decisions about the nature of their personal giving or contribution to social causes. In other words, they can decide whether to undertake personal giving or substitute their holding shares in CSR active firms for personal giving, as a means of creating value around social objectives. This focus on the strategic capabilities and market expectations of social entrepreneurs is worth exploring in specific strategic and operational contexts.

See also: Agency Theory, Business Case for CSR, Corporate Social Responsibility, Risk Management, Social Capital

REFERENCES

Austin, J., Stevenson, H. and Wie-Skillern, J. (2006) 'Social and Commercial Entrepreneurship: Same, Different, or Both?', *Entrepreneurship Theory and Practice*, 30 (1): 1–22.

Baron, D.P. (2007) 'Corporate Social Responsibility and Social Entrepreneurship', *Journal of Economics & Management Strategy*, 16 (3): 683–717.

Certo, S.T. and Miller, T. (2008) 'Social Entrepreneurship: Key Issues and Concepts', *Business Horizons*, 51: 267–271.

Friedman, M. (1970) 'The Social Responsibility of Business is to Increase its Profits', *New York Times Magazine*, 13 September, pp. 32–33.

Sahlman, W.A. (1996) 'Some Thoughts on Business Plans' in Sahlman, W.A., Stevenson, H., Roberts, M.J. and Bhide, A.V. (eds), *The Entrepreneurial Venture*. Boston, MA: Harvard Business School.

Seelos, C. and Mair, J. (2005) 'Social Entrepreneurship: Creating New Business Models to Serve the Poor', *Business Horizons*, 48: 241–246.

Stevenson, H.H. (1983) 'A Perspective on Entrepreneurship', *Harvard Business School Working Paper No. 9–384–131*. Boston, MA: Harvard Business School.

Townsend, D.M. and Hart, T.A. (2008) 'Perceived Institutional Ambiguity and the Choice of Organizational Form in Social Entrepreneurial Ventures', *Entrepreneurship Theory and Practice*, July: 685–700.

Weerawardena, J. and Sullivan Mort, G. (2006) 'Investigating Social Entrepreneurship: A Multidimensional Model', *Journal of World Business*, 41: 21–35.

Social Partnerships

NEW MODELS FOR COLLABORATION

Social partnerships refer to a wide range of inter-organisational, cross-sector mechanisms designed to address issues such as the environment, health and education (Seitanidi and Crane, 2009). Partnerships between NGOs and other not-for-profits (NPOs) and business organisations and between government and business are increasingly seen as key to responsible management. Such partnerships may also be tripartite and involve business, government and NPOs, as shown in Figure 5. They may involve contractual arrangements between two parties, looser agreements between two or more organisations or collaborative relationships between organisations of all sectors. What is termed 'partnering' may, in fact, involve diffuse or overlapping networks.

Business enters into partnerships that have social or environmental objectives partly as a result of external industry and market forces and partly to bolster internal resources and competitive strategies. Numerous benefits associated with more responsible corporate behaviour are claimed for partnerships. Those between business and government, for example, represent a new form of governance for corporate social responsibility and corporate sustainability. Partnerships formed to promote sustainability or corporate responsibility goals are not a substitute for government regulation but they may be the only realistic first step

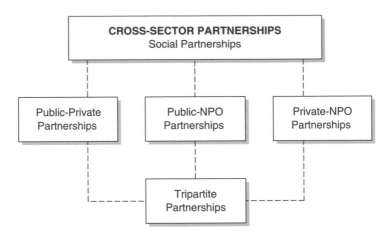

Figure 5 *Cross-sector partnerships*
Adapted from: Seitanidi and Crane (2009), 'Implementing CSR Through Partnerships: Understanding the Selection, Design and Institutionalisation of Nonprofit-Business Partnerships', *Journal of Business Ethics* 85: 414. With kind permission from Springer Science + Business Media.

towards effective governance until national and international government organisations can be involved. They can encourage the development of a set of accountability requirements that will be shared by the company and key stakeholders, while allowing for some flexibility and certain economic efficiencies. Alberto and Sharma (2003) suggest that regulations may be more important drivers of corporate environmental practices in the initial stages but that eventually other external and internal drivers will become more important influences on corporate environmental strategies. Companies may start with compliance-based relationships and then shift to more voluntary forms of relating to regulators. The emergence of various partnership models highlights a new approach by governments away from rules-based compliance. Local authorities, for example, can act as network brokers and managers or as 'knowledge banks', a role seen as very important in moving SMEs towards more responsible and sustainable practices.

As consumers pressure both companies and governments to act more responsibly in relation to human rights issues, the environment and the use of resources, reputation can be enhanced by environmental or social involvement. Thus, partnership initiatives boost legitimacy and act as significant contributors to strengthening society's perception of the corporation. By contributing to the relationships with technical expertise and financial resources, companies can leverage the experience, knowledge networks, know-how and legitimacy of being associated with the public sector. Partnerships can enable knowledge sharing and a distribution of competencies across the contributing organisations, as well as allowing government participation in a relationship that is based more on discussion and trust rather than a more punitive mindset.

An often quoted example of a partnership is the one formed in the 1990s between McDonald's and the Environmental Defense fund around the promise made by McDonald's to phase out Styrofoam. Ten years into the partnership, the CEO of McDonald's announced that the firm had reduced packaging by 150,000 tonnes, purchased $3 billion of recycled materials and recycled more than one million tonnes of cardboard. But as Brown (2005) inquires, has McDonald's taken control of the conversation between the partners or is it an equal collaboration?

GREENWASH OR LEARNING OPPORTUNITY?

Partnerships with NGOs can offer attractive returns to companies in the form of publicity. Some well-known NGOs have the legitimacy and links with the media that, as Bendell notes, 'are the envy of corporate PR departments. To have these impressive environmental PR machines working for business is an attractive bonus' (1998: 5). However, some corporations may see this as the real objective, not just a bonus. Both government and NGO versions of corporate partnering are vulnerable to accusations of greenwashing. A leading environmental NGO, The Nature Conservancy, for instance, claims that by finding common ground with communities and developers, ranchers and farmers, government agencies and corporations, it can also find more creative and practical solutions that balance human needs with conservation goals (Nature Conservancy, 2010). However, in doing so, the fact that it has partnered with leading corporations such as ARCO, BHP, BP, Chevron, Chrysler, Coca-Cola, Dow Chemical, DuPont, General Electric, General Mills, General Motors, Georgia-Pacific, McDonald's, Mobil, NBC, Pepsi-Cola, Procter and Gamble, Toyota, and Pfizer has drawn criticism for the NGO.

On the other hand, Ahlstrom and Sjostrom note that the Swedish Society for Nature Conservation (SSNC) in 2005 was 'looking for opportunities for joint action with business' (2005: 234). The SSNC believes that a collaboration with 'worst cases' – that is, worst environmental offenders – was a fitting role for environmental groups who would be able to develop a green consciousness in these corporations that would ultimately help bring them into an era of better environmental practice.

ALONG THE SUPPLY CHAIN

The formation of partnerships along the supply chain is a recent trend. As often highly complex relationships these can carry ecological, social and business advantages, especially in an age where national governments may have their hands tied and can be overridden by, say, the World Trade Organisation with its emphasis on barriers to trade. Supply chain partnerships primarily involve businesses at different levels of the supply chain, as has happened with the production of coffee under Fair Trade conditions. But, increasingly, NGOs with concerns focused on ecology, workers' rights or other social justice issues, are playing a role.

While such partnerships may offer the double advantage of environmental improvement and a certainty of knowledge about supply, de Man and Burns (2006) argue that claims for enabling a more responsible or sustainable supply chain would be more credible if various checkpoints to expose links in the chain that are not meeting their obligations under the agreement were initiated. Such partnerships represent a form of self-regulation within the supply chain, a rather different form of self-regulation from that undertaken within an organisation. To some degree, every partner's reputation depends on the ability of each other partner to abide by the principles and commitments of the contract. This tends to build in demands for transparency and traceability, even if there are no guarantees of these occurring.

CHALLENGES FOR PARTNERS

There are numerous challenges in establishing and maintaining credible partnerships around corporate responsibility. Trust is clearly a key operating principle in any partnership, and trust takes time to develop. Governments may find it difficult to maintain high levels of scrutiny as they attempt to accommodate their business partners and build these high levels of trust and communication. Real and meaningful partnerships appear to require the development of social relations, through commitment and through establishing mutual understanding and consideration. To be effective, partnerships need clear, quantifiable goals, simple management structures and appropriate governance rules to consider the needs of external stakeholders. At their worst, partnerships may present some businesses without a commitment to sustainability (but perhaps with the intention of appearing to be green by employing a number of finely tuned skills in projecting this image) a way to obviate their responsibilities.

While much is made of the benefits of partnerships, there are likely to be costs if the contributing organisations do not acknowledge the precise purpose of a partnership. A fundamental and recurring critique is that the voluntarism that underpins partnerships between businesses and governments risks reducing or compromising a government scrutiny of business in the area of pollution and other environmental concerns. There is also considerable debate over whether voluntarism stimulates innovation more than stringent regulation, with evidence in the literature for both sides of the argument.

See also: *Corporate Citizenship, Governance, Greenwash, Social Capital, Voluntary Regulation*

REFERENCES

Ahlstrom, J. and Sjostrom, E. (2005) 'CSOs and Business Partnerships: Strategies for Interaction', *Business Strategy and the Environment*, 14 (4): 230–240.

Alberto Aragón-Correa, J. and Sharma, S. (2003) 'A Contingent Resource-Based View of Proactive Corporate Environmental Strategy', *The Academy of Management Review*, 28 (1): 71–88.

Bendell, J. (1998) 'Beyond Self-Regulation: An Introduction to Business-NGO Relations and Sustainable Development', *Greener Management International*, 24, Winter: 4–9.

Brown, M. (2005) *Corporate Integrity*. Cambridge: Cambridge University Press.

de Man, R. and Burns, T.R. (2006) 'Sustainability: Supply Chains, Partner Linkages and New Forms of Self-Regulation', *Human Systems Management*, 25 (1): 1–12.

Nature Conservancy, The (2010) 'Corporate Partnerships'. Available at www.nature.org/joinusanddonate/corporatepartnerships/ accessed 17 September 2010.

Seitanidi, M. and Crane, A. (2009) 'Implementing CSR Through Partnerships: Understanding the Selection, Design and Institutionalisation of Nonprofit-Business Partnerships', *Journal of Business Ethics*, 85: 413–429.

social partnerships

HISTORY OF SRI

Socially responsible investment (SRI) (as described in the USA) or ethical investment (as described in Europe) can be defined as the 'integration of personal values, social considerations and economic factors into the investment decision' (Michelson et al., 2004: 1). SRI is another concept that is problematic due to its lack of a consistent terminology. As an instance, ethical is not always environmentally sustainable: an ethical fund, for example, may be one that selects according to Biblical criteria or Sharia law.

Pre-1980s, corporate environmental and social performance was controlled through legislation, the so-called 'command and control' model. As market-based incentives have grown in importance as a means of reducing corporate externalities, so SRI has emerged as the market response to CSR.

In 2005, in a process coordinated by the United Nations Environment Programme Finance Initiative (UNEP FI) and the UN Global Compact, the Principles for Responsible Investment (see http://www.unpri.org) were developed in order to provide suggestions as to how to incorporate environmental, social and governance considerations into investment decision making. The Principles apply across the financial investment sector and it is expected that signatories engage with companies in order to improve their environmental, social or governance performance.

According to the most recently available report from the Social Investment Forum (SIF), from 2005–2007, SRI assets increased more than 18 per cent compared to the less than 3 per cent increase in general professionally managed assets. Roughly 11 per cent of assets under professional management in the USA – nearly one out of every nine dollars – are now involved in SRI. SRI assets rose more than 324 per cent from $639 billion in 1995 (the year of the first *Report on Socially Responsible Investing Trends in the United States*) to $2.71 trillion in 2007 (Social Investment Forum, 2007). During the same period, the broader universe of assets under professional management increased less than 260 per cent from $7 trillion to $25.1 trillion. According to the Investment Management

Association, in 2009 more than £5.6 billion was invested in green and ethical funds in the UK, up from £2.5 billion ten years ago (UKSIF, 2010).

The SRI volume is still small compared to the total capital market. However, with one in every $8 or $9 now in this type of fund, it is exerting pressure and growing at a faster pace than other types of investment funds. Both supply (e.g. managers of investment funds identifying new market opportunities) and demand (e.g. the emergence of ethical investors as a market segment, with concern over such factors as climate risk) are now driving the emergence of SRI. Although SRI now occupies only approx 11 per cent of the total investment market, its growth rate has been rapid. As an example, the recent growth of SRI in Australia is shown in Figure 6. Despite retractions in 2008 and 2009, the figure shows the sector has sustained a long period of relative growth.

TYPES OF SRI FIRMS

There are now large and growing not-for-profit organisations dedicated to responsible investment. In the USA, the Social Investment Forum membership includes investment management and advisory firms,

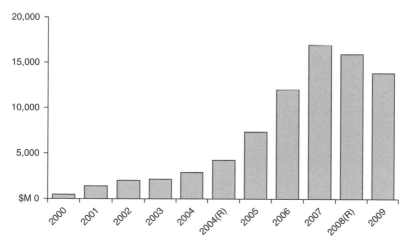

R = Reinstated in the following study.

Figure 6   *Long-term growth trends in responsible investment managed portfolios*

Modified from: The Responsible Investment Association Australasia (2009) *Responsible Investment*, November 2009:16.

socially responsible investment

mutual fund companies, research firms, financial planners and advisors, broker-dealers, banks, credit unions, community development organisations, non-profit associations, and pension funds, foundations, Native American tribes and other asset owners. Some funds identify themselves as responsible investment funds on the basis of including firms who have reduced their impact on the planet, for instance resources companies.

HOW THEY WORK

The Social Investment Forum's 2007 Trends report identifies $2.71 trillion in total assets under management using one or more of the three core socially responsible investing strategies: screening, shareholder advocacy and community investing (Social Investment Forum, 2007).

Screening is the process whereby companies are excluded or included in investment portfolios according to certain designated social and environmental criteria. Screens can be negative (such as avoiding stocks from certain sectors whose activities, such as gambling, or products, such as tobacco, they do not support) or positive (where companies are included only if they accord to certain criteria, such as improved social or environmental performance, or if they have a positive effect on society or the environment). Other selection methodologies used by fund managers include sustainability analysis, best of sector and thematic analysis (see www.responsibleinvestment.org for more details).

Clearly, it is not difficult to fit well-managed companies into one or another of these categories. BHP Billiton, for instance, may be excluded from some funds because of its mining interests but feature in others because of its award-winning sustainability management schemes. An interesting aspect of defining this area of investment is that industry reports note environmental, social, governance (ESG) criteria are increasingly used as screening mechanisms for mainstream non-ethical funds, on the grounds that they simply reflect good management practice.

Shareholder advocacy involves shareholder activists putting pressure on companies to change their investment strategies. It often involves filing shareholder resolutions on ethical, sustainable or governance topics. As with accountability, investment requires a determination of issues of materiality – that is, the relevance and significance of an issue to an organisation and its stakeholders. NGOs, for example, play a role in influencing materiality decisions on SRI by using shareholder activism to put pressure on companies. CEOs need the good esteem of shareholders, and responsible investors as activists can be very influential. Faith groups, for instance, are highly active responsible investors. The Interfaith Centre on Corporate Responsibility (ICCR), for example, files hundreds of shareholder resolutions or written shareholder requests to management concerning ethical issues each year and lists them on their website together with the sector ranking of each company in terms of their greenhouse gas emissions compared to the average in their business sector (see http://www.iccr.org/shareholder/trucost/index.php). The ICCR now consists of a coalition of 275 groups that represent an estimated $110 billion in capital. Its members support environmental justice, access to health care, diversity on boards of directors and an end to global warming and sweatshop abuses.

Community investing is financing that creates resources and opportunities for economically disadvantaged people who are underserved by traditional financial institutions. This form of investing requires a decision to conduct banking only with a community bank or a credit union, such as Bendigo Bank, in Australia. Many of these organisations have specified relationships with community aid programmes. Community investing is the fastest growing area of SRI in the USA. Over the past decade, community investing has grown over 540 per cent, from $4 billion to $25.8 billion in assets.

SRI PERFORMANCE

Despite this growth, studies of SRI performance have been mixed. While some studies have found no statistically significant relationship between returns of SRI funds and conventional funds (e.g. Bauer et al., 2005), the picture is complex and analysis may be different according to the type of methodology or screening involved. For instance, a 1992–2007 study by Statman and Glushov (2008) found that stocks rated as socially responsible by KLD Research and Analytics gave a positive return, while excluding those stocks of companies associated with tobacco, alcohol, gambling, firearms, military and nuclear operations was a disadvantage. Barnett and Salomon (2006) found different social screening techniques affected financial performance differently. For example, they discovered that funds which screened on the basis of community relations showed relatively stronger financial performance, while those that screened on the basis of environmental and labour relations showed decreased financial performance. They suggested the debate should move away from an emphasis on the relationship between social responsibility and financial performance and focus more on the screening criteria.

See also: *Business Networks, Codes of Conduct, Corporate Responsibility Reporting, Corporate Social Responsibility, Corporate Sustainability*

REFERENCES

Barnett, M.L. and Salomon, R.M. (2006) 'Beyond Dichotomy: The Curvilinear Relationship between Social Responsibility and Financial Performance', *Strategic Management Journal*, 27 (11): 1101–1122.

Bauer, R., Koedijk, K. and Otten, R. (2005) 'International Evidence on Ethical Mutual Fund Performance and Investment Style', *Journal of Banking and Finance*, 29 (7): 1751–1767.

Michelson, G., Wailes, N., van der Laan, S. and Frost, G. (2004) 'Ethical Investment Processes and Outcomes', *Journal of Business Ethics*, 52: 1–10.

Social Investment Forum (2007) *Report on Socially Responsible Investing Trends in the United States*. Available at www.socialinvest.org/resources/research/, accessed 2 April 2010.

Statman, M. and Glushov, D. (2008) *The Wages of Social Responsibility*. Available at www.socialinvest.org/resources/research/documents/2008WinningPrize-Moskowitz.pdf, accessed 2 April 2010.

UKSIF (2010) Ethical Investment on the Rise: ISA Opportunity. Available at http://www.uksif.org/about/Latest_news/News_Archive, accessed 13 July 2010.

Stakeholder Theory

THE NOTION OF STAKEHOLDER THEORY

Stakeholder theory aims to explain the nature of relationships between organisations and those persons with a 'stake' in the operations and outcomes of business activity. Freeman provided a broad definition of a stakeholder as any group or individual that 'can affect or is affected by the achievement of an organization's objectives' (1984: 46).

Although this definition has become widely used, there is still ongoing debate about its content, boundaries and relevance. Donaldson and

Preston (1995) note that stakeholder theory has been developed in a variety of ways in the management literature. Sometimes it is used *empirically or descriptively* to outline critical relationships of the firm with groups that impact on its fortunes. Alternatively, it is used *instrumentally* to identify effective business practices concerning stakeholder management in increasingly complex and shifting environments. It has also been used *normatively* to critique the role and purpose of business, with Fassin (2009) suggesting that in this latter manner the theory of stakeholder management has become an important tool to transfer ethics to management practice and strategy. Key contributors to the debate (Carroll and Buchholtz, 2006; Donaldson and Preston, 1995) have used stakeholder theory normatively to explore the appropriate role of business in society, including associated standards of accountability for the economic, environmental and social impact of business operations.

Donaldson and Preston note that these three aspects of stakeholder theory, i.e. descriptive, instrumental and normative, are at once interrelated and distinct, using 'different types of evidence and argument and hav[ing] different implications' (1995: 65). This is also an important framework for a critical consideration of the economic benefits and ethical imperatives associated with CSR.

Noland and Phillips (2010) more recently suggested that stakeholder theory has not adequately focused on the nature of stakeholder engagement. They have highlighted the tension between stakeholder theorists who favour what they describe as the 'Habermasian approach' (suggesting business has *either* exclusive moral *or* strategic relationships with stakeholders), and those who uphold the Aristotlean view, described as ethical strategists (who hold that the nature of business should always be aligned with the pursuit of the good or virtuous life manifest as societal wellbeing). They argue that such strategic and ethical concerns can be aligned, organisations having always had ethical obligations to all stakeholders as a matter of course. They support the latter view on the basis that it appreciates the 'confluence of conceptual and practical concerns' (2010: 39).

THE ORIGINS OF STAKEHOLDER THEORY

Carroll (1979), one of the earlier yet still contemporary commentators on stakeholder theory, noted the increasing relevance of stakeholder management to a pluralistic society (one that exhibits a diversity of power concentration) in which increasing numbers of special interest groups are capable of challenging business about its ethics. Carroll and Buchholtz (2006) believe that understanding and responding to stakeholder perspectives concerning CSR is a critical managerial function because 'in the long run, those who do not use power in a manner which society considers responsible will tend to lose it' (Davis and Blomstrom 1975, cited in Carroll and Buchholtz, 2006: 19).

A useful starting point to explore and critique stakeholder theory is to consider how the stakeholder view of the firm evolved from production and managerial views of the firm.

A DEVELOPING VIEW OF THE FIRM: FROM INPUT/ OUTPUT TO STAKEHOLDER MODELS

Production views of the firm recognised only inputs, processes and outputs, perceiving two groups of stakeholders, i.e. suppliers (inputs) and customers (outputs). A subsequent managerial view of the firm identified the separation of ownership from control of the firm, as a result of which owners had to be considered as investor stakeholders. Employees also became recognised as an important stakeholder group that could influence market performance (Donaldson and Preston, 1995; Fassin, 2009). However, the managerial approach still assumed *mainly unilateral interactions* based on the centrality of the firm's strategic decisions and interests.) These two perspectives are numbered 1 and 2 in Figure 7, the weak feedback links being indicated by transparent arrowheads.)

Freeman's (1984) stakeholder model provided a powerful visualisation of the *more realistic multilateral relationships* that existed between a broader range of players with perceived stakes in the operation of the business (number 3 in Figure 7). By identifying governments, civil society and competitors as stakeholders, he drew attention to the increasingly dynamic social, economical and political environment in which firms were operating and the growing diversity of stakeholder expectations and consequent risks to the business.

As the business world has experienced a proliferation of internal and external pressures for change, managers have recognised the need to identify, evaluate, prioritise and align the interests not only of those groups that had a direct stake in the firm, but also those groups who perceive they have a stake in the firm, possibly through the impact of the business on their community. As the media have successfully drawn attention to the negative externalities or impacts of business and associated costs to

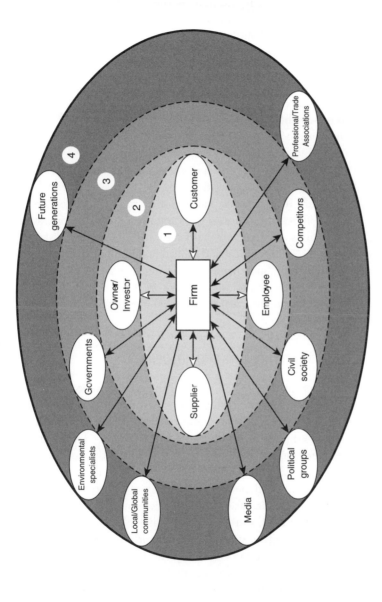

Figure 7   *An evolving stakeholder model*

society, more complex stakeholder models have emerged that have included stakeholders with no direct stake in the firm but which could influence an organisation's reputation in the community. Calls have increased for the natural environment to be considered as a stakeholder (Starik and Rands, 1995). Political considerations also now include the perceived impact of current activity on future generations, thus introducing ethical considerations around intergenerational equity. Figure 7 historically represents the expansion of stakeholder models over four iterations, i.e. from production to managerial to multilateral to sustainable concepts of stakeholder groups, and thus might represent a contemporary stakeholder model.

Figure 8 exemplifies the areas for business attention as the result of a proliferation of stakeholder interests and associated expectations (as illustrated in Figure 7). It also suggests the need for increased attention to global and local shifts in community values, for example: those concerned with the responsibilities of businesses with abundant resources, operating in developing nations experiencing hardships such as natural disasters, wars and disease; the philosophical and ethical underpinnings of business/stakeholder relationships; and changing community expectations around the sustainability agenda and its implications for CSR. Finally, Figure 8 illustrates the need for the firm to include stakeholder engagement as part of its risk management strategy.

TYPES OF STAKEHOLDERS

There has also been prolific debate around the categorisation of stakeholders. Kaler (2002) suggested there were two major types of stakeholder: 'claimants' who have some claim on the services of a business, e.g. financiers and employees, and 'influencers' who have a capacity to influence the operations of the business, e.g. critics, the media, special interest groups, etc. Clarkson differentiated between 'primary' stakeholders, who have an interdependent relationship with the firm 'without whose continuing participation the organization cannot survive as a going concern' (1995: 106), and 'secondary' stakeholders, who influence or are affected by the organisation's activities and may represent legitimate special interests or public concerns. The latter do not engage in transactions and are not critical to organisation survival. Mitchell et al. (1997) developed a theoretical framework that helped organisations not only to identify stakeholders but also their 'salience' or prominence based on their power to influence, their legitimacy of relationship and

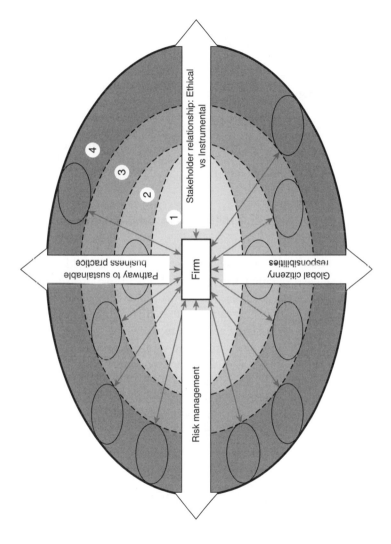

Figure 8 *Implications for business of evolving stakeholder groups and expectations*

the urgency of their claim. Phillips (2003) distinguished between 'normative' stakeholders, to whom the organisation has a moral and ethical obligation (e.g. employees), 'derivative' stakeholders, who can harm the organisation but to whom the organisation has no direct obligation (e.g. the media), and 'dangerous' or 'dormant' stakeholders, who can affect the organisation but to whom it has no obligation (e.g. thieves). Capron (2005) (cited in Branco and Rodrigues, 2007) recognises that 'silent' or 'absent' stakeholders, such as future generations, need to have their concerns represented by existing groupings of stakeholders or they will remain unrepresented.

These categorisations can help leaders and managers to identify stakeholder claims and influences. Freeman maintains that any business is about creating value for stakeholders and consequently '[m]anaging the stakeholders is about creating as much value as possible for stakeholders without resorting to tradeoffs, fraud or deception' (2008: 166).

CRITIQUE OF STAKEHOLDER THEORY

Critics of stakeholder theory have commented on the confusion surrounding its nature and purpose. As noted earlier, Donaldson and Preston (1995) have detailed the empirical/descriptive, instrumental and normative dimensions of stakeholder theory. This categorisation has elicited significant debate. For example, Branco and Rodrigues (2007) note that normative approaches attempt to prescribe the way things should be and are therefore not easily related to descriptive and instrumental approaches which describe the way things are.

A key debate is around which stakeholders have prominence. The 'classical/neo-classical' view of business maintains that the purpose of business is to maximise the wealth of its owners or shareholders while operating honestly within a society's rules (Friedman, 1962). Proponents of the classical view generally maintain that it is inappropriate to use business resources to meet social objectives, as this is considered to be the role of government.

Jensen argues that the role of business is to 'maximise the total long run value of the firm' (2008: 167) as a means of producing maximum value for society. He cautions against a myopic focus on short-term shareholder value. He argues that maximising the equity of the firm does not lead to maximising the value of the firm in the long run, and that stakeholder theory should recognise that society needs to set rules to achieve desirable community outcomes, rather than assume that 'managers [will] do the right thing so as to benefit society as a whole' (2008: 168) without appropriate rules to regulate behaviours.

STAKEHOLDER THEORY AND CSR: AN INTEGRATED MODEL?

In stating her case for a 'normative' ethical basis for stakeholder theory, Wood (2008) also challenges neo-classical models of business. She offers valuable insights around the relationship between CSR and stakeholder theory, noting that originally CSR 'was framed as a voluntary social control mechanism whereby business organisations would fulfil all their duties in the absence of, or without a need for, overly restrictive government intervention' (Frederick, 2006, cited in Wood, 2008). Wood sees the benefits of stakeholder theory as detailing specifics concerning the interested parties to whom a company should be responsible, together with characteristics of interests and rights that might be at risk. She concludes that although both stakeholder theory and CSR are very limited in their potential to redress the problems of business in society, 'they can ... point to a need for social control to encourage the beneficial effects of institutional behaviours and to regulate or prevent the harmful effects' (2008: 162).

Freeman's instrumental approach to stakeholder management embraces some of Wood's concerns within the pragmatic framework of 'what good management is' (2008: 166). He concludes that it is no longer useful to separate questions of business and ethics by pursuing the development of either a normative (prescriptive) or an empirical/instrumental (descriptive) stakeholder theory. He argues for an integrated model that combines business and ethics around responsibility for ourselves and our actions, i.e. around the corporate social responsibility of a business. Noland and Phillips affirm the Freeman approach by arguing for an ethical strategic approach by business that includes an 'honest, open, respectful engagement of stakeholders *as a vital part of a firm's strategy*' (2010: 49).

See also: *Civil Society, Community Relations, Corporate Responsibility Reporting, Corporate Social Responsibility, Corporate Sustainability Strategies, Employee Engagement, NGOs, Triple Bottom Line*

stakeholder theory

203

REFERENCES

Branco, M.C. and Rodrigues, L.L. (2007) 'Positioning Stakeholder Theory within the Debate on Corporate Social Responsibility', *Electronic Journal of Business Ethics and Organization Studies*, 12 (1): 5–15.

Capron, M. (2005) 'L' Economic Ethique Drivée: La responsabilité des enterprises á l'épreure de l'humanisation de la mondialisation', Paris: United Nations Educational,

Carroll, A.B. (1979) 'A Three-dimensional Conceptual Model of Corporate Social Performance', *Academy of Management Review*, 4: 497–505.

Carroll, A.B. and Buchholtz, A.K. (2006) *Business and Society: Ethics and Stakeholder Management*, 6th edition. Mason, OH: Thomson South-Western.

Clarkson, M.B.E. (1995) 'A Stakeholder Framework for Analysing and Evaluating Corporate Social Performance', *Academy of Management Review*, 20 (1): 92–117.

Davis, K. and Blomstrom, R.L. (1975) *Business and Society: Environment and Responsibility*, 3rd edn. New York: McGraw-Hill

Donaldson, T. and Preston, L.E. (1995) 'The Stakeholder Theory of the Corporation: Concepts, Evidence and Implications', *Academy of Management Review*, 20 (1): 65–91.

Fassin, Y. (2009) 'The Stakeholder Model Refined', *Journal of Business Ethics*, 84: 113–135.

Frederick, W.C. (2006) *Corporation Be Good!: The Story of Corporate Social Responsibility*. Indianapolis, IN: Dog Ear Publishing.

Freeman, R.E. (1984) *Strategic Management: A Stakeholder Approach*. Boston, MA: Pittman.

Freeman, R.E. (2008) 'Ending the So-called "Friedman-Freeman" debate', in Agle, B.R., Donaldson, T., Freeman, R.E., Jensen, M.C., Mitchell, R.K. and Wood, D. (eds), 'Dialogue: Toward Superior Stakeholder Theory', *Business Ethics Quarterly*, 19 (2): 153–190.

Friedman, M. (1962) *Capitalism and Freedom*. Chicago, IL: University of Chicago Press.

Jensen, M.C. (2008) 'Non-rational Behaviour, Value Conflicts, Stakeholder Theory, and Firm Behaviour', in Agle, B.R., Donaldson, T., Freeman, R.E., Jensen, M.C., Mitchell, R.K. and Wood, D. (eds), 'Dialogue: Toward Superior Stakeholder Theory', *Business Ethics Quarterly*, 19 (2): 153–190.

Kaler, J. (2002) 'Morality and Strategy in Stakeholder Identification', *Journal of Business Ethics*, 39 (1–2): 91–100.

Mitchell, R.K., Agle, B.R. and Wood, D. (1997) 'Toward a Theory of Stakeholder Identification and Salience: Defining the Principle of Who and What Really Counts', *Academy of Management Review*, 22 (4): 853–886.

Noland, J. and Phillips, R. (2010) 'Stakeholder Engagement, Discourse Ethics and Strategic Management', *International Journal of Management Reviews*, 39–49.

Phillips, R. (2003) *Stakeholder Theory and Organizational Ethics*. San Francisco, CA: Berrett-Kohler.

Starik, M. and Rands, G.P. (1995) 'Weaving an Integrated Web: Multilevel and Multisystems Perspectives of Ecologically Sustainable Organisations', *Academy of Management Review*, 20 (4): 908–935.

Wood, D.J. (2008) 'Corporate Responsibility and Stakeholder Theory: Challenging the Neo-classical Paradigm', in Agle, B.R., Donaldson, T., Freeman, R.E., Jensen, M.C., Mitchell, R.K. and Wood, D. (eds), 'Dialogue: Toward Superior Stakeholder Theory', *Business Ethics Quarterly*, 19 (2): 153–190.

Stewardship

WHAT IS 'STEWARDSHIP'?

Stewardship is a relatively new approach to effective governance of business. Davis et al. (1997: 20) recognise that its theoretical contribution is in its early stages, having developed principally in contrast to economic approaches to governance. An example of such an economic approach is agency theory that purports that organisational actors (agents) who are ultimately responsible to owners and investors will behave in an 'individualistic, opportunistic and self-serving' manner and thus will need incentive schemes and governance structures appropriate to these underlying motives and behaviours in order to align their behaviour with the goals of the owners. By contrast, stewardship theory (derived from psychological and sociological theory) assumes that human nature is more aptly reflected in 'a steward whose behavior is ordered such that [his/her] pro-organizational and collectivist behaviors have higher utility than individualistic self-serving behaviors. Given a choice between self-serving behaviour and pro-organizational behavior, a steward's behavior will not depart from the interests of his or her own organization' (1997: 24).

ETHICAL STEWARDSHIP AND STAKEHOLDERS

Caldwell and Karri (2005) have noted that despite an increasing societal disillusion with business mismanagement and ethical misconduct, many management scholars have advocated that business leaders can create both long-term wealth and build organisational trust by leading and managing as ethical stewards. Caldwell et al. (2008) suggest that the concept of ethical stewardship has arisen from stakeholder theory, managers being stewards who are aligned with the goals of several stakeholders. To operate in this manner, managers need to be trustworthy and collaborative, seeing such behaviour as synonymous with putting the interests of the organisation foremost. According to Davis et al., stewards are not operating merely on the basis of ethics by substituting self-serving behaviour for collaborative action, rather 'the steward perceives greater utility in cooperative behavior and behaves accordingly, [thus]

stewardship

205

his or her behavior can be considered rational' (1997: 26). Caldwell and Karri (2005) state without reservation that the fundamental assumption underpinning stewardship theory is that the maximisation of long-term economic wealth is in the interests of all stakeholders and of the social and economic welfare of society. These collaborative behaviours are increasingly regarded by business leaders in global institutions such as the World Business Council for Sustainable Development, World Economic Forum and The World Bank as fundamental to achieving responsible business behaviour that supports long-term, integrated commercial, social and environmental business outcomes.

STEWARDS AND STAKEHOLDERS

A steward's role may not only involve treating stakeholders ethically, it may also require the resolution of conflicts of interest between the organisation and its stakeholders. Caldwell and Karri (2005), in discussing the 'stewarding' of the interests of these different stakeholders, consider the contractual basis or the 'covenantal relationship' between employee and organisation as important. A covenantal relationship suggests a mutual and positive commitment to agreed organisational and individual goals, and to treat parties ethically, not abusing relative power advantages. Thus this relationship is both transactional and psychological. Solomon (1993) suggests that covenantal duties operate within a framework of virtue ethics that aligns benefits to business, public good and individual interests. The role of the steward is to create and manage such covenantal relationships by balancing shareholder value, professional development, purposiveness and security of employment, and a corporate social responsibility that respects the community values and expectations around business practice.

Solomon (1993) identified the 'virtues' that support ethical business in contemporary and complex environments. These include: developing a communitarian culture focused on cooperation not competition; rewarding excellence on the basis of contribution around both technical excellence and social relevance; providing opportunities for aligning organisational and individual values; adopting a synergistic approach to growth and development that appreciates sustainable and long-term outcomes; and a consistent integration of virtue and ethics into an organisational culture and resource capability that can deal with paradox and tension in roles without compromising principles.

Caldwell and Karri (2005) suggest that the stewardship model of governance based on covenantal relationships is superior to either agency theory or stakeholder theory 'because it honors the societal obligations and the duties to all stakeholders' and achieves cultures of trust. To support their claim they compare the characteristics of stewardship theory, agency theory and stakeholder theory in relation to organisational assumptions concerning covenantal duties. These characteristics include the ethical focus, the managerial role and motivation, the basis of organisational and individual trust, the moral position, the key values and organisational goals, the manager's personal goals and motivational drivers, the organisational vision and so on.

STEWARDSHIP, LEADERSHIP AND CULTURE

A key contribution to leadership theory in the context of CSR is made by Caldwell et al. (2008). They suggest that ethical stewardship requires leadership that is characterised by:

- one-to-one relationships with followers
- transformational and transactional leadership practices
- the delivery of both explicit and implicit contracts (the latter supporting unspoken covenantal understandings of commitment and performance between leaders and followers)
- a culture that helps individuals perceive the conditions appertaining to fairness, justice and trust within an organisationally contextual ethical framework
- a commitment to long-term value creation for all stakeholders
- a capability to sense-make purpose and meaning that help create trust and respect that in turn help employees deliver beyond minimum levels to create value for all stakeholders.

Other commentators have reported on the capability that might underpin ethical stewardship and covenant management relevant to the integration of CSR into corporate and business-level strategies. As discussed in the entry on Responsible Leadership, Waldman et al. (2006) found that CEO intellectual stimulation (rather than charisma) was significantly related to the firm's propensity to engage in strategic CSR and hence ethical stewardship. This might be seen as being associated with both transactional and transformational leadership that can sense-make and manage meaning as well as lead the strategy associated with long-term value creation. Bolton (2004) explores the management of change to achieve long-term and integrated commercial, social and environmental business outcomes, providing related insights into 'covenantal management' in the context of ethical stewardship. She argues that management (stewards) have responsibility for helping individual employees build a coping capability in complex environments such as that described in developing stakeholder cultures. Sense-making change challenges for employees in ambiguous environments by stewards facilitate the alignment of organisational goals and values with the development of social and human capital. This approach emphasises the one-to-one relationship between leader and follower through the management of 'meaning' also illustrated in Caldwell et al.'s (2008) leadership framework. It is also consistent with Solomon's (1993) suggested virtues for business in contemporary complex environments.

The practice of ethical stewardship and its approach to governance demonstrates an important challenge to a key premise of agency theory, i.e. concerning the need for tight and prescriptive delegations around the agent/manager in order to curb self-serving behaviour. As pointed out by Jones (1995), in order to support a stewardship role, corporate governance structures need to allow a high level of discretionary behaviour for managers as stewards, thus assuming a culture of trust that encompasses managerial as well as other employee behaviour. In other words, as Davis et al. note, 'a steward's autonomy should be deliberately extended to maximise the benefits of a steward because he or she can be trusted' (1997: 25).

See also: *Agency Theory, Business Case for CSR, Complexity Theory, Governance, Responsible Leadership, Stakeholder Theory*

REFERENCES

Bolton, D. (2004) 'Change, Coping and Context in the Resilient Organisation', *Mt Eliza Business Review*, 7 (1): 56–66.

Caldwell, C. and Karri, R. (2005) 'Organizational Governance and Ethical Systems: A Covenantal Approach to Building Trust', *Journal of Business Ethics*, 58: 249–259.

Caldwell, C., Hayes, L.A., Karri, R. and Bernal, P. (2008) 'Ethical Stewardship – Implications for Leadership and Trust', *Journal of Business Ethics*, 78: 153–164.

Davis, J.H., Schoorman, F.D, and Donaldson, L. (1997) 'Towards a Stewardship Theory of Management', *Academy of Management Review*, 22 (1): 20–47.

Jones, T.M. (1995) 'Instrumental Stakeholder Theory: A Synthesis of Ethics and Economics, *Academy of Management Review*, 20: 404–437.

Solomon, R.C. (1993) *Ethics and Excellence: Cooperation and Integrity in Business*. New York: Oxford University Press.

Waldman, D.A., Siegel, D.S. and Javidan, M. (2006) 'Components of CEO Transformational Leadership and Corporate Social Responsibility', *Journal of Management Studies*, 43 (8): 1703–1725.

Sustainable Development

WHAT IS MEANT BY SUSTAINABLE DEVELOPMENT?

The most commonly used definition of sustainable development refers to development that meets the needs of the present without compromising the ability of future generations to meet their own needs, and is drawn from the Brundtland Report, formally the report of the World Commission on Environment and Development (WCED, 1987). The Brundtland Report was named for the chair of the Brundtland Commission, called by the United Nations (UN) in response to the 1983 General Assembly call for nations to work together to find long-term strategies to address the environmental and other concerns of sustainable development.

An action plan for the implementation of these principles, termed 'Agenda 21', was adopted by more than 178 governments at the UN Conference on Environment and Development (UNCED) held in Rio de Janeiro, Brazil, on 3–14 June 1992. Agenda 21 provides a series of actions to be taken globally, nationally and locally by organisations of the UN system, governments and other major groups in every area in which humans impact on the environment (see www.un.org/esa/dsd/agenda21/). A number of sustainable development topics are specified in Agenda 21. They include sustainable production and consumption, climate change, partnerships, industrial development and a range of others, each of which has long-term as well as short-term implications for all organisations, including corporations.

A key goal of the Brundtland Commission and the declaration made at Rio de Janeiro in 1992 was to bring about shared understandings and enable effective responses across developing and developed nations in relation to the need to balance social, environmental and economic needs and interests. The concept has since been popularised as the first attempt to reconcile the environment with development, offering a vision of a mutually reinforcing relationship between economic growth, distributive justice, environmental protection and the sustainability of the planet.

Hence, what is referred to as 'sustainable development' entails the integration of environmental protection, social advancement and economic prosperity. Organisations of all types across the world are now required by national legislation and intergovernmental agreements, or encouraged by a range of economic incentives, to address its principles. Its discourse applies at global, regional and local levels and draws on the fields of politics, economics, development and environmental studies, as well as a host of other sub-disciplinary areas. Given its lack of definition, breadth of application and highly political post-colonial associations, it is not surprising that sustainable development is the subject of a wide and ongoing debate. Its influence on the global stage is such that writers have likened it in importance (and in the degree of contestation) to democracy (e.g. Dryzek, 2005).

GLOBAL PERSPECTIVES

Sustainable development has global, regional and local applications. Globally, the UN has played the key role in its promotion to government agencies, multinational business organisations and international NGOs. As described in the entry on Business Networks, the impact of the concept on the business community has been evaluated, articulated and promoted by such institutions as the World Business Council for Sustainable Development and the Global Compact. Overall, however, its discourse delivers a message of cooperation and the integration of all aspects of society, including social and biological systems.

KEY PRINCIPLES

Implementing sustainable development agendas can entail juggling three key objectives: intergenerational equity, intragenerational equity and the precautionary principle. Addressing these core objectives requires decision makers to balance three sets of relationships: between humans and the rest of the biosphere; between present and future generations; and between the developing and developed worlds. For instance, to implement intergenerational justice, as discussed in the entry on that topic, means ensuring that future generations have access to a quality of life at least equivalent to that of the present generation. The question is how to decide what share of finite resources should be consumed or exploited now and what should be left for the future. One interpretation of this principle is that no one generation should leave the next generation worse off.

CRITICAL APPRAISAL OF SUSTAINABLE DEVELOPMENT

Critics of sustainable development argue that it is an anthropocentric concept, privileging immediate human needs over the long-term preservation of nature. In that sense it has been classified as a reformist rather than a radical environmental discourse, as discussed in the entry on environmental discourses (Dryzek, 2005). In this account, sustainable development promotes an instrumentalist approach to nature and endorses the mutually dependent relationship between economic growth and environmental protection, underpinned by techno-scientific rationality and market-based mechanisms. Furthermore, there has long been criticism that sustainable development justifies a form of green imperialism, and that the discourse has marginalised local practices and needs and so cannot counter the destructive effects of global economic expansion on local cultures and traditions (Shiva, 1993). One argument in this vein is that interpretations of sustainable development are made by an international elite, led by the UN and the World Bank, who are intent on promoting free trade and continuing the capitalist agenda of business expansion, rather than a serious attempt to accord any intrinsic value to the natural environment and hence maintain intergenerational equity in terms of access to natural resources.

One of the problems with this concept is that balancing the key principles of intergenerational and intragenerational equity can be very difficult in practical terms. The debate over greenhouse emissions, for example, is one aspect of the wider issue of whether richer nations have the right to intervene to prevent poorer communities overexploiting natural or human resources to ensure survival. On the positive side, the principles of sustainable development have been drawn on to prevent richer nations externalising the costs and consequences of pollution or hazardous by-products associated with industrial activity to developing countries. For example, the Basel Convention, the major international treaty concerning the transport of hazardous waste, is now ratified by 151 countries and emulated in other intergovernmental arrangements. Its immediate purpose is to prevent developed countries reacting to tightened environmental legislation at home by dumping hazardous wastes in developing countries.

FUTURE DIRECTIONS

One of the great achievements of sustainable development is that it has succeeded in bringing different stakeholders to the negotiating table. The very looseness of its terminology has enabled it to draw support not only from different sectors and levels of society but also from very different philosophical traditions. To resolve the criticisms noted above, further research is needed to develop a more political understanding of sustainable development principles in relation to collaboration and cooperation between organisations, nations and sectors.

In addition, it should be noted that one of the great advances since the publication of the Brundtland Report is wider recognition of the social dimension of environmental problems; that the environmental crisis is constructed and mediated by social institutions. While the future seen through the lens of sustainable development appears by many to rest on technological solutions, it also espouses an equally important and previously unrecognised social vision and understanding (Benn, 2008).

See also: *Business Networks, Environmental Discourses, Intergenerational Equity, Intragenerational Equity, Postcolonialism, Systems Approaches*

REFERENCES

Benn, S. (2008) 'Sustainable Development', in S. Clegg and J. Bailey (eds), *International Encyclopaedia of Organization Studies*. Thousand Oaks, CA: Sage, pp. 1491–1494.

Dryzek, J. (2005) *The Politics of the Earth*, 2nd edn. Oxford: Oxford University Press.

Shiva, V. (1993) 'The Greening of the Global Reach', in W. Sachs (ed.), *Global Ecology*. London: Zed Books, pp. 149–156.

World Commission on Environment and Development (WCED) (1987) *Our Common Future* (The Brundtland Report). Oxford and New York: Oxford University Press.

DEFINITION

'Sweatshops' is a widely used term that describes conditions in which workers earn very low wages, often in dangerous working environments. Arnold and Hartman define sweatshops as:

> Any workplace in which workers are typically subjected to two or more of the following conditions: systematic forced overtime; systematic health and safety risks that stem from negligence or the wilful disregard of employee welfare; coercion; systematic deception that places workers at risk; underpayment of earnings; and income for a 48 hour work week less than the overall poverty rate for that country (one who suffers from overall poverty lacks the income necessary to satisfy one's basic non-food needs such as shelter and basic health care). (2005: 207)

There are many debates concerning whether workers are being 'exploited' in these conditions and whether human rights are being violated. Arnold (2003) notes that this debate is complicated because the term 'exploitation' has received little attention compared to other concepts relevant to labour market conditions such as 'equity' and 'distributive justice'. He distinguishes between non-exploitative practices whereby an object is effectively utilised, and exploitative practices that take unfair or illegitimate advantage. A Marxist view holds that capitalism exploits workers by 'expropriating' a significant level of value generated through productivity, the opportunity for such exploitation being extended through globalisation of the economy. The focus in this entry is on whether or how the term 'exploitation' might apply to sweatshop activity.

ARE SWEATSHOPS 'EXPLOITATIVE'?

'Willingness' to work

Fukuyama (1999) rejects the Leftist assertions that globalisation necessarily exploits workers. He argues that exploitation does not occur merely because workers are 'coerced' into the work because they might have few alternatives. Rather, his approach (reflecting that of the school of free-market economics) argues that sweatshop wages still benefit the poor when they are *willing* to take the work. In this vein, Maitland (1997) suggests that fair wages should not be determined by a minimum set level, but rather that the notion of 'fairness' depends on whether wages are accepted freely by workers who are reasonably well-informed of the terms of their labour contract.

Zwolinski (2007) supports this approach by arguing that the act of choosing to work in sweatshops is morally significant, i.e. the *exercise of autonomy* is 'morally transformative' and should be recognised as such. In other words, workers exercise a *preference evincing choice* to work in sweatshop conditions, even if it appears there is no choice because they have to work to survive. This autonomous act, to work in a sweatshop rather than survive by other means, e.g. crime or prostitution, is sufficiently autonomous to imply that employers, consumers or rights activists should not work to take away this option.

Mutual advantage

Other commentators have concluded that there are grounds for perceived exploitation even if a mutual advantage is identified. One argument put forward is that if one person takes advantage of another's weakness or vulnerability in order to derive some benefit from the latter, then exploitation takes place. Wertheimer (1996) suggests that, even where there is a mutually advantageous exchange, exploitation can still occur when one person takes unfair advantage of another relative to an explicitly defined baseline. His moral baseline is a 'hypothetical market price' that reflects 'neither party tak[ing] *special* unfair advantage of particular defects in the other party's decision-making capacity or special vulnerabilities in the other party's situation' (1996: 245). In other words, he believes that there is no right to use the concept of choice, i.e. autonomy to exploit or to agree to be exploited, because both types of behaviour incur consequences for future generations of the same class.

In accord with Wertheimer's (1996) argument, Meyers (2004) suggests that unfair wages do in fact exist and that it is incumbent on the community and business to find out what the notion of 'unfair' might constitute. Concerning global economic development, he questions whether open markets are the best way for a developing nation to prosper, noting that in Latin America wages had only increased 6 per cent in the prior twenty years and wages had fallen in Soviet bloc countries consequent upon the introduction of a free market economy. He concludes that exploitation can occur when a person is wronged whilst receiving benefit. He calls this '*wrongful beneficence*', thus posing the question as to whether there is a limit to low wage levels, whilst still being able to claim that they are morally acceptable.

Mayer (2007) agrees with Meyers (2004) that mutually advantageous transactions are on occasion both wrongful and exploitative. Yet Mayer argues that Meyers' critique is flawed in that it fails to distinguish between 'discretionary' and 'structural' exploitation. Structural exploitation takes advantage of circumstances for which the exploiters are not totally responsible and in which exploitation might be the lesser evil. Discretionary exploitation is morally different in that the exploiters are responsible for creating exploitative practices and therefore should avoid this on moral grounds.

SO WHAT ARE THE RESPONSIBILITIES OF BUSINESSES, CONSUMERS AND GOVERNMENTS?

Zwolinski (2007) asks how businesses, consumers and governments should act if sweatshops are unjustly exploiting; or conversely, if this is not the case, how should they then respond.

Meyers (2004: 329), operating from the premise that sweatshops are operating unjustly, concludes that it is certainly possible and desirable for sweatshop workers to be paid more, but asks 'whose responsibility is this?' He concludes that the competitive pressures on local entrepreneurs and the nation inhibit action, and this leaves the responsibility with the multinational corporation who can be held responsible for 'the morally objectionable practices of their agents (those who operate the sweatshops for them)'. This increase in wages might impact on the profit maximisation goals, but he denies the implication that companies pay workers as much as they can without significantly hurting profits. He argues they generally pay workers as little as they can, often less than a morally acceptable wage. He gives the example of producing a pair of Reebok shoes: at US$1 labour cost per pair, to double or even triple wages might only increase the price of shoes from US$100 to $US101. He argues that this would hardly impact on competitiveness or market share.

Zwolinski (2007) is more guarded, concluding that the worker's choice to accept sweatshop conditions rather than other choices of survival establishes a moral claim against many forms of interference with sweatshop wages (without implying that sweatshop employers are doing all that is morally justifiable). In contrast to Meyers (2004), however, he suggests that it is the managers of sweatshops who are in the best position to improve conditions, but that moral responsibility might differ in accordance with their levels of awareness of the nature of abuse and their power to act. He also acknowledges that multi-national enterprises (MNEs) also have a strong reason to act, but he cautions against the 'methods and scope of change that the MNEs [might] seek to bring about' (Zwolinski, 2007: 713), e.g. a shift from voluntary regulation to industry standards might create economic disincentives that will diminish the scale of sweatshop employment.

There is, however, some agreement that the best way to move forward from dogmatic debates (around economic efficiency versus increased regulation of worker rights) is to focus on positive models of organisations that are proactive in addressing what might be categorised as 'exploitative' practices in global labour markets. Arnold and Hartman (2005) categorise this type of pro-activity as 'positive deviance', providing examples in the apparel and footwear industry, including the health management and safety audits introduced by Nike, consequent upon pressure from human rights organisations in 1998 to accept corporate responsibility for the questionable treatment of labour by Nike suppliers. Adidas also committed to programmes to improve global labour management, with some initiatives requiring collaboration with competitors. Some argue that Levi Strauss set a new standard in 'positive deviance' by allowing children in its employment, who were discovered to be under the age of 14, to continue to receive their wages whilst completing their school education at the factory. Tuition, books and uniforms were paid for by the company. The children were then offered work when they turned fourteen (Varley, 1998).

These examples invite further research into whether such initiatives can in fact increase the competitive advantage in organisations rather than merely constitute efficiency deficits. Such findings might better inform the debate between advocates of sweatshops as a manifestation of economic efficiency and those who purport labour market reform in sweatshops on moral and ethical grounds.

See also: Corporate Citizenship, Human Rights, Intragenerational Equity, Postcolonialism

REFERENCES

Arnold, D.G. (2003) 'Exploitation and the Sweatshop Quandary', *Business Ethics Quarterly*, 13 (2): 243–256.

key concepts in corporate social responsibility

Arnold, D.G. and Hartman, L. (2005) 'Beyond Sweatshops; Positive Deviancy and Global Labour Practices', *Business Ethics: A European Review*, 14: 206–22.

Fukuyama, F. (1999) 'The Left Should Love Globalization', *The Wall Street Journal*, 1 December.

Maitland, I. (1997) 'The Great Non-debate over International Sweatshops', *British Academy of Management Annual Conference Proceedings*, September. Reprinted in Beauchamp, T. and Bowie, N. (2000) *Ethical Theory and Business*, 6th edn. Englewood Cliffs, NJ: Prentice-Hall.

Mayer, R. (2007) 'Sweatshops, Exploitation and Moral Responsibility', *Journal of Social Philosophy*, 38 (4): 605–619.

Meyers, C. (2004) 'Wrongful Beneficence: Exploitation and Third World Workshops', *Journal of Social Philosophy*, 35 (3): 319–333.

Varley, P. (1998) *The Sweatshop Quandary: Corporate Responsibility on the Global Frontier*. Washington, DC: Investor Responsibility Research Center.

Wertheimer, A. (1996) *Exploitation*. Princeton, NJ: Princeton University Press.

Zwolinski, M. (2007) 'Sweatshops, Choice and Exploitation', *Business Ethics Quarterly*, 17 (4): 689–727.

Systems Approaches

SYSTEMS THINKING

A systems approach presupposes that most of our thinking, experiencing, practices and institutions are interrelated and interconnected. (Werhane, 2008: 467)

Systems thinking has been applied in the sciences for many years but was only taken up by organisation theorists in the 1960s when scholars of management and organisational studies recognised the relevance of Bertalanffy's (1969) 'general systems theory' to their own field of endeavour. On this account, biological systems are recognised as open systems that cannot be reduced to the workings of a machine. Numerous scholars and practitioners have applied this understanding of an open system to society and the social systems of which it is comprised, including organisations of all types.

PARALLELS BETWEEN NATURAL ECOSYSTEMS AND BUSINESS NETWORKS

Systems approaches to organisations see the organisation as a whole system, and one which is open to the social, political, economic and environmental systems in which it is nested. The implication for the study of organisations is that focussing on just one aspect may result in distorting other dimensions of the system.

There appear to be numerous parallels between business networks and natural ecosystems. The analogy is drawn because of the mutual interdependence of the entities within the business networks. Mirroring the complexity of the interrelationships within nature, individual entities in the business system have little meaning outside the context of the system in which they are embedded. Similar to the communities that make up natural ecosystems, business networks and their component organisations are in the process of ongoing change. This has two key implications for business: first, the importance of innovation, and second, the health of the components of the system cannot be separated from the health of the overall system.

IN RELATION TO CSR AND SUSTAINABILITY

Proponents of applying systems approaches to the implementation of CSR argue that single-solution approaches are particularly susceptible to failure because of the underlying interconnectedness of the various elements within business, organisational systems and sub-systems, and their ultimate dependence upon the social and natural systems they are embedded within. Given the complexity of social and environmental challenges that contemporary organisations face, richer, more holistic and systemic understandings of corporate responsibility are required. Systems approaches to the implementation of CSR focus on interrelationships rather than on specific entities. As Werhane (2008) points out, for example, how Wal-Mart interacts with its suppliers has implications for the suppliers' employees, for the communities in which they live, and for the natural environment.

Complex social problems, such as how to ensure sustainable development through more responsible corporate action, requires an understanding of how natural systems intersect with social systems. How we perceive and address these problems has psychological, philosophical

key concepts in corporate social responsibility

218

and social dimensions that go beyond the technoscientific systems which have been typically engaged to address sustainability problems.

Systems approaches which incorporate an interconnectedness of the components of a system therefore underpin many environmentally and socially proactive organisational processes and tools. For example, corporations and their stakeholders are increasingly requiring that suppliers comply with certain environmental and social standards, many of which require a knowledge of lifecycle impacts. Whether driven by a concern for managing liabilities or to accord with changing community values, firms are now looking to whole systems approaches.

Complex problems can be classified according to what sort of approach they require (Hector et al., 2009). For some problems, systems-based analytical approaches utilising techniques such as computer simulation, for example, are appropriate. Other problems such as those typically associated with the domain of corporate sustainability and CSR involve multiple stakeholders with different value sets and conflicting viewpoints and hence cannot be addressed by 'hard' or mathematically-based systems approaches.

Porter and Cordoba (2009) argue that systems approaches to sustainability and CSR need to be considered to apply at a number of levels. At the functionalist or techno-analytical level, specific quantities and functions are traced through such processes as lifecycle analysis. In a similar vein to Hector et al. (2009), these writers argue that an interpretative approach using such techniques as stakeholder participation and values identification needs to be applied to address the complexity of the meaning of sustainability and CSR. Based on observations that contemporary organisations display such typical characteristics as self-organisation, emergence and bottom-up change, another systems-level approach looks to the organisation operating as a complex adaptive system (see the entry on Complexity Theories). Recognition that organisations may be behaving according to such characteristics, and that they may be doing so against a background of uncertain physical phenomena and limits to human cognition, has resulted in a new emphasis on learning networks and multiple stakeholder dialogues around addressing CSR and sustainability.

There are many other implications for managers attempting to implement CSR or sustainability programmes. For example, because an organisation may be in a continual state of moving from low to high levels of organisation, it may not be possible for a leader to definitively bring about change in a certain direction because of the multiple actors and interactions involved (Wempe, 2009).

APPLYING SYSTEMS APPROACHES

Systems approaches underpin numerous programmatic attempts to introduce the environmentally-related dimensions of CSR and corporate sustainability. Implementing systems design across the supply chain is dependent upon innovations that ensure cyclical material and energy flows, and thereby upon lifecycle analysis as a process tool.

For example, the Natural Step organisation promotes a well-known systems approach that employs a lifecycle-based process to implement sustainability. Numerous companies, such as IKEA, have utilised and promoted this approach as a means of addressing their interpretation of CSR.

In this framework, the 'four system conditions' of the Natural Step are interpreted as the 'four principles of sustainability' that are held to be essential if we are to develop a sustainable society:

1. We must eliminate our contribution to the progressive build-up of substances extracted from the Earth's crust (e.g. heavy metals and fossil fuels).
2. We must eliminate our contribution to the progressive build-up of chemicals and compounds produced by society (e.g. dioxins, PCBs, and DDT).
3. We must eliminate our contribution to the progressive physical degradation and destruction of nature and natural processes (e.g. over-harvesting forests and paving over critical wildlife habitats).
4. We must eliminate our contribution to conditions that undermine people's capacity to meet their basic human needs (e.g. unsafe working conditions and not enough pay to live on).

While such redesign features enable environmental gains, critics argue that the lifecycle approach remains linear and does not necessarily encourage the cyclical processes of sustainable manufacture and re-use that we must engage in if we are not to deplete the world's natural resources, including energy. Nor does it necessarily apply the form of system thinking that expands the world-view of organisational stakeholders so that their impact on wider social and natural systems can be understood and integrated into their decision making. An example of a systems approach as it is applied to CSR and corporate sustainability which also incorporates the interpretative and complex adaptive systems levels of systems thinking is cradle-to-cradle design. Cradle-to-cradle design enables the creation of wholly beneficial industrial systems driven by the synergistic pursuit of positive economic, environmental and social goals and involves a multiple perspectives point of view. An example might be nutricars that contribute positively rather than negatively to the environment by emitting substances such as nitrogen compounds which enable plant growth (Braungart et al., 2007: 1343). Such an approach to design is linked to eco-effectiveness in that it goes beyond the elimination of pollutants and on to a more radical redesign of products that will contribute positively to ecological and social systems. While still operating at functional and analytical levels, it attempts to gauge the values and preferences of different social actors and incorporate these into redesign concepts.

In sum, implementing CSR and sustainability requires firms to take a systemic approach by interacting with multiple actors and different stakeholder values and perceptions, and hence to engage in an ongoing learning process that may involve many ways of knowing. It also requires a level of acceptance of ambiguity and uncertainty by managers, and for a firm to engage with external and internal stakeholders that will include the natural environment. It is critically important for managers to understand systems-based approaches at each of the levels we have described above as these underpin a number of emergent and forward-looking business models. One of the most significant of these models promises to be the 'business at the bottom of the pyramid' model, and it is only systemic approaches, it is argued, that will be successful in such markets (Werhane, 2008).

See also: *Business at the Bottom of the Pyramid, Complexity Theory, Corporate Sustainability, Pollution and Waste Management, Product Stewardship*

REFERENCES

Bertalanffy, L. von (1969) *General System Theory*. New York: George Braziller.
Braungart, M., McDonough, W. and Bollinger, A. (2007) 'Cradle-to-cradle Design: Creating Healthy Emissions – a Strategy for Eco-effective Product and System Design', *Journal of Cleaner Production*, 15 (13–14): 1337–1348.
Hector, D., Christensen, C. and Petrie, J. (2009) 'A problem-structuring method for complex societal decisions: Its philosophical and psychological dimensions.', *European Journal of Operational Research*, 193: 693–708.

systems approaches

Porter, T. and Cordoba, J. (2009) 'Three Views of Systems Theories and their Implications for Sustainability Education', *Journal of Management Education*, (33): 323–346.

Wempe, J. (2009) 'Industry and Chain Responsibilities and Integrative Social Contracts Theory', *Journal of Business Ethics*, 88: 751–764.

Werhane, P. (2008) 'Mental Models, Moral Imagination and System Thinking in the Age of Globalization', *Journal of Business Ethics*, 78 (3): 463–474.

Triple Bottom Line

DEFINING THE TRIPLE BOTTOM LINE

The triple bottom line (TBL) framework is intended to provide a mechanism through which businesses can review and report on the overall impact of their operations, rather than limiting this activity to financial performance. Elkington coined the term 'triple bottom line' in the mid-1990s. He regards the TBL as conceptualising the ways in which 'companies and other organizations create value in multiple dimensions ... [through] ... economic, social and environmental value added – or destroyed' (2006: 523). A common feature of the TBL framework is the measurement and reporting of corporate performance concerning economic, social and environmental outcomes and impact. Note, however, that Brown had earlier discussed the expansion of business goals by calling for a shift 'from an organization conscious of a single purpose (profit) to one conscious of a multiplicity of purposes (economic, social, psychological, educational, environmental, and even political)' (1979: 20). More recently a number of institutions have added corporate governance to environmental, social and economic outcomes as a 'quadruple bottom line' approach to their reporting frameworks. Bendell and Kearins (2005) suggest that a 'political bottom line' should also be included, measuring the impact of progressive corporate political activity and influence on the overall goal of achieving more effective governance for sustainable development.

STRENGTHS AND WEAKNESSES OF THE FRAMEWORK

Robins (2006) notes that a key strength of a TBL reporting framework is that it requires a company to take into account a much broader range of stakeholders. He also draws attention to assumptions that underpin a TBL model, i.e. that companies go beyond a culture of regulatory compliance in accepting moral responsibility for environmental and social impacts associated with their organisational operations. Yet he also perceives major weaknesses in the framework, noting 'it provides no standard of account, that is, of measurement; either within one single dimension of account, or across all three' (2006: 2). Neither does it offer a means of prioritising stakeholder needs.

In retrospect, Elkington's comments appear prescient and contemporarily relevant: 'We should ask whether it is even possible to measure progress against the Triple Bottom Line. The answer is yes but the metrics are still evolving in most areas – and need to evolve much further if they are to be considered in an integrated way' (1999: 72).

So how have measurement and reporting mechanisms developed since Elkington's observations?

MEASUREMENT AND REPORTING MECHANISMS

Historically, there have been a number of management systems that could be brought to bear on the task of measuring the dimensions of a TBL, including ISO 14000, BS 8900, ISO 9004, the Balanced Scorecard, and various levels of social and people regulation around health, safety, EEO and human rights. Milne et al. note that, arguably, 'among the initiatives to evolve in support of non-financial reporting the Global Reporting Initiative (GRI) represents the predominant development' (2005: 11). As discussed in the entries on Corporate Responsibility Reporting and Business Networks, the GRI is a not-for-profit, multi-stakeholder network of 'experts' world-wide. Members participate in GRI's working groups and governance bodies, report on GRI Guidelines by drawing upon GRI-based reports, and contribute in various ways to the further development of the GRI's Reporting Framework. Application of the GRI *Sustainability Reporting Guidelines* (2006) is intended to facilitate the transparent and reliable exchange of sustainability information in order to promote an organisational disclosure of economic, environmental and social performance as a contributor to organisational success. The GRI and its reporting

triple bottom line

guidelines were recognised at the 2002 World Summit on Sustainable Development in its Plan of Implementation and are promoted by the UN Environment Programme (UNEP). A 2008 survey conducted by KPMG indicated that the GRI guidelines were used by 77 per cent of G250 companies and 69 per cent of others, with about 20 per cent of companies in both groupings using internally developed standards.

Elkington (1999: 94) suggested that social accounting, auditing and reporting will probably take longer to refine than the first and second bottom lines (economic and environmental). Nevertheless, he was adamant that the importance of the social bottom line should not be downplayed in progressing toward sustainable societies, stressing the need to revisit the significance of social as well as human capital in measuring the social bottom line: 'If we fail to address wider political, social and ethical issues, the backlash will inevitably undermine progress in the environmental area' (1999: 84). His definition of 'the social' included public health, welfare and education and other wider measures of society's health and wealth creation potential.

SUSTAINABILITY WITHIN THE TBL: LIMITATIONS AND CHALLENGES

It is now widely accepted that sustainability is a holistic multi-dimensional concept and that the 'three pillars' are interrelated. The environmental, economic and social dimensions of sustainability are highly interconnected, so attempting to measure individual actions and impacts will lead to an oversimplification of such a complex concept. In addition, taking a reductionist TBL approach may only encourage companies to trade off one dimension against another. One simple way around this is to use integrated indicators, or footprint or wellbeing studies, or more place-based impact studies, as discussed in the entry on Corporate Responsibility reporting.

TOOLS FOR INTEGRATING TBL INTO STRATEGIC BUSINESS PRACTICE

As stated earlier, traditional performance measurement systems, such as the 'balanced scorecard' (Kaplan and Norton, 1992) have tried to link non-financial corporate activities to the organisation's longer term strategy. Figge et al. suggested that:

Sustainability Management with the Balanced Scorecard helps to overcome the shortcomings of conventional approaches to environmental and social management systems by integrating the three pillars of sustainability into a single and overarching strategic management tool. (2002: 269)

Hubbard (2009) puts forward a stakeholder-based sustainable balanced scorecard with a performance index to integrate the measures of sustainability outcomes and to make them accessible to stakeholders. He acknowledges the simplicity and limitations of the approach, but sees it as a useful start to develop a stakeholder perspective on sustainability performance.

CONCLUSION

Although there are many criticisms of the framework, the TBL still presents an influential framework for conceptualising the challenges associated with transitioning to sustainability. Many commentators note how quickly it has been adopted by business. However, attention has also been drawn to tensions in developing measurement systems in an extremely dynamic and often paradigmatically shifting economic, social and political environment. The WBCSD (2010) highlighted this reality when they concluded that the transformational changes they forecasted to be associated with a stable population 'living well and within the limits of the planet' would require a new agenda for business driven by the need for new solutions at a global and local market level, one reflecting the 'true values and costs'.

This challenge will require the identification and development of new measures of success that will indicate progress towards often ambiguous, iterative and rapidly changing sustainability objectives. The TBL has initiated such a model, creating an awareness of the urgency and value of both accruing social and environmental capital and accounting for the impact of business in these domains. However, as UNEP/SustainAbility (2004: 5, 39) note in relation to the GRI framework, an increased standardisation of reporting risks can promote the acceptance of gaps in understanding and responding to the challenge of the Reporting Principles. Such a methodology can condone less innovative and relevant approaches by organisations. The challenge for 'committed leadership' is to encourage a contextual application of the kind of guidelines that will overcome these problems.

See also: Business Case for CSR, Corporate Responsibility Reporting, Corporate Social Responsibility, Resource-Based View, Stakeholder Theory, Voluntary Regulation

triple bottom line

REFERENCES

Bendell, J. and Kearins, K. (2005) 'The Political Bottom Line: The Emerging Dimension to Corporate Responsibility for Sustainable Development', *Business Strategy and the Environment*, 14: 372–383.

Brown, C.C. (1979) *Beyond the Bottom Line*. New York: Macmillan.

Elkington, J. (1999) *Cannibals with Forks: The Triple Bottom Line of 21st Century Business*. Oxford: Capstone.

Elkington, J. (2006) 'Governance for Sustainability', *Corporate Governance*, 14 (6): 522–529.

Figge, F., Hahn, T., Schaltegger, S. and Wagner, M. (2002) 'The Sustainability Balanced Scorecard – Linking Sustainability Management to Business Strategy', *Business Strategy and the Environment*, 1 (11): 269–284.

GRI (2006) *Sustainability Reporting Guidelines*. Amsterdam: Global Reporting Initiative.

Hubbard, G. (2009) 'Measuring Organizational Performance: Beyond the Triple Bottom Line', *Business Strategy and the Environment*, 18: 177–191.

Kaplan, R. and Norton, D. (1992) *The Balanced Scorecard*. Boston, MA: Harvard Business School.

KPMG (2008) *International Survey of Corporate Social Responsibility – 2008*. Amsterdam: KPMG.

Milne, M.J., Ball, A. and Gray, R. (2005) 'From Soothing Palliatives and Towards Ecological Literacy: A Critique of the Triple Bottom Line', *Working Paper Series*. Accountancy and Business Law, University of Otago.

Robins, F. (2006) 'The Challenge of TBL: A Responsibility to Whom?', *Business and Society Review*, 111 (1): 1–14.

UNEP/SustainAbility (2004) *Risk and Opportunity: Best Practice in Non-Financial Reporting*. London: UNEP/SustainAbility.

World Business Council for Sustainable Development (2010) *Vision 2050: The New Agenda for Business*. Geneva: WBCSD.

Voluntary Regulation

THE EXAMPLE OF VOLUNTARY ENVIRONMENTAL PROGRAMMES

'Voluntary regulation' refers to a system whereby firms can pledge to take continuous environmental or social action beyond that which is required by government regulation. Such regulation may involve commitments to reducing environmental pollution or addressing unsafe working environments or social exclusion, such as those associated with various equal opportunity initiatives. For example, the SA 8000 Social Accountability Certification Standard focuses on workplace values and human rights. Its elements refer to such issues as child labour, discrimination and discipline.

In this entry, we use the detailed example of voluntary environmental programmes. These have become a standard aspect of environmental policymaking since the 1990s – stimulated by a number of events, but most particularly by the high levels of participation by international business in the 1992 Rio Earth Summit. As an aspect of the global trend away from command-and-control forms of environmental legislation, elaborated on in the entry on Environmental Policy Tools, voluntary environmental programmes seem to offer efficiency advantages to governments and business alike. In addition, critics argue that governments cannot necessarily be relied upon either to develop or enforce effective policy, and nor may they have the capabilities or resources to do so. Importantly for environmental regulation, command-and-control mechanisms are essentially end-of-pipe and do not incentivise companies to prevent pollution. The effectiveness of the voluntary alternative, however, rests on clear mechanisms to monitor and enforce the 'rules' associated with the particular voluntary scheme.

ISO 14001

The dominant example of this form of voluntary environmental legislation is the ISO 14001 standard. In 1996, the ISO 14000 series of standards was launched by the Geneva-based International Organisation for Standardisation (ISO). The ISO is an NGO made of up other NGOs in the form of national standardisation associations from around the world. Leading multinationals collaborated with the ISO in developing the ISO 14000 series.

The ISO 14000 family of standards is based on the ISO or quality management standards, and is process-based rather than outcome- or performance-based standards. While this means no set environmental performance criteria have to be met by participating organisations, it does mean that a commitment to continuous improvement and ongoing compliance is required. Basically, it is this system of ongoing audits that sets it aside from traditional environmental management systems. Since 1996, ISO 14001 has spread to become the dominant voluntary environmental regulation system. Although not outcomes-based, a key component of the scheme is that participating firms must have an environmental policy and a documented means for improving environmental outcomes.

EMAS

While ISO 14000 is the dominant standard for assessing environmental management processes, many firms in Europe are also registering their environmental management systems with the Eco-Management and Audit Scheme (EMAS). EMAS is the European Union (EU) voluntary instrument that acknowledges those organisations that improve their environmental performance on a continuous basis. EMAS-registered organisations must be legally compliant, run an environment management system and report on their environmental performance through the publication of an independently verified environmental statement. Such performance-based measures distinguish EMAS from the process-based ISO 14000 series. They are recognised by the EMAS logo, which guarantees the reliability of the information provided. Participation is voluntary and extends to public or private organisations operating in the EU and the European Economic Area (EEA). The primary aim of this voluntary-membership organisation is to acknowledge organisations that go beyond the minimum legal compliance and are willing to produce transparent environmental performance reports. These reports are then independently audited, a feature that gives EMAS members credibility.

When established in 1995, EMAS was only available to industrial companies, but after the 1997 revision known as EMAS II was released in 2001, it became open to all public and private companies in the region. Small and medium enterprises (SMEs) are also encouraged to participate. Another advantage of EMAS II is the integration of EN/ISO 14001 as the required environmental management system. EMAS has fewer members than ISO 14001 because it requires greater detail in terms of reporting against objectives and making these reports publicly available.

As explained on the EMAS website, there are four steps involved in registering with EMAS:

1. Conducting an environmental review.
2. Establishing an effective environmental management system.
3. Carrying out an audit which assesses the effectiveness of the environmental management system.
4. Producing a publicly available statement of environmental performance.

MOTIVES FOR PURSUING VOLUNTARY REGULATION

According to Epstein (2008), companies will pursue EMAS and ISO 14001 for a range of reasons:

- a strategic framework for establishing and implementing an environmental management system
- supply chain pressure as companies attempt to manage their supply chain against the possibility of social and environmental risk
- the expansion of foreign trade, with ISO 14001 for example, being widely taken up across more than 100 countries
- the reduction of regulatory burdens as a result of improved practices
- stakeholder interests and reputation.

EFFECTIVENESS OF VOLUNTARY REGULATION

Prakash and Potoski's (2006) research indicates that, at least in the USA, joining ISO 14001 reduces the amount of time companies are non-compliant as well as reducing the amount of toxic emissions. These researchers also argue that their work shows that this form of regulation enables a firm's private business motives to align more closely with societal benefits. Importantly, their work also seems to indicate that it is the mid-range firms in terms of any potential negative environmental impact who see most benefit in such regulation. This indicates wide benefits if utilised as a policy tool.

Other research indicates that the longer a facility operates under ISO 14001, the lower its emissions (Russo, 2009). The wider implication of this work is that environmental management skills may be thought of as a dynamic capability, requiring high levels of flexibility as well as the ability to integrate a number of organisational processes and resources. The suggestion is that such a system, backed by mandated information gathering requirements, might therefore replace the expensive and inefficient command and control systems, which, after all, seem to provide for scant learning as an aspect of their rulemaking.

While both EMAS and ISO 14001 are generated through the activities of supranational organisations (one regional and one international), researchers have found that the firms' perceptions of their costs and benefits are largely determined by domestic factors, such as how they are promoted nationally and how they are supported by other stakeholders such as government, suppliers and environmental NGOs. This sort of

voluntary regulation

research points to a need for more government support if the schemes are to have universal effect.

The overarching message from recent research is that government-directed command-and-control mechanisms can be very usefully complemented with voluntary regulations such as ISO 14001 and EMAS. However, the potential exists for an institutional failure due to these schemes acting as de facto green clubs and in such a context, not offering enough value to firms to join these clubs constitutes failure. Another source of institutional failure comes with the company that joins the scheme but shirks its responsibility. Prakash and Potoski (2006) suggest that these limitations can be avoided if the 'club' backing the voluntary regulation either sanctions the shirking, publicises it or, more positively, instigates third-party certification schemes.

See also: *Codes of Conduct, Corporate Accountability, Environmental Policy Tools, Pollution and Waste Management*

REFERENCES

Epstein, M. (2008) *Making Sustainability Work*. Sheffield: Greenleaf.

Prakash, A. and Potoski, M. (2006) *The Voluntary Environmentalists*. Cambridge: Cambridge University Press.

Russo, M. (2009) 'Explaining the Impact of ISO 14001 on Emission Performance: A Dynamic Capabilities Perspective on Process and Learning', *Business Strategy and the Environment*, 18 (5): 307–319.

key concepts in corporate social responsibility

Index

Please note that references to Figures and Tables will be in *italic* print

index

233

index

243

index